PINSTRIPED SUMMERS

PINSTRIPED SUMMERS

Memories of Yankee Seasons Past

by

Dick Lally

ARBOR HOUSE
New York

Library of Congress Cataloging in Publication Data

Lally, Dick.
Pinstriped summers.
1. New York Yankees (Baseball team)—History.
I. Title.
GV875.N4L35   1985   796.357'64'097471   84-24478
ISBN 0-87795-670-7   (alk. paper)

PROLOGUE

Here at NBC there is just one more reason to hate the Yankees.

—CHET HUNTLEY, NBC commentator

WHEN CBS promoted Mike Burke in 1962 to the position of vice-president, he was thrown the task of exploring new areas of financial diversification for the network conglomerate. Had he merely gone out and made a few small acquisitions—Albania, for instance—his position at CBS would have been secure. So would his place in history.

Burke was not your ordinary television executive. Having graduated with honors from the University of Pennsylvania, where he had achieved a certain amount of gridiron fame as an outstanding halfback, he found his first full-time employment as a marine cargo inspector for an insurance firm. This had little to do with the life he had envisioned for himself, but that was of little consequence. He was young and had the confidence of youth. He knew something else would come along. Something did. It was World War II.

The renowned Italian philosopher in Mario Puzo's *The Godfather*, Don Vito Corleone, espoused the theory that a man had only one destiny and that this fate was inevitable no matter how circuitous the path he took to reach it was. Michael Burke's route started with a stint in Wild Bill Donovan's OSS and a particularly active role with the French Resistance. His escapades behind German lines had brought him the Navy Cross for "conspicuous gallantry and intrepidity in action." Life was the sort of stuff celluloid dreams were made of, something Warner Brothers recognized when it transformed his adventures into the 1946 spy thriller *Cloak and Dagger*. The film starred Gary Cooper, playing a character based on Burke.

Burke spent the first three years following the war as an intelligence adviser to the U.S. high commissioner in Germany. Perhaps tired of all this high-level intrigue, he decided to join the circus—Ringling Brothers—as its general manager in 1950. He held sway there until 1956 when he joined CBS as head of its European operations based in London. Six years later he was brought to New York.

CBS was an expanding empire and an executive like Burke—bright, energetic, and extremely charismatic—was viewed as the perfect choice to assist in its growth. His OSS experience pointed to him as a man able to make decisions under duress and equipped to carry out clandestine operations. These assets were deemed invaluable in the corporate world. In addition to these virtues, the young Burke (as he did in later life) carried with him the air of a child of destiny, though there would be times when even he may have been tempted to question the legitimacy of his celestial parentage.

As part of his new duties, Burke lunched weekly with William S. Paley, the network's chairman of the board, and Dr. Frank Stanton, its president. It was at one such meeting in May of 1963 that Burke casually asked, "What about the Yankees?" The question was rhetorical. He wasn't wondering about the team's chances in the current pennant race (excellent), or inquiring about the condition of Mickey Mantle's knees (terrible). He was suggesting them as a possible acquisition. The thought of owning the most glamorous franchise in baseball was certainly intriguing. When Paley inquired about the team's actual availability, Burke suggested he call the chairman's friend Dan

Topping. Dan Topping just happened to be part owner of the New York Yankees.

As it turned out, not only was the team available, an agreement had already been reached to sell. Topping had tentatively accepted an offer from Lehman Brothers, a giant investment firm in New York. The deal hinged on a very complicated tax ruling which would make the acquisition much more attractive. CBS was thanked for its interest and assured that if the Lehman deal did not pan out, the Yankees would give them a call.

On July 1, 1964, that is precisely what happened. The tax ruling was not favorable to the Yankees or their prospective buyers. Suddenly, Dan Topping had a ball club to peddle. So he got back to Bill Paley and, after a little bit of haggling, sold 80 percent of the Yankees to CBS for $11.2 million. Under terms spelled out in the agreement, Topping and his partner, Del Webb, retained 20 percent of the club and would remain with the team in the front office.

To understand the tempest in a ball park that followed the sale's announcement, one has to realize at least one thing: Buying a sports franchise is not like buying a toaster. For one thing, there are the feelings of other people, besides the principals, to be considered. These people can be divided into three groups. The first group comprises wealthy and powerful members. They are called owners, and they treat their leagues like exclusive men's clubs. They claim to be very particular about whom they let in. Members of the second group are not thought of as being as rich as members of the first (though many of them are), and in matters governing baseball they do not have much power. What they do have are a lot of opinions. These are worth weighing because these people are senators. Every time someone whispered about even the possibility of buying, selling, or (God forbid!) moving a baseball team, a small mob of senators could be counted on to start raising the Capitol dome over baseball's immunity to antitrust edicts. They do all this posturing to impress a third group. Members of this faction are, on the average, neither wealthy nor powerful. But they can do two things that greatly affect the lives and prosperity of the first two groups: buy tickets and cast ballots. These people are called fans, a.k.a. voters. While few members of the first two groups feel it is important to give the opinions of this third group any real value, it is extremely important to have the fans/voters think their views carry some weight. For the owners, this comes under the heading of sound business policy. To the senators, it's just politics.

The first order of business in completing the sale of the Yankees was to get majority approval of the transaction from group one, the American League owners. This permission is usually sought at a face-to-face sitdown of the type held in Chicago only forty-eight hours prior to the eventual poll. Since there were far more pressing matters to be discussed, like whether pitcher Masanori Murakami's contract belonged to the San Francisco Giants or the Naukai Hawks, a little thing like the sale of the New York Yankees never came up. It was left to league president Joe Cronin to send a telegram to each owner and request a vote by telephone. Carrier pigeon was thought to be too risky.

Voting was conducted on a level of secrecy usually reserved for the auction of classified information vital to the security of the free world. Any rumor of a sale was speedily quashed. Baseball commissioner Ford Frick was vacationing in Colorado Springs. When reached for comment about the supposed sale he said, "I know nothing about it." Which didn't exactly surprise anyone. All possible leaks had been sealed up, the owners had anticipated everything. Well, almost everything. They forgot about Charles O. Finley.

Charlie O. was the owner of the Kansas City Athletics and he was not terribly pleased with the way the vote on the sale had been handled. He felt it had been sneaked through and was further evidence of typical "Yankee shenanigans." So he blabbed, and, before the evening was over, the news of the proposed sale was being broadcast throughout the nation. The customary denials were issued right up until the next afternoon when Cronin announced that the sale had been approved by a vote, via telephone, of eight to two. Finley had been joined by Chicago White Sox owner Arthur Allyn in casting the two negative votes.

Whereas Finley didn't like the way the vote had been railroaded through (an opinion that was fueled, one might suspect, by his flat-out hatred for the lordly Yankees), Allyn had reasons for opposing the sale that were a bit more far-reaching. Like Finley, he pointed out that a telephone vote was constitutionally valid only if it resulted in a unanimous decision. Good point. His next point was even better. Given its new position in the league, CBS would now have an active voice in deciding what role television would play in baseball. This could set up a conflict of interest. Allyn also argued that the network would have an educated advantage in competing with its network rivals for the broadcasting rights to the All-Star Game and the World Series. Finally, there was the matter of pay-TV, glimpsed by the White Sox owner and a few other farsighted individuals as having an unimaginable potential as a source of future revenues. CBS was pay-TV's natural rival. By buying into the American League for what amounted to a piddling 1.9 percent of its total revenues for 1963, the network could choose to mount a formidable defense against cable's entry into the baseball business.

Despite these protests, the other owners could not be swayed. Backers of the sale pointed out that at least three major league owners—the Detroit Tigers' John Felzer, the California Angels' Gene Autry, and the Houston Astros' Roy Hofheinz—were in the television and radio business, albeit on a local level. Ford Frick came back from his holiday to give the deal his blessing. It seems that, contrary to his earlier disavowals, Frick had known about the proposed transaction ten days prior to its announcement. He had checked out the principals involved and had been "satisfied on all counts," those counts being:

1. The identity of the Yankees would be maintained.
2. The sale did not represent a conflict of interest.
3. The sale would not reduce the competition in the bidding for baseball's TV rights.

Frick also guaranteed that he had been "assured orally by Dan Topping and Will Paley that the Yankees would be operated as a separate corporation under the management of Dan Topping and Del Webb for a period of at least five years."

This may have satisfied Frick, but it didn't assuage Finley or Allyn. When told of the commissioner's assertion, the White Sox owner exploded, "When the hell did he ever take a position on anything? If you find out let me know and I'll start the whistles blowing and the smoke flying!"

The answer to that query was a very, very long silence, followed by calls from Senator Phillip Hart of Michigan and Senator James Pearson of Kansas for the launching of federal inquiries into the national pastime's antitrust exemptions. The Justice Department started an investigation of its own, and Senator William Proxmire went so far as to suggest that baseball should lose its exclusive territorial rights unless it agreed to pool and divide evenly all radio and television receipts, an idea about as appealing to the owners as a kick in the groin.

Of course, all of this turned out to be so much smoke-blowing. There wasn't a cabdriver in the five boroughs who didn't know that the Big Guy (CBS) would come out on top. The Big Guys always did. When the initial furor was over, CBS emerged unscathed and in firm possession of its latest acquisition. The only result of all the threatened legalities was that five American League owners and executives were ordered to divest themselves of CBS stock. One of those so ordered was Arthur Allyn. No wonder he was so enraged. On the day the sale was announced, his stock in the network dropped almost two full points on the New York Stock Exchange.

When the transaction was completed on November 1, 1964, it was anticlimactic. The Justice Department, after long and careful consideration, decided against an antitrust action, just as CBS counsels predicted it would. When the Senate hearings concluded on February 24, 1965, they had accomplished next to nothing. By the time the hearings adjourned, even Arthur Allyn admitted he could live with the deal. Only the maverick Finley remained in opposition, and he had been reduced to the role of a lonely Cassandra. The only other vocal opposition to the sale, except for a few sportswriters, came from the Soviet newspaper *Izvestia*, which lamented, "In the best traditions of trade in human bodies, the Yankees were not even told about the deal."

That was not quite true. The players had been told about the sale. When Charlie Finley first decided to talk, he unknowingly provided this little black comedy with its first indication of the bungling about to come. As CBS prepared to play a leading role in the biggest sports story of the year, one major network scooped the nation with its bulletin informing the country and most of the Yankee players of the impending sale. That network was NBC.

Chapter
ONE

You know every baseball man dreams of being connected with the Yankees.

—LELA KEANE, wife of Yankee manager Johnny Keane

"GENTLEMEN, I've been in this game for over thirty-five years. I've seen a lot of things in that time and if there is one thing I can guarantee all of you, it's this: You can't show me anything I haven't seen already." The speaker was Johnny Keane and the occasion was his first day as manager of the American League champion New York Yankees. As speeches go, it wasn't bad. He was succinct. He was also wrong. What Johnny Keane had failed to realize on that balmy Florida morning of February 25, 1965, was that he had never, ever seen anything like this team.

He had expected a few of the usual obstacles managers confront during spring training, but he had also expected to tackle them with a group of mature athletes who understood the role of discipline in the preparation for a successful season. Upon his arrival at the Fort Lauderdale camp, Keane had quoted liberally from the catechism of Vince Lombardi. "Winning," the new skipper reminded everyone, "isn't everything; it's the only thing." Unfortunately, on the Yankees, the more popular slogan was "Work hard; play harder." With a strict company man like Keane, this informal approach to the rites of spring was bound to create a problem.

This should not give the impression that the manager didn't expect some ballplayers to break curfew. He wasn't Peter Pan flown in on strings. Curfew infractions are common in spring training and rather easy to handle. You simply deputize a coach to stay up a few hours and read a paper in the hotel lobby. As recalcitrant players come straggling in, the coach jots down a few names and the proper action is taken. Nothing serious. Maybe a stern reprimand or a light fine for the first offense. On any other team it might have worked.

But this was not any other team. Certain players on the Yankees took a more creative view of the situation. Since returning to the hotel late would get them into nothing but hot water, they decided to add a unique wrinkle to the idea of curfew. They just didn't show up at all. They would crash wherever or with whomever they ended up and then proceed the next morning to the ball park, ready (more or less) to get the old body prepared for another winning year. It wasn't the whole team that was doing this. It was just a few, or slightly more than a few, enlightened individuals who were starting to convince their manager that he had stepped into some sort of baseball Gomorrah. And it was driving him out of his gourd.

Keane was in a situation filled with pressure. He had quit the world champion St. Louis Cardinals to manage their World Series opponents. He had replaced a manager who was a big favorite with the fans and who, almost impossibly, had helmed the team to the pennant. When Keane appeared quoting Lombardi, he wasn't messing around. He had to win. There were no other options.

Keane found himself in this position as the result of the most unlikely chain of events in the history of managerial merry-go-rounds. Yogi Berra had led the Yankees in 1964. He could have told Keane that sometimes even winning wasn't enough.

Berra had been a great player. He also had an off the field image, created and promoted in part by boyhood chum Joe Garagiola, that caused a number of people to see him in two lights: clutch hitter and clown. The reputation as a hitter gained him a great deal of respect around the leagues. But it was, to a degree, in the guise of clown that Yogi got his shot at managing the Bronx Bombers.

Just prior to the Yankees' World Series victory over the San Francisco Giants in 1962, New York general manager Fred Hamey told club owner Topping of his decision to retire immediately following the 1963 season. This was not the sort of news the owner expected to hear on the eve of the Fall Classic, and his first reaction was to openly wonder who in the organization could possibly succeed the sixty-one-year-old executive. Hamey had the answer. Fellow by the name of Ralph Houk, the present Yankee manager. With Topping's blessings, Hamey proposed the idea to Houk, who did not exactly stand on his head and spit nickels. Houk was known affectionately by his charges as the Major. He had been a hero in the Battle of the Bulge and preferred to stay close to the action in the trench that was the Yankee dugout. Hamey would not be deterred. After talking Houk into accepting the front-office post by appealing to his sense of loyalty to the organization, they started the process of determining Houk's successor as manager. Topping had a candidate.

The owner was sick of watching the New York Mets outdraw the Yankees, despite the fact that the National Leaguers were offering an inferior product in a dilapidated stadium, the old Polo Grounds. He was determined to hire a manager who would be able to compete with the team's biggest box-office attraction—Casey Stengel. So he pushed for Berra. Houk and Hamey resisted the idea, but to no avail. A press conference was called on October 22, 1963. On that day, amid the shimmering majesty of the Sheraton Plaza's Crystal Suite, Lawrence Peter Berra became the eighteenth manager in the history of the New York Yankees.

What followed is a part of baseball lore. The Yankees stumbled out of the gate under Berra. Whenever it appeared they were about to get their act together, someone would turn up lame. Players began to rush to Houk, crying that Berra had lost control of the club. By mid-August, the Major had reached a decision: Yogi would be canned. The undercover search for a replacement started and eventually zeroed in on three possibilities: Alvin Dark, Leo Durocher, and Johnny Keane.

Dark had worn out his welcome with the San Francisco Giants when he reportedly made repugnant remarks about black and Latin American ballplayers. He might have gotten the Yankee post if CBS hadn't acquired the team. The network's big eye wasn't about to risk being blackened by hiring a suspected racist. After all, they had just acquired a club whose past record in the support of non-Caucasian ballplayers was not about to earn it any Nobel Peace Prizes.

Durocher was the next choice. He was quickly ruled out because (or so everyone thought) he was about to take over as manager of the St. Louis Cardinals, a job held by the third choice, Johnny Keane.

Keane and Berra didn't know it at the time, but their lives were entwined by a cosmic cord. They both managed muscular squads that were expected to cakewalk through the opposition. It didn't happen. Their teams were trapped on a treadmill maintained by injury and fueled by bad breaks. Their bosses, being men of extreme compassion and patience, decided to present them both with gifts: small slips of pink paper. By some unexplainably wacky piece of logic, this made Keane, who was about to be fired, the perfect choice to ascend to the Yankee throne about to be torn from under Mr. Berra. Baseball thinking being what it was (and is), this was ultimate sense. A manager, after all, is hired to be fired. And vice versa. Before this master plan could get under way, however, two tiny flies took dips into the ointment. The cosmic twins, Yogi and Johnny, fooled them. They both won pennants.

Berra made up for this breach by not winning the World Series. Not exactly a crime punishable by death on most ball clubs, but his club was the Yankees and, by gum, pennant or no pennant, Berra was gone.

Keane's victory had quite the opposite consequence. It drove a block-long limousine up to his door and placed him firmly in the driver's seat. Cardinal owner Gussie Busch was so elated over his newly minted world championship that he offered his manager a new contract with a hefty raise. That wasn't exactly a surprise. Most owners would gladly part with their firstborn in exchange for a World Series ring. What was surprising was Keane's response to this benevolence. With the Yankee job practically in his pocket (he had already been approached about it), Keane became an early candidate for working-class hero. He waited until one half-hour before the October 17 press conference called by the Cardinals to announce his rehiring to turn to his boss and say, in so many words, "Take this job and shove it!" With this declaration came a letter of resignation dated September 28, 1964. It had been written when the Cards were one and a half games out of first place. When asked why he waited until October 17 to present it, Keane explained, "I didn't want to upset the players while we were still in the pennant race."

While Keane's resignation was a cause for celebration— everybody loves it when an employee gives his employer a good swift kick in the ass—Berra's firing that same afternoon was a woeful melodrama with tinges of the seriocomic. Houk solemnly announced that Berra had been dismissed because he couldn't communicate with the players.

Since the team had reached the seventh game of the World Series, no one quite understood what this meant. Would the next manager have to be multilingual? Would Norman Vincent Peale be a candidate for the job? He was a pretty fair communicator.

With the news of Berra's ouster thus handled, the club turned its attention to the question of his future. Berra, it was announced, would be retained by the club for the next two years at an annual salary of $25,000. His title would be "special field consultant." No office came with the position. This made sense because no position came with the position either. As one wag observed, "Yogi isn't being kicked upstairs, he's sort of being kicked sideways." In just one more example of how the Yankees got and maintained their cold corporate image, Berra hadn't been invited to his own wake. He had learned of the firing the day before. While on the golf course. By phone.

On October 20, only three days after the dual earthquakes had struck, the Yankees called another press conference. There it was officially announced that John Keane had been hired to manage the Yankees for the 1965 season. The proclamation was made at the Savoy Plaza, which had also served as the site of Berra's dismissal. The plush red carpeting served a double purpose. It gave the coronation a regal setting and also kept hidden the sight of Yogi's still-warm blood.

As tremors go, this one kicked up only a mild rating on the Richter scale. Joe Trimble of the *New York Daily News* had already reported Keane's pre-selection as manager on the occasion of Yogi's professional demise. Despite this earlier scoop, the story still managed to share the front pages with the news that Mr. Joseph (Joe Bananas) Bonnano had been kidnapped. Mr. Bonnano was a gentleman who was led by journalistic etiquette to believe that his first name was Reputed, as in "Reputed Mafia Chieftain." Before very long, Keane would feel a certain amount of kinship with Giuseppe. Both would have spent what seemed like forever in a place they did not want to be.

Keane's difficulties started immediately. Many of the Yankees had complained about Berra, but after he won the pennant, most of the squawking disappeared. It was assumed by the players that Yogi would be rehired. When he wasn't, they were flabbergasted. When Keane was hired they went beyond shock. It was as if Rod Serling had unlocked some door with the key of their imaginations and shoved them into a room with this guy from another planet. They just couldn't get used to him. He wasn't big. He wasn't tough-looking. He wasn't a "real Yankee." Most of all, he wasn't Ralph Houk. That was precisely what Yogi's problem had been the year before, but there was a difference. Berra had been a Yankee, had paid his dues as a player in the system. Sure, they made fun of him. In a typical display of clubhouse humor, one wit pinned up a half a dozen pictures of a chimpanzee with captions like "Yogi gives sign to third base coach." But they felt he was one of them. And he had won. Keane was a National Leaguer and, worse than that, he had beaten them in the World Series only last October.

When spring training got under way, Keane was a target. The players didn't like the way he ran camp. His meetings were too long. One of his coaches, Vern Benson, was nicknamed Radar because the players thought he was always trying to eavesdrop on their conversations. As each day passed, the bitching got a little worse. Finally the *World Telegram* published a story claiming, in essence, that the Yankees thought their new manager was a joke. The players denied it and, a few days later, the paper took it back. Items like this tended to create enemies, the sort of enemies who could make a sports department's summer a long and miserable one. Still, in spite of the retraction, the allegation was true.

If Keane's problems had been limited to an off the field arena, he may have been able to cope with them. As he said, winning is the only thing. But he would have on the field problems that would eventually prove to be fatal.

Mickey Mantle's health was one. On February 15, 1965, the Mick had signed his third consecutive $100,000 contract. He commented, "My legs feel better than ever." Perhaps they did at that moment. But signing a contract did not put the same strain on them as playing the biggest center field in baseball.

When spring training opened, Mantle looked wobbly on defense and seemed to lack balance at the plate. His sweet swing, once an instrument of savage beauty, had been replaced by a cruelly imperfect caricature. The thoroughbred swiftness that had seemed to defy the realms of human possibility existed only as a memory. For fourteen years center field had been his position. Now it was beyond his physical ken. It was heartbreaking. The year before, several pitchers confided to the *New York Post*'s Vic Ziegel that Mantle wasn't getting to balls like he used to, and some of them allowed as how it might have, just might have, cost them a few games. But, they were quick to point out, he won so many games with his bat. The early fear of spring training was that he might not even be able to do that anymore.

Whitey Ford, the cornerstone of the pitching staff, also had his share of the miseries. The circulatory problems that had limited Ford's World Series participation against the Cards to five and one-third innings had forced him to accept an offseason operation. The surgery performed by Dr. Denton Cooley was deemed a success, but whether Ford could pitch competitively or not remained conjecture. Complicating this were the numbers on his birth certificate. Whitey was thirty-six years old and would have to be brought along carefully. With 216 wins in the bank, including 17 the season before, he was one valuable piece of porcelain.

Other physical problems started to crop up in camp. Catcher Elston Howard complained about a perpetually sore right elbow, and shortstop Tony Kubek had suffered a variety of ailments over the last several seasons. Kubek reported to Florida with a stiff shoulder that was pestering him, sapping strength and accuracy from his throws. Both missed early exhibition games.

These minor hurts began to point out a new area of vulnerability for the Yankees, one that should not have gone unnoticed. The bench, which had helped to give the team a decided edge over their opponents, had greatly eroded. Phil Linz could still sub for Kubek and do an adequate job, but when Howard sat he was replaced by the platoon of Bob Schmidt, a thirty-two-year-old who had played with four teams in the last four seasons, and Johnny Blanchard, who would have been a tremendous designated hitter, had that position existed at the time.

Mantle's ills forced a juggling in the outfield. Tom Tresh traded places with him, going from left to center. Mantle really shouldn't have been playing at all, but if he didn't, who was there to take his place? Hector Lopez? He was adequate in the field, but he certainly couldn't replace even an infirm Mantle at the plate. There was nobody else.

The pitching staff did not have a similar problem. Ford's rehabilitation was a luxury the team could afford. If Whitey wasn't ready by Opening Day, the Yankees could open with a still-solid starting rotation: Jim Bouton, Mel Stottlemyre, Al Downing, Bill Stafford, and Rollie Sheldon. That group had compiled a record of 50–26 in 1964, and of the five, Sheldon was the "old man" at twenty-seven. The club appeared to be pitching rich.

The rest of the personnel were in equally good shape. Joe

Pepitone, the team's Errol Flynn, at first base and Bobby Richardson at second were All-Stars. Third baseman Clete Boyer was, with Brooks Robinson of the Baltimore Orioles, one of the best third basemen in the business. In right field, Roger Maris may not have been much of an interview, but he was the most complete player in the league.

Backing up the starting pitching was a superb bullpen manned by Steve Hamilton, Pete Mikkelsen, Hal Reniff, and last year's pennant saver, Pedro Ramos. The fact that Ramos, who had been a late August acquisition from the Cleveland Indians, was going to be with the club from the beginning of the season was considered an additional plus.

It was really not astounding that this crew was being picked by almost everyone to win another league championship. Even a computer tabbed the Yanks to play another World Series (against the Philadelphia Phillies). When the team got off to a ragged start in spring training, nobody gave it a thought. Spring training was never important for the Yankees. As far as the players were concerned, its main purpose was to let the league know they were going to show up for the regular season. Keane had a different view.

In 1961, as manager of the Cardinals, he released his best left-handed reliever—in fact, his only left-handed reliever—Mickey McDermott, over a curfew violation. It was common knowledge that he had fined at least one other pitcher for "not trying." Keane was not viewed as being the most flexible of men. He had a certain way of looking at things, and he wasn't shy about letting people know what his opinions were. His conviction about spring training was simple. He felt that it was important because it helped establish the habit of winning.

Well, the Yankees didn't quite think they had to establish the habit of winning. They had won fourteen pennants in the last sixteen years, thank you kindly, and just who did this busher think he was anyway? The players' initial resentment toward Keane started to fester into an open sore.

Keane called a clubhouse meeting, the gist of which was later immortalized in the marvelous collaboration by Jim Bouton and Lenny Shecter, *Ball Four.* One is reminded here of a scene from the movie *The Caine Mutiny*, where the Queeg/Bogart character calls a meeting of his officers in order to clear the air. Choosing his words too cautiously, he loses them in a fruitless attempt to draw them closer. In a similar vein, Keane attempted to set things straight. The team had lost a few early exhibition games. The manager took note of this and proceeded to point out that a number of players, about three or four, had gotten "a little bit careless" in their training habits. He called several such meetings as the losses piled up, and each time the number of players who had gotten "careless" grew, until finally it was in the neighborhood of the population of Rhode Island. The guilty players could not keep a straight face. "Are we being too careless tonight?" became the in joke of the spring and was usually uttered at a time when "tonight" invariably meant "this morning." Keane had been relegated to the role of clubhouse comedian and the season hadn't even started.

When it did start, the team came north in reasonably sound mental shape. They had compiled a losing record in the Grapefruit League, but that was of little consequence. The Yankee veterans were correct about that. Spring training is usually a barometer of nothing.

What was worrisome, besides the dissension that nobody would admit to, was the number of question marks that rode with the team. Ford had done reasonably well, enough to be counted on as part of the regular rotation, albeit a fragile one. He still had some problems on unusually cold days and would have to be monitored. Stottlemyre, Bouton, Downing, and the rest of the pitchers looked exactly the way they were supposed to look: awesome. The hitting and fielding, however, were another matter.

During the final weeks in Florida, Mantle had begun to show brief, promising flashes of his former hitting eloquence. In an exhibition game on April 9, he christened the newly opened Astrodome with its first home run. It was a moonshot that represented the Yankees' only tally in a 2–1 loss. The problem with the Mick was that he wasn't hitting or playing often enough. When he didn't start the effect on the lineup was devastating:

WITH MANTLE:	WITHOUT MANTLE:
Tresh, cf	Richardson, 2b
Richardson, 2b	Kubek, ss
Maris, rf	Tresh, cf
Mantle, lf	Maris, rf
Pepitone, 1b	Pepitone, 1b
Howard, c	Howard, c
Kubek, ss	Lopez, lf
Boyer, 3b	Boyer, 3b

Keane would have preferred to bat Tresh first. He was quick, a switch-hitter, and showed an ability to do the one thing a leadoff man must accomplish: get on base. Over the last three seasons only Mantle had had a higher on-base percentage. In addition, Tresh could hit home runs, and the very idea of starting a game with a quick lead before the contest was more than a few pitches old has been known to move most managers to the limits of rapture. With Mantle in the lineup batting fourth, Keane could afford the luxury of a leadoff man named Tresh. An absent Mantle made the price of putting Tresh's power at the top of the batting order too dear. This put the skipper in a "catch-22" position. In order to place Mickey in the lineup, Keane had to let him play the field. That area of Mantle's game had not improved. Indeed, it seemed that Mantle was getting a ton of ink whenever he caught fly balls. Ordinary fly balls.

Ellie Howard's elbow, reinjured during an exhibition stint in Puerto Rico, wasn't getting any rave reviews either. Base runners, used to regarding his arm with the same respect that hamburger has for a meat grinder, were now brazenly stealing second. Maris had a pulled hamstring that was hampering his outfield play and baserunning. Kubek was in and out of the lineup, and Ramos had a virus.

The team was forced to leave Florida with three rookies: nineteen-year-old pitcher Gil Blanco, twenty-seven-year-old outfielder Art Lopez, and twenty-year-old outfielder Ross Moschitto. This group in no way resembled the Yankee freshman class of '62 that included Tresh, Pepitone, and Bouton. It was another sign that the once-inexhaustible bank of talent that was the Yankee farm system had defaulted.

These portents of doom went unheeded, so the baseball deities provided one more. The Yankees opened their season against the Minnesota Twins in Bloomington, Minnesota, on April 14. The evening before, the Great Baseball Commissioner in the Sky must have visited the owners of both teams and said, "I want you to build an ark. A big one. On it place two of every infielder, nine of every pitcher..." because he blessed the stadium and surrounding regions with a good, old-fashioned Minnesota flood. Four Twins—Jim Kaat, Dick Stigman, Rich Rollins, and Bill Bethea—had to be flown into the stadium by helicopter. The whirlybirds were then used to dry the playing field. Before the game was very old the Yankees probably wished they hadn't gone to all the fuss. The record shows that the Yankees lost that afternoon, 5–4. Jim Bouton started for New York, Jim Kaat for the Twins. Neither was involved in the decision. The two pitchers threw well but they had the misfortune to be supported, in the loosest sense of the word, by eight fielding miscues (five by the Yankees) and countless mental flubs. Both teams' offensive maneuvers were being conducted by a group of innocent bystanders. The plug was pulled on this circus in the eleventh inning when Twins rookie Cesar Tovar, who earlier had permitted the Yankees to tie the score on an error of his own, came up with a runner on second and hit a short fly ball off the still-sniffling Ramos to Tresh in center. Tresh dove and came up with the ball. On one bounce. End of ball game. Ramos took the loss. The winner was a young rookie named Jerry Fosnow. It was one of three games he would win all season. It was one of three games he would win in his entire major league career. After the game, Keane remarked, "I have never seen anything like it in thirty-five years of baseball." This was not the sort of thing his players wanted to hear. It wasn't the sort of thing Ralph Houk would have said. Ralph would have blamed the loss on the weather, opined that it was only one game, and pointed out that the three wild pitches Yankee hurlers had thrown provided them with excellent opportunities to practice covering home plate. What the records don't show was the first major blow to the Yankee season. It wasn't the loss of a mere game. It was the loss of a pitcher.

Bouton was injured. If throwing a baseball at ninety miles an hour is an unnatural act, then doing it under wet and freezing conditions is insanity. Frank Lary, the former Yankee-killer of the Detroit Tigers, ruined his career pitching under a similar set of circumstances in an earlier season opener. Sixteen years after the fact, Bouton recalled, "It was a funny kind of injury. I didn't notice any problems while I was out there on the mound or even after the game. But the next day I woke up with a small toothache in my biceps. That's what made the injury so unusual. Sports medicine wasn't as advanced back then as it is now. I'm sure they didn't even call it sports medicine. Whatever, when there was a pain in the area of the biceps, the usual diagnosis was that the muscle was tired. That's what they told me. They also said that throwing wouldn't make things any worse. So I tried to throw through it. That opener was the last good game I pitched all year. The arm just got worse. At first it didn't bother me except when I was pitching, but by midseason I couldn't lift a half-gallon of milk. Yet I still thought I could throw. I guess the Yankees thought I could too because pretty soon they started to wonder if maybe my problems really were in my arm. They figured maybe they were in my head. Isn't that great? Only six months earlier I had beaten the Cardinals twice in the World Series, but now suddenly I was supposed to be afraid to pitch against the Kansas City Athletics. Unbelievable!"

Taking the mound armed only with the fortitude that had won him the nickname bulldog, Bouton pitched in 30 games and compiled a record of 4 wins against 15 losses.

In the wake of the controversy that was *Ball Four*, it is not often remembered what a fine pitcher this Bulldog was. In 1963 and 1964 he won a total of 39 games. During that same span, only Whitey Ford, Juan Marichal, and Sandy Koufax won more. It was not unreasonable to argue that Bouton was the best right-hander in the American League. The injury erased all that. In the last seven years of his career, including a brief comeback with the Atlanta Braves in 1978, Bouton won a total of 16 games.

He also wrote a book with Lenny Shecter, the afore-mentioned *Ball Four*, that helped change the range of sports literature and forever earned him the reputation of a baseball gadfly.

Bouton's mishap served as the starter's pistol for a marathon of injuries. Maris reinjured his hamstring in an outfield tumble, Kubek began missing time with an assortment of nagging hurts, and in late April Howard finally had to submit to surgery on his elbow. A bone chip the size of an adolescent splinter was unearthed. He was expected to miss four to six weeks. It was right about this time that Old Man Panic decided to pay the Yankees a visit.

The Schmidt-Blanchard backup catching platoon was rushed into action and found to be woefully inadequate. Nothing rash about that judgment; it was reached after an entire week. The front office decided to shop around for a replacement and they found one with the Kansas City Athletics: Doc Edwards. Edwards was a twenty-seven-year-old journeyman with occasional power and an adequate defensive reputation. It was a deal that never should have been made.

It's true that Blanchard was not really a catcher. But Schmidt was at least as good defensively as Edwards and a much better hitter. The statistics bore that out. The Yankee management didn't bother to look at the stats, and they certainly didn't waste much time looking at Schmidt. They gave Kansas City Blanchard and pitcher Rollie Sheldon in exchange for Edwards.

Blanchard was that rare commodity, a ballplayer who was perfectly content to fill a role on a good ball club. He may not have been the answer behind the plate, but he could play a little first base and some outfield and pinch-hit; with Yankee Stadium's right field porch and his left-handed power he was always a threat to hit the ball out. He was also "one of the boys," and his value in the clubhouse was immeasurable. Sheldon, though not a great pitcher, was an insurance policy. With Bouton hurting, Ford still a question mark, and Bill Stafford joining the walking wounded with a sore arm, it was ill-advised to let him go. Especially for a commodity they did not need. That season, pitching for a last-place club with a record of 59—

103, Sheldon won 10 games while losing only 8. He was missed.

The panic in the executive suite was directly related to the news from the playing field. The season was shaping into a catastrophe. By June 1, the team was in eighth place with a record of 19–26, nine and a half games behind the Twins. No Yankee pennant winner had ever been so far back that late in the season. The club was last in the major leagues in hitting and runs scored. Only Tresh, Mantle, and Richardson were hitting with anything approaching consistency. The rest of the lineup's numbers suggested a Murderers' Row that had spent too much time in the death house: Pepitone, .198; Boyer, .197; Maris, .194; Kubek, .192; and Edwards, .181. This sort of offensive impotence puts a tremendous strain on pitchers who begin to feel that every pitch has to be perfect because there is no margin for error. Of the Yankee starters, only Stottlemyre, en route to his first 20-victory season, seemed able to rise above the lack of firepower.

The team was taking these bad times rather well. Keane, to his credit, maintained his cool. He acknowledged that it was a long season, and that it was only "a matter of time" before his hitters began to strut their stuff. He wasn't far wrong. In the first week of June, the Yankees started to look like the Bronx Bombers reborn. Five wins in three days will do that for a team. The high point of that mini-campaign came on June 6 when the Yankees executed a 6–1, 12–0 doubleheader sweep of the second-place Chicago White Sox in the Bronx. 50,364 of the stadium faithful saw a vintage Yankee performance: cold, systematic, and merciless.

When the carnage had ceased, the club was still nine and a half games behind Minnesota. But they were only four games out of third. It was a wonderful time to be starting a road trip against the lowly Athletics. As the bus bound for Newark International Airport pulled out, there was an electricity in the air. Yankee electricity. Something was about to happen.

When the players reached the airport, they found that due to a mechanical mishap there would be a two-and-a-half-hour delay before takeoff. One group, desperate to fill the time and crushed to learn the Newark Public Library was closed at 10

P.M., decided to enjoy some stimulating conversation at an airport cocktail lounge. Some time during the evening, the intoxicating mixture of victory and Coca-Cola proved to be a bit much. The boys got, well, careless. Not too careless. Just a few wolf whistles at the waitresses. That sort of thing. The whole episode wouldn't have rated a mention except the timing of it was wrong.

Why was the timing wrong? Four reasons:

1. The boys were imbibing in a public place where they were immediately recognizable.
2. The manager (who was seething) was present.
3. He was seated with his wife.
4. None of the five players involved was playing very well at the time.

If listed according to the priorities of baseball, the order would definitely be inverted.

Keane was furious. He was a religious man and it embarrassed him to have his wife see his players "out of control." The spring training gaffs were one thing. But this was the regular season. This was serious.

The next day, a clubhouse meeting convened. Three unnamed players (reportedly Mantle, Ramos, and Reniff) were fined $250 each. Two others (reportedly Maris and Mikkelsen) were severely reprimanded for "breaking training" and for having been seen "with one too many in a public place." "One too many" seemed to be a piece of newspeak around the Yankee organization. When Houk issued a release explaining the actions taken by the team, he used the term at least a half-dozen times. One puzzled Yankee later wanted to know what Houk meant by "one too many." Did he mean cases? The incident died a quick, painless death. But, to some observers, it seemed to completely reverse the clubhouse attitude toward the manager. The players started to look as if they were actually going to take this guy seriously. Like the current winning streak, it was an illusion.

This team was chasing its own tail. Lose two, win two. Win

three, lose four. Howard and Kubek came off the disabled list on June 13. Mantle was benched. Roger Repoz was brought up from the minors and immediately took over center field. He hit like a banshee for about two weeks. Nothing helped.

On July 2, the American League All-Star lineup was announced. For the first time in the thirty-three-year history of the event, not a single member of the New York Yankees was elected as a starter. One week later, the club went to Minnesota for the start of a four-game series that the Yankees hoped would put them back in the pennant chase. Empty dreams. Their record stood at 40–43 and they were 12½ games behind the league-leading Twins.

Minnesota took the first two games 8–3 and 4–1. Bouton and Ford had lost to Dave Boswell and Jim Perry. Minnesota led the third game 5–4 when Boyer hit a grand slam off Twins reliever Johnny Klippstein to give the Yankees the lead in what would be an 8–6 victory. The final game of the set was on Sunday, July 11. It featured what was later voted by hometown fans as "The Greatest Moment in Twin History."

The Yankees had started the ninth inning of the contest tied 4–4. With one out, Ellie Howard singled and went to third on a base hit by Hector Lopez. Pepitone hit a ground ball to Bernie Allen forcing Lopez, but failing to score Howard who remained at third. Repoz followed with a high chopper down the first base line that was speared by pitcher Jerry Fosnow. Fosnow lunged for the ball, lunged for Repoz, and wound up with neither, Howard scoring on the play.

Or did he? Umpire Ed Hurley called Repoz out for interference, a call which did not endear him to John Keane. Keane calmly walked out of the dugout and did his best impersonation of a man trying to swallow another fellow's head. Since this was a departure from John's usually placid demeanor, Hurley decided to consult with first base umpire John Flaherty. Hurley then did something that got the Twins and their 35,263 supporters a trifle upset. He reversed himself. Repoz was ruled safe and the Yankees had a 5–4 lead. Now it was Minnesota manager Sam Mele's turn to take the stage. He did his fans proud with a lovely interpretation of a man attempting to cut a baseball in two. With his teeth. He grimaced. He scowled. He raged. He called his team off the field. All to no avail. Finally, after umpire Hurley refused to re-reverse himself, the Twins came back to their positions. But not without first having it announced that they were playing the game under protest. In five minutes that protest would be moot.

The top of the ninth ended with Tom Tresh unsuccessfully pinch-hitting for Pedro Ramos. As the Twins were about to take their turn at bat in the bottom of the inning, Pete Mikkelsen took the mound to protect the New York lead. He retired shortstop Zoilo Versalles on a ground ball to Clete Boyer. Third baseman Rich Rollins walked. Tony Oliva, the previous season's batting champion, hit a long fly ball that was hailed down by Repoz in center field. Up came Harmon Killebrew. With the count full, Mikkelsen threw a fastball toward the inside corner. A fastball that never reached its destination. It was intercepted by Killebrew's bat and promptly deposited some 360 feet away into the left field bleachers. The game and the Yankee season were over.

The loss left the Yankees with a record of 41−46, 14½ games out of first place. It also sent a message to the Twins, their fans, and the rest of the league. The Yankees weren't going to do it this year. There would be no amazing comebacks. No Frank Merriwell phenoms would come out of the minors to save the day. The kings were dead, et cetera and so on.

Oh yes, there would be another spurt in late August that would leave them at .500 on September 1. That was followed by a seven-game losing streak. On September 9, despite a 6−5 win over the Washington Senators, the team was officially eliminated from the pennant race. When the final numbers were in, the Yankees, the mighty Yankees, were in sixth place, 8 games under .500 and 25 games out of first place. First division, the upper half of the meridian line separating the contenders from the pretenders, was 10 games away. It was the worst finish by a Yankee ball club in forty years.

On an individual basis, the numbers game wasn't any better. Tresh led the club with 26 home runs, 74 runs batted in, and a .279 batting average. No one else on the club was close to those statistics. Mantle, Maris, Howard, Kubek, Richardson, and Pepitone were part of an epic season-long slump that resulted in eleven Yankees having the worst years of their lives. Stottlemyre, at 20–9, was the best pitcher in the league, and Ford managed to win 16 games after a horrendous start. Al Downing was 12–14. They were the only pitchers in double figures in wins.

The bullpen was inconsistent, while the fielding, even with the Gold Glove performances of Tresh, Pepitone, and Richardson, and the nonpareil efforts of Boyer, was something less than what it had been in the past. The collapse was a group effort.

To the players, it seemed a sudden thing. They acted as if the disintegration had struck the club with the ferocity of a car crash, swift and deadly. They were wrong. An insidious cancer had gripped the team and had ravaged its guts. The pissing and moaning about Keane which, except for that brief spell in July, went on for the entire season, was just a part of the problem. The team had gotten old and aching. When they looked to the minor leagues to take up the slack, they found it populated by invisible men. In trying to make deals, they found they didn't have the stock to pull off a swap of any consequence. What trades they could make saw them fleeced by their own blind fear.

At least one player wasn't dazed by the "sudden" decline. After the All-Star break, he had managed to tack 70 points onto his batting average. His numbers were quite respectable: .251, 18 home runs, and 58 RBI. This hitting did not net him much publicity. It wasn't out of insensitivity that his second-half performance was ignored. It was just that anything he accomplished with his bat had to be resigned to living in the shadow of what he did with his glove. Pure magic. For eight years he was the sole proprietor and performer of an aerial circus that guaranteed a miracle every day, no two miracles alike. In 1965 he was one of the few things in pinstripes still worth getting excited about. His name—Clete Boyer.

Clete Boyer had a reputation as a maverick magician who had built a rapport with the media, who appreciated his wit and baseball knowledge, along with a candor that was rare in his generation of athletes. It was the last quality that got him in Dutch with the baseball hierarchy. In 1971 he was allegedly blackballed by the Atlanta Braves for taking on their front office in the press. He spent the next few years playing baseball in Japan and running his saloon in Georgia. Boyer returned to the major leagues in 1980 as a coach with Billy Martin's Oakland A's. It was a hot Sunday afternoon in July when he sat down in the visitor's dugout in Yankee Stadium and recalled, "I wasn't surprised by our collapse in 1965. Hell, I didn't think we were the best team in '64. We were lucky to be in it at all. I thought Baltimore had the better club that year, so what happened in 1965 wasn't much of a shock. Baltimore and Chicago led most of '64, and I think we just sort of snuck by them. It got tight at the end and we knew how to win. But you could see that we didn't have the young stars like we used to. That new draft rule had a bad effect on the Yankees and they didn't know how to cope with it. You know they used to have their choice of thousands of ballplayers all over the country, the best ballplayers in the world. The Yankees usually signed a good share of them. When it came time to pick up a spare part like a Bob Cerv or a Pedro Ramos, they always had some good young prospects to offer in a deal. Hell, we had a ton of guys like Deron Johnson and Norm Siebern. But with the new draft rules they just couldn't stockpile talent like they used to. When we needed help we didn't have much to offer anymore in the way of young talent.

"Johnny Keane was a hell of a man, extremely religious, just a beautiful guy. He would have made a hell of a college coach, you know what I mean? But he wasn't the right guy for our club. First he was not from our organization, he was from the organization that kicked our ass in the World Series. Going outside the organization to replace Yogi was not a good idea. Then, he had a funny way of managing. He used to have us bunt in the first inning. Bunt! We were the fucking Yankees, we didn't bunt. A manager's got to utilize his personnel according to what they can do, what they're comfortable doing. We had a veteran ball club built for power, not the hit-and-run. He didn't understand. I remember times when we would be behind in a game, you know three or four runs behind, and he would give the take sign to Mickey Mantle on 3 and 0! Mickey Fucking Mantle! This was a Hall of Famer and Keane's giving him the take sign. Mickey would look at him like he couldn't believe it. You just don't do something like that....It's simply a matter of knowing your personnel. Keane didn't."

Chapter
TWO

Fans in other cities started to cheer for us. It was as if they felt sorry for the Yankees. That really used to make me mad.

—STEVE HAMILTON, Yankee reliever

DURING the winter, the Yankee management tried to shrug off the debacle of 1965 as "just one of those things." The party line held that the reason for the sixth-place finish could be summed up in that too-familiar refrain, "if not for the injuries." Loser talk. Generally, injuries are quite common on winning ball clubs. Participants in a pennant race tend to play hard, and nagging injuries are bound to pop up. It is why the game is played with a twenty-five-man roster. On the Yankees, while it was true that they had had an unusually high casualty list, it is also true that none of the lame or walking wounded bounced back very quickly. This inability to recover rapidly is one of the tariffs demanded by age. The tissues lose their elasticity, and the bones become more brittle than they were a short time ago. The decay was compounded by the after-hours habits exhibited by some members of the team. In this regard, Keane's approach to spring training may have been correct. The team needed work. A pulled hamstring is the body's way of saying,

"We'd better not miss curfew tonight." That Keane could not communicate this, or much else, to his players had a small hand in his eventual downfall. He couldn't change their habits, and he certainly couldn't change the year they were born.

Since, at the time, the Yankee management seemed scarcely aware of the team's real problems, the next series of errors could hardly be seen as unexpected. Actually, they serve as a damning indictment of just how blind the front office was.

Their first bobble occurred before the 1965 season came to its conclusion. On Wednesday, September 8, the day before they excused themselves from the pennant chase, the club announced the rehiring of Johnny Keane. He was given a one-year contract. This aggravated the initial mistake of hiring him. At the press conference, Houk said, "We cannot blame our present position on the manager. We feel our present standing is the result of not having our club together for the entire season. While we don't like to use injuries as an alibi, it is true that we have not been able to play our club, as a unit, this season." Neither could the Minnesota Twins. During their season, they went for a long stretch of time without the services of the league's most prolific slugger, Harmon Killebrew. He had suffered a broken elbow and was out for six weeks. They also had to struggle without the services of their regular second baseman, Bernie Allen (torn knee ligaments), their best starting pitcher, Camilo Pascual (sore arm), and their most promising rookie, Dave Boswell (minor eye injury). These players missed parts of the 1965 season, but the Twins didn't call any press conferences to lament this. They were too busy clinching the American League pennant. Before Houk finished his speech, he assured everyone that "Johnny [Keane] and I are not concerned with this ball club..."

They should have been. Playing the winter trading game with this philosophy of unconcern, the Yankees made the following moves:

NOVEMBER 12—Traded Phil Linz to the Philadelphia Phillies for Ruben Amaro.

DECEMBER 10—Traded Pete Mikkelsen to the Pittsburgh Pi-
    rates for Bob Friend.

JANUARY 4—Traded Doc Edwards to the Cleveland Indians for
    Lu Clinton.

What was on their minds? Obviously they thought that they
really were just the victims of bad breaks, and that the club
was still a contender. The deals were evidence of that. They
were just the sort of trades made by clubs who were only missing a few pieces.

On the surface, Linz for Amaro was not a bad deal. It should
have been one of those famous "trades that help both clubs."
Amaro was a twenty-nine-year-old shortstop who was probably
as good as any shortstop not named Luis Aparicio. He had hit
.264 as recently as 1964, while sharing the Philadelphia shortstop's chores with Bobby Wine. Unfortunately, that respectable
mark was sandwiched between two seasons in which he batted
.217 and .212. The thinking of the Yankee chain of command
was that anything he did offensively was so much gravy. The
"big" Yankee bats would carry his glove. That those bats had
conspired for a lofty .235 batting average the past season must
have gone unnoticed. Perhaps the front office was too busy
watching reruns of the 1961 Yankee highlights film. Giving up
Linz was considered no risk, which betrayed a certain insensitivity to the club's needs. Linz had earned the nickname
Supersub and was one of the few real pros left on a bench that
had been whittled by termites. He was three years younger
than Amaro, and he had never hit less than .250 until 1965.
The Yankees, though, were mindful that Tony Kubek was considering retirement, and so they felt they had no choice. They
needed a shortstop.

The Mikkelsen-Friend deal offers evidence that the den these
swaps were dreamed up in was probably filled with a golden
haze and run by proprietors who resembled Fu Manchu. Bob
Friend was a thirty-five-year-old right-hander who had pitched

grandly for some of the worst Pirate teams in history. As soon as the team surrounded him with personnel who could play, he became a big winner. During the last two seasons, however, he had won 21 games while losing 30. The Pirates were no longer a bad club.

Mikkelsen was a twenty-six-year-old right-handed reliever who had thrown well during his two-year stay in New York. Dealing him for Friend was the sort of swap the Yankees could (and often did) make in the fifties: young pitcher with a lot of promise for the grizzled, established veteran. The theory was that the veteran would come from a mediocre club and automatically be rejuvenated as soon as he put on pinstripes. As for the youngster with all the promise? "Well, hell," the Yankees thought, "we've got plenty of them." The problem with that sort of thinking was that it was no longer true. Now it was the Yankees who were the mediocre club. Going to them was no longer a step up; it was no longer a guarantee of improvement through osmosis. Trading away a twenty-six-year-old pitcher at that point was a no-no. In *Casablanca*, Claude Raines admonishes Humphrey Bogart "How extravagant you are, throwing away women like that. Someday they may be scarce." That should have been the Yankees' attitude toward their young hurlers.

Sending Edwards to Cleveland for Lu Clinton was an exercise in pursuing someone else's fantasy. Clinton was a twenty-eight-year-old outfielder who had displayed enough power (52 home runs from 1962 to 1964) to make the deal interesting. A close examination of the record, though, reveals that most of those homers were hit while Clinton was in the employ of the Boston Red Sox, a team whose home games were played in Fenway Park. That was the place that turned right-handed pull hitters (Dick Gernert, Felix Mantilla, Rico Petrocelli, etc.) into Beantown versions of Superman, able to leap tall pitchers with a single bound. Yankee Stadium had the opposite effect. It had a Kryptonite-laced stretch called Death Valley that turned right-handed hitting Men of Steel into a feeble collection of Clark Kents. And then broke their glasses.

There was one right-handed power hitter who could have solved the Stadium dimensions, and he was available. Frank Robinson had fallen out of favor with the management of the Cincinnati Reds and was being aggressively shopped around. One potential customer was the Yankees. They intimated that they might be willing to let go of Joe Pepitone in exchange for Robby. The Reds were interested, but their main object in trading Robinson was to beef up their pitching. They asked that Jim Bouton be included. That was the deal: Bouton and Pepitone for Robinson. New York, which ascribed to the theory that you can never have too many sore-armed pitchers, came back and asked for pitcher Jim O'Toole. Things get a bit foggy here, but apparently the Reds started to make noises about Mel Stottlemyre or Al Downing and the deal was aborted. It was precisely the sort of trade the Yankees needed to make. At the time, it was a calculated risk. Bouton and Pepitone were both in their mid-twenties, and 1965 was the first off-season either of them had ever experienced. Robinson was, according to the legendary assessment of Cincinnati general manager Bill DeWitt, an "old thirty." What DeWitt forgot to mention was that Robinson was also the kind of competitor who could elevate an entire team with his mere presence. Had the Yankees acquired him it would not have been a cureall, but it would have been a good start. He would have kept them respectable while they rebuilt. It was the sort of move the club seemed incapable of making anymore. Perhaps Pepitone's guardian angel was watching over him and derailed the exchange. The idea of Pepi, with his hair dryer, hip-huggers, shoulder bag, assorted wigs, and Don Juan reputation, playing for baseball's most conservative team, in one of the country's most conservative cities, opens up a Pandora's box of possibilities, none of which boded well for Pepitone's physical or mental well-being.

The new year was not even a month old when the transaction for Amaro took on its full dimensions. On January 25, 1966, Tony Kubek announced his long-rumored retirement. He was twenty-nine years old. Kubek had told Houk of his decision at the end of the 1965 season, a campaign he had played with a backache which had caused him considerable distress. Houk apparently talked him into delaying his decision.

In November Kubek was examined at the Mayo Clinic. The final report showed that he had suffered damage to a nerve at the top of his spinal column, the result of improper healing of a neck injury. The shortstop thought the mishap might have occurred during a touch-football game he had played in the Army following the 1961 season. He remembered that during the course of the game, "I got racked up and lost a couple of teeth." Whatever the cause, X rays revealed he had suffered the medical equivalent of a broken neck without knowing it.

Kubek hadn't hit consistently for two seasons, and observed, "My reflexes are unreliable and erratic. A sudden, jarring movement could result in paralysis." Shortstop is a series of sudden, jarring movements choreographed into a silken fandago. Faced with the prospect of permanent disability, Kubek let his earlier decision become final.

Kubek's partner at second base, Bobby Richardson, also wanted to call it quits. He was tired of the endless road trips and the time spent away from his family. But he had entered into a pact with Kubek. They had agreed not to retire at the same time. Both realized it could be too rough on the organization. One of them would have to remain on the job for at least a year in order to help the infield make a smooth transition.

Kubek wasn't the only Yankee at the Mayo Clinic. Mantle was there. Surgeons excavated the outfielder's right shoulder and unearthed a loose particle from the tendon sheath. This was the malicious pest that had wreaked so much havoc with the strength and accuracy of Mickey's throwing arm and had hampered him at the plate. After the operation, the doctors reported no complications and said that Mantle would be ready for the start of spring training in late February.

When the team assembled in Florida, the feeling was the club would make amends for 1965 and that, despite the loss of Kubek, they would come back just as strong as ever. They were missing the point.

Baseball had legislated against the eventuality of another Yankee dynasty. They didn't make it illegal, they just placed enough obstacles in the way to make it almost impossible for the Bombers, or any other team, to be that powerful again.

Under the new regulations, a team could only control forty players on their roster at a time. In the past they could control many times that number. For a team with the Yankees' reputation, this had been a solid advantage. Everyone wanted to play for them. If they signed a hundred of the top-shelf amateur players in the country, the odds were excellent that 10 percent of them would reach the major leagues and have viable careers. That's an incredible number. With the forty-man-roster rule, the front office had to take care in deciding whom to protect and whom to risk losing to another club in the draft. Do you give sanctuary to the veteran who might have one or two good seasons left in him, or do you discard him and give the roster spot to an untried rookie? Either way there were hazards involved.

The rule also cut down on the total universe of talent the Yankees had to draw from and decreased the margin of error allowed in assessing that talent. This assessment was crucial. Once an unprotected player was claimed by another club, he was lost. No talent was received in return. The Yankees had some great scouts, but they also had some who had made their reputations because of the club's ability to stockpile talent. In their cases, nobody remembered the thirty guys they signed who went bust; they were too busy raving about the one who didn't. None of this was helped when the club fired George Weiss in 1960. Weiss had forgotten more about baseball talent and how to gauge it than the rest of the Yankee organization could ever hope to know.

The second set of rules to be utilized to "break up the Yankees" were those covering the free-agent draft, not to be confused with the "millionaire's lottery" of today. This draft came into being in 1965, and it was seen not only as a measure taken to stop the Bombers, but as a method to restore sanity to teams caught in the clutches of "bonus baby" madness. Prior to its inception, teams could compete for the rights to sign any prospect who caught their fancy. This meant the top talents could choose from any one of twenty major league teams. Just the name New York Yankees conjured up enough romantic visions of Ruth, Gehrig, DiMaggio, et al. to give the team a decided edge over, say, the California Angels, before the Yankees even had to check their bank balance. Now teams didn't have to compete at all. Instead, they would take part in a draft, choosing in reverse order of the previous year's standings, for the right to negotiate with a particular individual. The player would only be allowed to deal with the club drafting him, unless he chose not to sign. In that case, he would wait for next year's draft where, once again, he would be chosen by a club. This not only kept the big bonus payments in check, it also kept the rich from getting richer by padding their farm system with all the best talent. That this system is probably illegal is another matter.

When CBS began to get involved with the ball club on a more active level, they found they had bought a pig in a poke. With the emphasis on *pig*. Mike Burke recalled, "When we really got into the ball club, we found out that there was no farm system left. There was only one player coming up who was of any quality, and that was Bobby Murcer. The whole system had been left to go to seed." New York, under Dan Topping, had stopped spending money. The pre-draft bonus babies they should have signed were gobbled up by the other clubs. It was a way of keeping the club's ledgers in the black. That was becoming increasingly hard to do.

The Yankees, despite their successes on the field, had not been a big draw at home. Their attendance had been spiraling downward since 1961. They were the league's best road draw, but they received a miniscule share of those revenues. As soon as the team started to lose badly, home attendance got worse. People still turned out to see them in other cities, but in their own ball park many games seemed to be attended only by a few intimate friends. A lot of the problem stemmed from the club's corporate image. Rooting for U.S. Steel was fine, but not when they were in the process of declaring bankruptcy.

The New York Mets, on the other hand, weren't having any problems drawing crowds. They were in a National League town, whose baseball appetite had been limited to starvation rations since the defection of the Brooklyn Dodgers and New York Giants to Paradise West. They had a sparkling new stadium, a courteous staff, and a location convenient to mass transit. More importantly, they were fun. Part of the reason they were fun, and the Yankees weren't, was the way the two clubs were perceived by the fans. This perception was aided by the sportswriters. Vic Ziegel was working for the *New York Post* during this time and had an opportunity to cover both clubs. He observed, "When I first covered the Yankees in 1964, they were still big winners, and, yes, you could say there was an arrogance or smugness about them. It was a different time. It doesn't seem like that long ago, only eighteen years, but the relationship between writers and players and writers and clubs was very different from what you have today. And that is to say you had a lot of flat-out house men, guys who wrote stories that found favor with the Yankee management. I don't believe they wrote them because it got them a better seat on the plane, or an extra drink after the game. I think they wrote them because they were there during the team's good years, and they identified with the Yankees. They wanted to be with the Yankees and wrote the kind of stories the Yankees wanted to read only because those were the kind of stories they wanted to write. You know, when the team started to lose, those guys were much harsher on the club than the younger writers, like myself, who had no history with the team. The reason they came down so hard was because they were bitterly disappointed. They were crushed. They had to cover games all year, and the team wasn't good anymore. It made them furious. The new writers who came along, represented up to that point by Lenny Shecter, who I thought was the best sportswriter I had ever read, were tough on them too....

"Now, that doesn't mean that sportswriters or their editors got together and said, 'Let's promote the Mets' or 'Let's build

Shea Stadium.' But writers were thrilled when the Mets came along. For one thing it was Casey [Stengel], and for another it wasn't the Major and Mickey Mantle cursing you and turning away. The Mets were a godsend. Their first spring training they were covered by Bob Lipsyte, George Vecsey, and Lenny. This was crème de la crème stuff. There were a lot of reputations made that spring, and the writers had fun. You can't overplay how important that was to the Mets because writers help shape the attitudes of fans. If they had written 'Mets Lose!' all the time and nothing else, the fans would have been turned off. Instead, the way it was written, the hipper fans said, 'Hey, we can celebrate losing,' because nobody was taking winning very seriously. The atmosphere was laid back. The Met players were extremely cooperative—they had no reason not to be—and, for a couple of years, it spawned a golden age. The writers were perfect. It gave us some of the best sportswriting ever seen in New York."

The Yankees took the offensive to combat this Met fever. They passed out thousands of free tickets to the New York cabbies, designed new promotions, and embarked on a new advertising campaign. None of it worked. Spontaneity and fun, by their very nature, cannot be manufactured. They simply have to *be*. At Yankee Stadium, they weren't.

Johnny Keane didn't give a hoot about any of this. He had a team to get in shape and a reputation to salvage. As spring training wore on, both objectives seemed within reach. Lu Clinton and Clete Boyer were leading an attack that looked ready to resume its pre-crash vitality. The pitching was mind-boggling, especially the work of the two veterans, Ford and Friend, and two rookies, left-handed starter Fritz Peterson and a right-handed reliever with the unlikely name of Dooley Womack.

Ruben Amaro was fitting snugly in the Yankee infield and Mantle was healthy. Keane wisely permitted him to take his time recovering from his off-season surgery. On April 8, Mantle started his first spring training game, playing left field. This was important; rumors of his switching to first base had already started circulating. The next afternoon, he started in center field for the first time in a year. With Mantle able to handle center on a regular basis, the team took on a different cast. The defense was improved and the club's confidence, which had taken a shellacking, was restored. When the exhibition season ended, the popular notion that the Yankees wouldn't be back for a long time was getting a revision. For the first time since 1962, the club won more than half its exhibition games. They finished 17–11, winning seven of their final eight games and finishing third in the overall Grapefruit League standings. The Chicago White Sox were the only American League team with a better record.

Keane, the evangelist on the virtues of "the winning habit," was ecstatic. What he didn't know was that, in a short space of time, his team was going to be like a group of disgusted smokers. They were going to kick the habit.

Most of these players, by the way, had not become any more enamored of Keane. They just figured they would win in spite of him.

On April 12, the club took the field at Yankee Stadium to start the 1966 season against the Detroit Tigers. They lost 2–1, as Mickey Lolich beat Ford before an Opening Day crowd of 40,006. That was the biggest mob to attend a Stadium opener since 1951. Apparently they believed in spring training too.

That first loss served as the opening page to a most painful April diary:

APRIL 14, HOME—Doubleheader loss to Detroit, 3–2, 5–3. Ramos loses first game in relief of Stottlemyre. Bob Friend KO'd by five-run fourth inning in the nightcap.

APRIL 16, BALTIMORE—Peterson wins first major league start, 3–2. Team record: 1–3.

APRIL 17, BALTIMORE—Orioles gouge Al Downing, 7–2, behind Dave McNally. Amaro hurt in collision with Tresh. Rookie Bobby Murcer to get shot at shortstop. Will have to play his way out of lineup.

APRIL 18, BALTIMORE—Murcer wastes no time in doing exactly
that. Commits three errors, including one in
the seventh inning that costs the Yankees a 5–
4 decision. Ford also charged with an error.

The Yankees had committed nine errors in six games; five
were committed at short. There was other bad news. Mantle
hurt his shoulder after his first hard throw of the season and
Richardson was spiked by new Oriole Frank Robinson during
the April 18 game and was forced to leave for treatment of his
wound. He was replaced by rookie Horace Clarke. After the
game, the Yankees announced that Boyer would be moved to
short, Tresh would come in from left and play third, and Roy
White would replace Tresh in the outfield. White had won the
James J. Dawson Award that spring as the team's most promising rookie. Roger Maris, who was not hitting, would be platooned in right with Lu Clinton.

This was the beginning of the end for Johnny Keane. The
moves made on April 18 were the type made while running
scared. It could be argued that moving Boyer to short made
sense; Boyer was the best infielder on the club. But by placing
Tresh at third, Keane was playing two men out of position.
Tresh should have been the shortstop. He had come up as a
shortstop, and his experience would have made him vastly
more comfortable there than at Boyer's position.

Also, consider that Murcer was supposed to be this club's
next star. What sort of thinking guides the decision to demote
a rookie after a one-game trial? Where was the regard for his
confidence? There wasn't any, just as there wasn't any concern
about the feelings of Maris, a player from whom the Yankees
absolutely needed a productive season in order to have any
chance of winning. Who platoons an essential player like that
after only six games? The answer is a manager who can only
see a 1–5 record and the vultures circling overhead.

The diary picks up:

APRIL 19, CLEVELAND—Yankees' first game with new infield alignment. Team plays well, but Sam McDowell beats Stottlemyre, 3–1.

APRIL 20, CLEVELAND—Friend pitches six and one-third innings. Allows one run, five hits. Strikes out two; walks none. Good news. The bad news is that he pulls a calf muscle and has to leave with a 2–1 lead. Ramos relieves. Gives up three runs. Yanks lose, 4–2. Ramos is 0–3. The Yanks are 1–7. Last place. After loss, club announces Ford has viral infection, will be sidelined indefinitely.

In the first eight games, Keane had used eight different lineups. For game number nine, he announced the following starters:

> Richardson, 2b
> White, lf
> Pepitone, 1b
> Tresh, 3b
> Mantle, cf
> Maris, rf
> Howard, c
> Boyer, ss

This was to be considered the starting lineup until further notice. They took the field on:

APRIL 22, HOME—Orioles and McNally beat the Yanks again, 4–2. Peterson gets his first major league loss. Boyer, who was one of the hitting stars of spring, is 2 for 29.

APRIL 24, HOME—Stottlemyre pitches third straight hard-luck game. O's beat N.Y. 3–2.

APRIL 25, HOME—Friend is racked up by Boston, 8–4. Ken Sanders gets first major league victory in relief of

Earl Wilson. No other New York American League club, including the Highlanders, had ever lost 10 of its first 11 games. Until now.

APRIL 26, HOME—Yanks beat Sanders, who had relieved Jim Lonborg, 7–6. Boyer homers. Womack gets W in relief of Ford. Club breaks seven-game losing streak. Mantle and Maris each get first rbi of season. Team record: 2–11.

The calendar shows the Yankees had a much-needed day of rest scheduled for April 29. They didn't enjoy it. Management had scheduled an exhibition game that day against the West Point team. That was a game New York managed to win. Barely. The final score was 1–0. The game was an indication of how far the team had fallen.

The Yankees played their "regular" lineup against West Point and started Jim Bouton. In a game they were apparently trying to win, they managed all of four hits off Army starter Barry DeBolt, who struck out eight. Eight. Mantle got the game-winning rbi in the fifth when he scored Bobby Richardson from third with a groundout to second. Womack got the save, but he needed the help of a game-ending double play. If the Yankees seemed embarrassed, it probably wasn't only because of the score. Apparently, before the game got under way, the Army and the Yankee management entered into an interesting agreement. The game was scheduled for seven innings, but if, after that time, the Yankees were trailing, they would play nine. It had reached that point. The Yankees were looking for an edge against a team of players that didn't have a Triple-A prospect among them.

The season resumed:

APRIL 30–MAY 1, HOME—One bright stretch. Yanks take two of three from Kansas City. The one loss is a 1–0 shutout, Rollie Sheldon beating Ford. Yanks climb out of last place.

May 3–May 5, home—Crawl back down. Lose three straight to Cleveland: 1–0, 2–1, 4–0. Murcer is optioned to Toledo.

May 6, california—Angels whip Ford 7–4. Yanks, 4–16, back in last place. *Keane is fired*. Replaced the next day by Ralph Houk.

Dan Topping made the decision. In a telegram to Houk, he declared:

> Have decided we simply must make a change, despite our efforts and hopes to snap out of this. As discussed, Johnny Keane will be relieved immediately, and you are appointed manager, on a four-year contract, through November 1, 1969. Internal management moves to be made in near future that will relieve you of your g.m. [general manager] duties, per your request. Daniel R. Topping Jr. to assume duties as acting g.m.

Keane rode the team bus, with the players, to Anaheim. Once there, he called his last team meeting and said his final farewells. Mantle summed up the team's public face by saying, "I feel I let this man down.... I think we all let him down." Privately, most of the club was glad to see him go, especially since it meant that Houk was back in the skipper's chair.

In truth, the team *had* let Keane down, but he never made an attempt to improve the situation. He had a very specific idea of how a manager was supposed to run a team and, in part, this was his undoing. He couldn't adapt. For a manager, there is only one worse failing: an inability to win.

As for the Yankees, they should have reacted as the professionals they were supposed to be. They didn't. Having said this, it becomes important to point out that had this situation been rectified, it wouldn't have made a bit of difference. With or without the convenient excuse of Johnny Keane, this was a bad ball club. Keane did not cause that. He had merely been the wrong man on the wrong team at the wrong time. Evidence that the club's poor showing was more an indication of its true caliber than of any managerial influence was provided not long after Keane's dismissal.

Houk took the reins of the team and immediately made some changes. He brought back some of the Yankee swagger and infused the air with his unquenchable optimism. To reporters who inquired about the team's grave state of affairs, he opined, "I still believe it [the team] can win the pennant. That may shake a lot of people up, but if I didn't [believe it], I wouldn't go back to managing. We still have 142 games to play. Right?"

Right. The first 16 of those games made Houk look like a genius. Under Keane, the Yankees had been getting good pitching, pitching that was being wasted. It was being undone by an offense that had managed only 6.4 hits per game and had a mere 12 home runs. It was immediately obvious to Houk that he had to get the offense going. His first move was to put Roy White into the leadoff spot, flip-flopping him with Richardson. Richardson would bat second. Mantle was returned to the third position. Pepitone would bat cleanup, and Tresh, who was slumping, was dropped to fifth. Maris followed. Houk was mindful that Maris's benching did not sit well with the right fielder or the club. By placing him back in the regular lineup, Houk was expressing the confidence he still had in the two-time Most Valuable Player. He was also making a known truth even clearer. If the Yankees were to have any chance of winning, a healthy, happy, and hitting Maris was an absolute necessity. Howard and Boyer filled out the order. With the attack set, a new batting coach was sought. His job was to bring the sickly Yankee sticks out of their coma. The new bat doctor was Wally Moses, an acknowledged master in the study of the mysterious movements of spherical entities.

The immediate results? Well, naturally, the Yankees went on a rampage, reeling off 12 wins in their next 16 games. All of a sudden, this was a scary team. They scored runs in clusters, played tight defense, and maintained the same level of pitching excellence they had established before the managerial change. By May 24, they stood 16–20, nine and a half games out of first, but only two out of fourth. Then, just as it did in 1965, the bottom dropped out. The team had merely been the benefactors of that unexplainable baseball alchemy that almost always works its spell whenever a managerial switch is made. Stottlemyre, who had earlier lost games due to bad luck and ill support, now lost them on merit. His earned run average hovered near 4.00. Downing continued to be an enigma. No one on the staff had as much stuff, and no one was as blatantly inconsistent. He would blow away the Frank Robinsons and the Boog Powells, and then get beaten by Andy Etchebarren. He could completely shut down powerhouses like the Twins and then, in his very next start, be mangled by the anemic Kansas City Athletics. He was like that all year.

Bob Friend, tabbed by the front office as that veteran fourth starter they needed, was sold to the Mets on June 15. His career was over. The two rookies, Peterson and Womack, did just fine. Peterson's first tour of the league served as a showcase for the best control in baseball. On a better team he would have been the league's Rookie of the Year. Womack proved valuable as a long reliever.

The most prominent name in that group, by reason of its omission, was Whitey Ford's. Ford had pitched well enough. He eventually finished with a record of 2–5, but his ERA was only 2.47. The problem was that he couldn't pitch very often. The circulation problems of the past had revisited. On August 25, he went back under Dr. Cooley's knife and had a six-inch vein from his leg transplanted into his shoulder. The operation was a success. When it was over, for the first time in several years, Whitey Ford had a pulse.

Sabermetrics is the mathematical and statistical analysis of the records of baseball. Practitioners of this sometimes exact science would find the Yankees of 1966 an excellent study in the real complexity of baseball numbers. The offense, centering around Mantle (108 games, .288, 23 homers, 56 RBI), Pepitone (.255, 31 homers, 83 RBI) and Tresh (.233, 27 homers, 68 RBI), scored the fifth highest number of runs (611) in the league. The defense, though not as quick as in their salad days, was still better than that of half the league. The pitching staff finished fifth in ERA (3.42), and allowed only one more run (612) than the team scored. All these numbers added up to a record of 70–89. Last place. This incongruity between the team's performance on paper and their position in the standings served as a final comment on a team whose inconsistency was its only consistent trait.

It was the first time since 1912 that a Yankee team had finished in the basement. There was no solace in the fact that their winning percentage (.440) was the highest for a last-place club in American League history. This was not a balm for the fans who, once again, did not exactly flock to the stadium in record numbers (1,124,648). The dwindling attendance figures provided the best editorial on a disappointing season that saw the club finish 26½ games behind Frank Robinson and the Baltimore Orioles.

The fans weren't the only ones upset. The players, many of whom still viewed winning as a birthright, were disgusted. Not just by the finish, but by the obvious lack of any foreseeable change in the situation.

Steve Hamilton had a special view of the results. Unlike most of his teammates, he had played on losing teams before joining New York in 1963. Upon joining the club, he immediately became a valuable asset to two championship teams. He was a left-handed pitcher with a wicked curve who could pitch long or short relief with equal effectiveness.

"The first day I joined this club," Hamilton said, "I just sat in the locker room and stared at everybody. I mean, I had never been in a room with so many great ballplayers. I mean, on the [Washington] Senators you had a pretty safe chance of keeping your job as long as you were breathing and could show up at the park every day. I had played professional basketball and so I really wasn't awed by professional athletes. But I was awed by the Yankees. They knew they were going to win and they were very loose. There was less pressure pitching for those champion Yankee teams than pitching for the Senators, because not only did they have supreme confidence, they also had guys who could make the plays. When you got guys like Boyer, Kubek, Richardson, and Pepitone, there wasn't any way anyone would get many by them. They caught everything that should be caught. Mantle was declining somewhat in his ability on balls going back or coming in, but sideways he could catch anything. Roger Maris was a much greater player than anybody ever gave him credit for in New York. And Tresh was playing well. We had great defense and a great attitude.

"I remember one night we were playing in Anaheim, and John Blanchard said we were going to win this game. Well, we were down three runs in the top of the ninth, and there were two outs when he said it, so I thought, 'This guy can't be serious.' As I remember it, Art Fowler was pitching for the Angels. He walked a batter. Then he walked another batter, and the next guy got a base hit. Then Roger hit a home run and we hang on to win the game 4–3. I couldn't believe it. This was the Yankee spirit that prevailed during that winning period. They felt like they could win every game. Everybody they played was aware of that. Any time a team would get a lead against us, and it would get into late innings, they started looking for the Yankees to come on. You could see it.

"That made the bad years very frustrating. It was terrible, knowing how great the team had been, and then playing badly. Everybody started beating us and that's when we started to get cheered on the road. I wanted so badly to make them boo us again. You knew you were good when people rooted against you.

"I knew we were down the tubes because Mickey was playing left and his legs were worse than ever. His arm was bothering him. Key players got injured or retired, and there went the ball club. Pepitone was very unstable. He drove in a lot of runs, but only when there were good people around him. When he had to take the responsibility he was no good. And the pitchers found out that Tommy Tresh was purely a fastball hitter. Now with our club, if you put Tresh in with all those good hitters, he got fastballs. Once you take Mantle, Maris, and all those other guys out of the lineup, you don't care if you walk Tom Tresh by pitching him breaking balls. And you had to see some of the kids they were bringing up from the minors. I couldn't believe it. I remember spring training with Washington. They didn't have many prospects. But when I got over and saw what the Yankees had coming up...well, it was bare. I mean, they had what they had in the big leagues, and that was it. They should have fired every scout they had. In 1971 I was with the Giants, and they were shipping guys like Garry Maddox, Gary Matthews, and Dave Kingman back to the minors! I looked at them and thought, 'My gosh, I can't believe this!' I had never seen so many good ball players in my life. They had George Foster sitting on the bench. But the Yankees of the sixties had nothing like that. They had no farm system.

"People talk about Ralph Houk being a great manager, and he was. He made his players feel confident by showing confidence in them. I learned a lot from Houk, the way he handled people, the psychology he used. He was great at working a pitching staff, especially the bullpen. It seems that no matter how bad we were we always came up with a decent staff. Part of the credit for that would go to the catchers.

"I threw to two great catchers in the time I pitched in the majors. One was Elston Howard. The other one will probably surprise you. It was Jake Gibbs.

"Jake was actually a better fundamental catcher, and he didn't catch until he got to Triple A. He came up as a third baseman. Jim Hegan, who is the foremost authority in the universe on catching, worked with him. Jake ended up breaking two or three fingers in the process, but he learned. He was great on fundamentals. Jake would shift his body on hitters and you couldn't throw a pitch by him. He was also an intelligent catcher. He worked a pitcher the way a pitcher should be worked, and he had a good arm. Pitchers liked to throw to Jake.

"You know, when Thurman Munson came up he was a hard catcher to throw to because he didn't set up well. Jake was there at the same time, and he was a much better catcher, but you had to play Thurman because you knew he was going to be great. Jake was very protective of Thurman; he wasn't resentful at all. He helped Thurman with his fundamentals. That was a Yankee trademark: guys teaching you how to improve yourself even if you may be a threat to their job. I remember Whitey Ford would show guys how to throw mudballs all the time. He would teach them all that illegal stuff. Or the legal pitches, too. The Yankees helped each other.

"The old feeling started to come back in 1970. Thurman came up and, oh, could he sting the ball. The ball would jump off his bat. He could hit a ball to right as hard as anybody. When you see a young kid come up, and he's a right-handed hitter who can hit the ball hard the other way, you know he's something special."

On September 19, two weeks before the season's end, Topping resigned as Yankee president, selling his remaining interest in the club to CBS. Topping had been spending less and less time with the team. He found the corporate structure of CBS too confining. When it became clear to the network that, as Mike Burke later put it, "Topping just wasn't going to function and wasn't happy," a decision was made to buy him out. A question immediately came up: "Who will run the club?" The final answer evolved through a process that was an excellent example of American corporate decision making at its best. Again, the recollection is Burke's: "As a working-stiff member of the board, I had begun to spend a great deal of time at the Stadium. There was the question of exactly who should take over the handling of the day-to-day operations. So I said, 'I'll do it.' And [William S.] Paley asked, 'Are you sure you want to?' I said, 'Sure.' That was in September of 1966."

Burke had seen enough of the baseball setup to understand that a lot of hard decisions were going to have to be made in order to bring the team back. The first changes would involve how the team was being presented to and perceived by the public. The Yankees were, after all, in the entertainment business.

Mel Allen, the team's popular radio-TV announcer, who had

become as closely identified with the Yankees as any player, had been fired in December 1964 and replaced by Joe Garagiola. The exact reasons for the dismissal remain murky, but it would be fair to say that management didn't think that Allen was what he once had been. When asked about the firing in 1982, Allen would only say, "I don't want to get into that, but I will say this: The Yankees didn't fire me. Perhaps they could have prevented it and didn't, but it wasn't their decision to let me go."

Allen's replacement, Garagiola, was teamed with Red Barber, Jerry Coleman, and Phil Rizzuto. During the next two seasons, rumors kept popping up that the Yankees were not all that pleased with the work of the quartet. These rumors were stoutly denounced as having no basis in fact. What they did have a basis in was some memos Topping had been passing out to Perry Smith, head of the radio-TV staff. In one dated May 27, 1966, Topping stated, "We have the best broadcast crew in baseball; however, of late all four have been horrible ... and it has gotten so bad that I am tired of answering all the letters of complaint. ... The club is coming out of its slump; tell the other four to get going, too."

On September 21, Burke was forced to issue a denial of the rumored firing of Red Barber. He stated he had no plans for any changes in the broadcasting staff. At this time.

Five days later, Barber joined the new team president for breakfast at the Plaza Hotel. Before the first coffee had been served, Barber was axed. Burke later said the decision had been made two weeks before he took over the club, and that it was just unfortunate that it fell to him to be the bearer of the bad tidings. No reason for the dismissal was given; Burke refused to elaborate on it. Barber, when asked, replied, "I don't know why I was fired."

It is popularly theorized that the firing was due to one incident. The day before the firing, the smallest crowd in the history of Yankee Stadium, 413 fans, turned out and watched the Yankees lose to Chicago 4–1. Barber, who refused to shill for any club he worked for, demanded the cameraman pan the rows of empty seats that went on forever. The director refused, and Burke, called at Barber's insistence, concurred with that decision. Things were bad enough without giving air time to the silent rebuke of a lost season. This is the event that many point to as the cause of Barber's firing, and the team was criticized for punishing him for his integrity. Once again, it was those heartless Yankees.

Burke refused to defend the move, preferring not to be drawn into a bloody public duel with the popular announcer. It was a gesture that cost the Yankees a lot of fans. Fourteen years later, Burke claimed, "I did have the unpleasant chore of sitting down with Red, and telling him he would no longer be with the Yankees. The reason was, Red had begun to think of his 'catbird seat' as a pulpit, and he began to preach to all of us, us and the fans, and everybody else. He also started to do what I thought was a very unattractive thing, and that was put down [Phil] Rizzuto and [Joe] Garagiola as being stupid guys. He would make comments like, 'Unless you're born in spikes, you can't get a job in the broadcast booth anymore.' That kind of thing. He resented the athletes so severely, he just couldn't resist the temptation to try and make them look bad. For instance, if we were in Chicago, during the broadcast he would ask a question like, "Do you know the date of the Chicago Fire?' and one of the guys would say, 'No.' And Red would reply, 'Well, of course it was May such-and-such.' Things totally unrelated to baseball. The athlete in the broadcast booth really got to Red, and it made him bitter."

At least one reporter tells a different story. "The way I heard it," stated the reporter, "is that Barber was fired because he told Burke, in so many words, that he was full of shit. Burke was trying to tell Red about how he knew so much about the broadcasting business, and Red told him that he, meaning Burke, knew nothing about the broadcasting business. Or at least not enough worth talking about. That supposedly pissed Burke off. Red was a consummate professional, but a guy in sales at CBS told me he was gone a year before it happened."

Whatever the reason, Barber was out. The broadcasting chores would be handled by the three remaining ex-ballplayers: Coleman, Rizzuto, and Garagiola.

The next moves were designed to give the trio a product that would prove attractive to their listening and viewing audience. The Yankee front office had decided to back up the truck. Richardson had retired, as expected, at season's end. On October 8, another familiar name was lopped off the roster: Roger Maris was traded to the St. Louis Cardinals for Charley Smith, a journeyman third baseman who had only once driven in as many as 60 runs. No single act could dramatize more vividly the drop in value of Yankee stock. Two years prior to the deal, the Yankees wouldn't have traded Maris for any other player in baseball. At the end of the 1966 season, after two dismal summers that saw his batting average and power totals tumble, Maris was placed on waivers. Nobody claimed him. The myth of how the Yankees got fleeced by St. Louis grew only in hindsight. It was common knowledge that Maris would retire rather than return for another Yankee season. He was thirty-two, hurting, and still carried a hefty salary. Charley Smith was the best New York could do.

Five days later, the team announced the signing of Lee MacPhail Jr. as executive vice-president and general manager. The forty-eight-year-old MacPhail had spent the previous year as special adviser to baseball commissioner William Eckert. Prior to that, he had put in seven years as the president and general manager of the Baltimore Orioles and was largely responsible for building their world championship club of 1966.

His father had been part owner of the Yankees, serving as their president and general manager from 1945 to 1947. MacPhail Jr.'s first statement to the press spoke of management's interest in getting the team back on track, but also warned, "It will probably take five years to rebuild the team."

There were other developments. Whitey Ford and Hector Lopez were released. It spelled the end of Lopez's career; in Ford's case, the action was a mere technicality. It had, in fact, been done at his suggestion. The left-hander had every intention of staying with the club but did not see the sense of taking up a spot on the roster that could be used to protect a prospect.

When the winter meetings convened in Hawaii in late November, the Yankees were determined to be bullish in the trade market. Houk announced that the team's weakness at short was a principal factor in the team's last-place finish. So they went out and traded their third baseman. For an outfielder. Clete Boyer was dispatched to Atlanta for Bill Robinson, a twenty-three-year-old who had led the International League in hitting, and was immediately tabbed as either the next Mickey Mantle or the next Willie Mays, and for a thirty-eight-year-old reliever named Chi Chi Olivo. Boyer was dispatched, it was said, because the Yankees could no longer afford to carry his bat. In his last six years as a Yankee, Boyer batted a .243, hit 81 home runs, and drove in 344 runs. In the next six years, before the arrival of Graig Nettles, the Yankee third basemen who followed him hit a collective .231, with 23 home runs and 213 RBI. Not one of them could carry Boyer's glove.

Ironically, the trade was made by Lee MacPhail. His last swap for Baltimore had been the Frank Robinson deal. Two outfielders. Both right-handed. Both with the same last name. As time would testify, the results of the two deals would be vastly different.

The Yankees also made a stab at getting Maury Wills, the thirty-four-year-old shortstop for the Los Angeles Dodgers. For seven years, Wills had been the igniter of what masqueraded as the Dodger offense. He was available because of his age and his refusal to accompany the team on a post-season tour of Japan. The Yankees offered the Dodgers any pitcher on their roster, with the exception of Stottlemyre. Los Angeles had an interest in Downing, but they felt they needed to get a shortstop in the deal. Of course, if the Yankees *had* a shortstop, they wouldn't have been quite so hot to make the deal. The Dodgers put the trade on hold, saying they would shop Wills around. They would come back to the Yankees if they didn't get a better offer. They did. The Pirates sent them Bob Bailey, their sometimes slugging third baseman, and a young minor league shortstop who was the key to the deal for the Dodgers: Gene Michael. The Yankees finished the week by trading Pedro Ramos to the

Phillies for a young right-handed pitcher named Joe Verbanic and promising their supporters that the new-look Yankees were just beginning to get their act together.

The fans would not buy it. Many probably ruefully thought back to the day the sale of the club was announced and the league was assured that the Yankees would be a separate entity within the network empire. The team would be an autonomous organization, independent of the conglomerate.

After two years of suffering through bad ball clubs, the fans wished the reverse were true. If CBS had only been able to exercise the same power over the club that they held over its sitcoms, the last two seasons could have been quickly and mercifully canceled.

Chapter
THREE

On my way home from my office in Dallas, I passed some kids starting to work out. I wanted to jump out of my car and take some swings with them. It's a feeling that comes over you. I can't describe it.

—MICKEY MANTLE

THE first year of the supposed new era of Yankee resurgence got under way with trumpets blaring and cannons firing. The heavy artillery belonged to New York. On April 10, the club opened the 1967 season in Washington with an 8–0 thrashing of the always thrashable Senators. Bill Robinson ("Nobody is more nervous than I am") made his regular season debut in pinstripes with a double in the first inning and a long opposite field home run off left-hander Pete Richert in the seventh. It was a fitting entrance for the outfielder who had been hailed as "the new Mickey Mantle."

The old Mickey Mantle was also making a debut of sorts. A press conference had been called on January 31 to mark the signing of yet another $100,000 contract by the switch-hitter. It was during this announcement that the club presented Mantle with a first baseman's mitt autographed by Joe Pepitone. This was Mantle's and the team's way of verifying rumors that had first surfaced two years before. The Commerce Comet was no longer going to bash the stuffing out of his fragile knees while cruising across the endless reaches of the Stadium out-field. The move made sense. It gave the Yankees an outfield of Tom Tresh, once again a full-time left fielder; Joe Pepitone, who had switched to center field; and Bill Robinson, the rookie right fielder who was going to lead everyone to the Promised Land. Defensively, this trio had the potential to be the equal of any alignment in baseball. It also gave the club a chance to keep Mantle's bat in the lineup. The season before, Mantle had the second highest home run percentage in the league, but he had played in only 108 games. A 145-game season from him could make a dramatic impact on the team's total offensive picture.

Mantle was the team's triggerman; the Yankee attack re-volved around him. It wasn't just how he did in any particular game against any certain pitcher. It was what he might do that made him so vital. With Mantle batting fourth, the number three hitter could count on getting more than the common allotment of fastballs from hurlers afraid to confront Number Seven with men on base. When he was up, base runners could afford the luxury of a slightly better lead because the pitcher's concentration was focused solely on the danger at the plate. Mantle's name was the primary topic of conversation during the opposition's pre-game meetings. Each of his at-bats carried with it an implied threat: "I can change this game with just one good swing." His was a force exerted even before the game's first pitch had been thrown. He *was* the Yankees.

That last fact made it especially desirable to get his name in the batting order as often as possible. Under Mike Burke's di-rection, the organization had embarked on a campaign to re-verse the exodus of fans that had begun in 1963.

The club's stuffy image was stuck in the deep freeze and replaced by a warmer model. Ticket-takers, ushers, and con-cessionaires were instructed to treat each fan as "they would treat a guest in our home." Security people were informed that smiling was not prohibited and that they were working a base-ball stadium, not the Berlin Wall. The new etiquette was in-troduced by Burke. The Yankee president became an omnipresent spirit of goodwill at the Stadium. He endeavored to turn everyone into a Yankee fan. One sportswriter characterized him as a man who "shook more hands and kissed more babies than an Irish ward boss." It was said with approval, and it was a fitting analogy. Like any politician, Burke thoroughly enjoyed social intercourse. He liked meeting people and pressing flesh as much as he relished meeting challenges.

The club also borrowed a page or two from the manual of old rival Bill Veeck. Veeck, while owner of several A.L. franchises, had realized long ago that you could not guarantee the fans a win; the best clubs lose 40 percent of the time. So, on occasion, he offered them something more than just baseball. Burke and MacPhail did not race out and put a midget in the lineup, as Veeck had done (though, at the time, it couldn't have hurt), or arrange for a cow-milking contest between Mickey Mantle and Al Kaline. They did, however, attempt to make the Stadium fun.

Promotional days, usually viewed with disdain by the previous administration, became common attractions. A Yankee Hall of Fame was erected, with admission free to anyone attending a game. These were just part of a $1.3 million facelift that included improvements in Stadium seating, clubhouse refurbishments, new lights in the ball park and the immediate surrounding area, and new parking facilities. The Yankees became involved with the community. They organized dropout programs, rewarding students who achieved certain academic standards with free tickets. An open house party was staged at the Stadium in early February. Thirteen hundred season ticket holders were fed, glad-handed, and given a tour of the ball park that allowed them a glimpse of their home-team heroes.

This new raising of Yankee consciousness may have annointed the House That Ruth Built with mass quantities of peace and love, but it didn't improve the ball club a hair.

Four days after the Opening Day celebration, the Yankees had their home opener against the Boston Red Sox. Opposing New York, in His first big league start, was a tall left-handed pitcher who looked more like an anorexic high school student than a professional ballplayer. The reed-thin rookie was twenty-one-year-old Bill Rohr. For eight and two-thirds innings he might as well have been Lefty Grove. During that time, he struck out two and allowed five base runners. All on walks. Not a single Yankee had gotten a base hit. With two men out in the ninth, the only thing that stood between Mr. Rohr and a no-hitter was the bat of a thirty-eight-year-old catcher who had started his professional career in the Negro Leagues when Billy Rohr was three years old. Elston Howard was coming to the plate.

Howard was one of the few remaining players on the team who knew something about winning. It had been ingrained in him throughout his Yankee career. Howard was not about to let his team suffer the humiliation of a no-hitter, especially at the hands of a rookie. Patiently, he worked Rohr to a 3–2 count and then proceeded to foul off what seemed like an eternity of breaking pitches. Finally Howard lined a shot to right, just before the lunging reach of a diving Tony Conigliaro. Base hit. The next batter, Charley Smith, ended the game with a soft fly to right field. Afterward, Howard said, "It was the only time I ever got a hit and got booed in New York." One week later, on April 21, in a game few remember, Rohr made his second start of the season. Once again, the opposition was provided by the Yankees. But this time the locale had shifted to Fenway Park, the left-handed pitcher's version of Cambodia. That evening Rohr gave up eight hits, but, in many respects, he pitched an even better game than he had the week before. He struck out six. The only man he got behind on in the count was the only man he walked. The lone run scored by the Yankees in a 6–1 loss was tallied when Bill Robinson scored from second in the eighth on a single by...Elston Howard. Despite these two overpowering victories, the lefty was not destined to take a position in the Parthenon of Pitchers. If a fan were to look up his name in *The Baseball Encyclopedia*, he would find a career record of three wins and three losses. It was Bill Rohr's misfortune that every team did not resemble New York. In 1967, it was New York's misfortune that almost every pitcher they faced resembled Bill Rohr.

The following statement is the sort of thing said in spring training, usually by the manager of a bad ball club: "We may not move up in the standings, but we're a better ball club than we were last year." On the Yankees the opposite was true. They did move up, from tenth to ninth, but they were worse than the previous season.

The problem was hitting, or the lack of same. The last two summers had seen a definite decline in the team's offensive vitality. The 1967 season saw a complete breakdown.

The first major blow occurred on March 12 when, as Tom Tresh later recalled, "we were playing an exhibition game against the Baltimore Orioles. [Mark] Belanger hit a ball down the third base line. I was in left, and I went over to the line to try to hold it to a single. That was a play I usually made very well because of my shortstop upbringing; it was really no different than going deep in the hole. Anyway, when I got to the ball, I backhanded it, spun around, and went to make the throw to second. As I came down to set myself, my knee gave out under me, and I collapsed. I had ripped the cartilage in my knee. That was the kind of injury you couldn't tell too much about without surgery. I had a choice: I could be operated on immediately, and miss the season or most of it, or I could wait until the season was over." Tresh was asked by Houk, who needed the switch-hitter's bat in the lineup, to continue playing if it would not lead to further injury. The choice was Tom's.

During the early sixties, four men began to gain pieces of baseball stardom while playing left field: Billy Williams of the Chicago Cubs, Lou Brock of the St. Louis Cardinals, Carl Yastrzemski of the Boston Red Sox, and Tom Tresh. If a poll had been taken in 1965 asking which member of this quartet was most likely to end up in the Hall of Fame, the consensus would have named Tresh. He was an athlete seemingly born to greatness. Baseball uses five categories to measure a player's physical abilities: running, fielding, throwing, hitting for average, and hitting for power. A player who can do any four of these things exceptionally well is elevated to the status of superstar. Tresh could do all five. He also brought other dimensions to the game. He was a switch-hitter capable of exploding from either side of the plate. Shortstop was the position he played in 1962, and he performed well enough to be named American League Rookie of the Year. Three seasons later, he won a Gold Glove while dividing time between left and center fields. There seemed to be no limit to his talents. To those who kept sacred the eternal flame of Yankee tradition, he was the heir apparent to a torch passed from Ruth to Gehrig, from Gehrig to DiMaggio, from DiMaggio to Mantle, and now from Mantle to Tresh. The knee injury ended all that. Tresh, thinking only of the team, elected to play. Over the next three seasons he never again hit more than 14 home runs and never batted higher than .219. The flame had gone out. He was traded in 1969 to the Detroit Tigers for outfielder Ron Woods. It was not a typical trade made in the interest of unloading some excess baggage. Tresh had requested the deal. He had suggested to Ralph Houk and Lee MacPhail that if a trade could be worked out that would be beneficial to the club, and that would also send him back to his hometown of Detroit, he would be most appreciative. In a compassionate move, rare in baseball, the deal was made. Tresh played well for Detroit, alternating between left field and shortstop. At the end of the season, he retired. He was thirty-two years old.

After the injury, nobody appeared on the team to replace the power Tresh had lost. Mantle, with a .245 batting average, was the only Yankee to hit more than 20 home runs, hitting 22. Even this total was not as good as it seemed to be. On May 14 he had hit career homer number 500 against Stu Miller, giving the Yankees a 6–5 victory over Baltimore. This clout came in the midst of a streak that saw Mantle smack eight home runs in 13 games. It left him two games ahead of Roger Maris's record-setting pace of 1961. Mantle hit 10 home runs the rest of the season. That did not dim the affection of his fans or deter Mantle from enjoying himself. On the occasion of that 500th homer, Mantle was interviewed by retired Dodger pitcher Sandy Koufax, a rookie broadcaster for the NBC Game of the Week. It provided the slugger with an excellent opportunity to have some fun at the expense of an old adversary. The scenario went something like this:

KOUFAX: Mickey, how did you feel when you hit the home run off [Stu] Miller?

MANTLE: I figured I had to be pretty lucky because I could never
hit that little bastard before.

The usually unflappable Koufax looked to be in severe dis-
comfort. Visions of millions of parents clicking off television
sets throughout the country and forbidding their children ever
to watch another ball game must have danced through his head.
Mantle, having kept a straight face throughout, finally doubled
over, engulfed by a villainous convulsion of laughter. Mantle
had prearranged with the TV technicians not to start the audio
until he gave the sign. Koufax was holding a dead mike; the
youth of America had been spared.

So had American League pitchers, at least when they played
the Yankees. Pepitone led the club in RBI with 64. Horace
Clarke had the highest batting average among the regulars, an
embarrassing .272.

Yankee pitchers had to make do with what few runs the
offense could scrounge up. Stottlemyre had a misleading 15–
15 record that could have been 23–5 if the Yankees had discovered some way to score just three runs a game for him. Bill
Monbouquette, a midseason pickup from Detroit, pitched ef-
fectively, as did Fritz Peterson and the bullpen chief, Dooley
Womack. Womack laughed at the sophomore jinx by grabbing
18 saves and compiling a neat 2.41 ERA. Then there was Al
Downing.

This was the season people stopped chattering about the left-
hander's unfulfilled promise. In 202 innings pitched, he allowed
158 hits and walked 61 while striking out 171. He compiled a
14–10 record for a team that finished 72–90. In the past he
had seemed capable only of the occasionally spectacular, a trait
that was as frustrating as it was tantalizing. In this, the summer
of his pitching maturity, Downing was able to add the element
of consistency to his exceptional pitching arsenal: a down-
breaking curve that broke with the suddenness of a striking
asp and a searing fastball that made the malicious breaking
pitch seem a more welcome death. When the American League
All-Star team was announced, the Yankees had two represen-

tatives: Mantle, a sentimental choice, and Downing. The lefty pitched two scoreless innings in a game the National League won 2–1. This was his golden season.

It was also the final season, in Yankee uniforms, for both Whitey Ford and Elston Howard. Ford had actually pitched well early on, despite a 2–4 record. His ERA was a dazzling 1.64, and the rest of his numbers were equally impressive. However, his continuing circulatory problems had been complicated by the appearance of a bone spur in his left elbow. At his age, he had no desire to put in another appearance under the knife. He retired on May 30, the winningest pitcher in Yankee history.

Howard was dealt to the Boston Red Sox on August 3, the Yankees receiving two minor league pitchers: Ron Klimkowski and Pete Magrini. It was a well-deserved piece of luck for one of the game's classiest gentlemen. Howard became the guiding light that led the young Boston pitching staff through a four-team battle for the pennant into the American League championship. Carl Yastrzemski was both a Triple Crown winner and MVP that season. During his club's flag-clinching party he remarked, "We couldn't have won it without Ellie [Howard]."

The trading of Howard for young pitching was a wise move, but it further weakened an already porous defense. Mantle's experiment had deprived the team of Pepitone's Gold Glove at first and placed pressure on the entire infield. Mantle was too formidable an athlete to embarrass himself at the position, but the truth was he was barely adequate. At the same time, Tresh's injury mugged him of his mobility in left, making Pepitone's task of playing the biggest center field in baseball a constant penance. Ruben Amaro never recovered his former dexterity at short, and Charley Smith was a third baseman in name only. Only Horace Clarke, Richardson's successor at second, and Bill Robinson excelled in the field. Robinson's success with the glove, however, was outweighed by his failure at the plate. After his scintillating debut on Opening Day, he managed only 5 hits in his next 75 at-bats. He finished the season hitting .196. In Atlanta, Clete Boyer enjoyed the greatest season of his career, batting only .245, but hitting 26 home runs and accounting for 96 RBI. Roger Maris also found happiness in St. Louis. His numbers were not as gaudy as Boyer's, but he was an integral part of the world champion Cardinals. To disappointed and frustrated Yankee fans, these numbers were not a comfort. Neither was the fact that when the results of the MVP voting were announced, not one Yankee got a mention. That had never happened before. Even Paul Casanova, catcher for the sixth-place Senators, got a vote, and he had batted .248.

When the following season got under way, Yankee loyalists were further discouraged. All signs pointed to another long summer of pop-ups, misplays, and wasted pitching heroics. The club had not made one significant addition during the off-season. Spring training did not nominate any rookie candidates for the position of folk hero. Nobody could be blamed for not knowing that this team would go farther on less talent than any baseball expert had any right to expect.

A perusal of the club's roster revealed an assemblage of twenty-five names brought together without apparent rhyme or reason. It was a shaky collection of green talent sprinkled in with the aged, the wounded, and the cast off. They were a team merely by the virtue of their mass availability. Yet they won ball games. Not enough to make people think that the dynasty was about to return. Mobs did not gather in the streets at season's end and rasp, "Break up the Yankees!" But, throughout the league, the club did manage to win back a tiny share of their rivals' respect.

It did not happen right away. The first two months of the season reinforced the pre-season view that this summer would be identical to the last three. The fans had little to cheer them. Mantle was good for an occasional spurt of homers, the obligatory last hurrah. But the team was having an embarrassingly hard time lifting the club batting average over .200. Only Roy White seemed unaffected by the offensive malaise. He was tattooing pitchers from both sides of the plate.

White had been signed by Yankee scout Tuffy Hashem in 1962. He was named the Southern League's MVP only three years later. After spending the entire 1966 season with the Yankees and batting a meager .225, White was demoted to Spokane in the Pacific Coast League. By the middle of the 1967 season, White was batting .343, a mark that prompted the Yankees to recall the switch-hitting outfielder. Once again he found major league pitching to be a puzzle. But, after the first six weeks of the following season, it was White who had become the mystery. Pitchers didn't have a clue what to throw him. By the end of May, the Yankees were three games under .500, and seven and a half games behind the front-running Detroit Tigers. Roy White was hitting 60 points over .300, and he wasn't running behind anybody. He was leading the league.

The rest of his teammates struggled. When they finally began to hit it didn't make any difference. The bullpen, always a strength on a Houk-led team, was in a shambles. No one could come out of it to protect a lead in the late innings. The Yankees had a talented starting pitching staff: Stottlemyre, Peterson, Monbouquette, and an amazing rookie, Stan Bahnsen, who got his chance in the wake of a sore arm suffered by Downing. It was driving Houk batty to watch them pitch inning after inning of terrific ball, only to have their work end up as so much dishwater the moment the bullpen went into action. This was doubly galling because a stingy relief staff was mandatory on a club that scored so few runs; it was going to be used and used frequently. By the All-Star break it looked as if no one on the team could do the job. Each fireman the Yankees turned to entered the game equipped with his own can of kerosene.

On July 12, with the club 37–43, MacPhail made a move to rectify the situation. He sent Monbouquette, who had cooled off after a feverish start, to the San Francisco Giants for relief pitcher Lindy McDaniel. This was one of those midseason deals that received little notice, if any. McDaniel had twice won the National League's Fireman of the Year Award, but he had just come off a mediocre season and had lost the star-status role of short man to Frank Linzy. It didn't take a genius to figure out why he was available. One look at his numbers at the time of the deal gives an adequate hint: 12 appearances, no wins, no losses, no saves. In 19 innings pitched he had allowed 30 hits and 5 walks. His ERA was an astronomical 7.58. The reason Lee MacPhail was willing to take a gamble on him was that the reports on the right-hander indicated his arm was sound.

His poor pitching was probably the result of inactivity and the haphazard way he was being used. Considering McDaniel's past accomplishments and the current state of the bullpen, the deal seemed a pretty good risk.

It took a month after McDaniel's arrival for the bullpen to get straightened out. In that time the team fell far below .500, but, during those four weeks, McDaniel established himself as the club's ace reliever. This enabled the rest of the bullpen to fall into line. Joe Verbanic, a failure in short relief, became a revelation as a swing man, starting or relieving depending on the club's needs. Dooley Womack was transformed into the ideal long man, holding the fort until McDaniel's entrance. And Steve Hamilton was allowed to return to his role of left-handed specialist, coming in to nip the Boog Powells, the Norm Cashes, and the Carl Yastrzemskis with the game on the line. As the relievers rose from the ashes, the starting pitchers became even stronger.

Stottlemyre had reached a point where he wasn't going to be bothered by the lack of scoring. He was going to win 20 games if he had to pitch a shutout every outing. Peterson inherited Stottlemyre's mantle as the hard-luck guy, constantly on the wrong end of a 3–2 or 2–1 score. Still, he managed to keep his head above .500. The rookie Bahnsen outpitched everybody. After his first tour of the league, batters were impressed, but wanted to see him again before they rendered a judgment. After a second taste they wished they hadn't bothered. Bahnsen couldn't have hired a press agent to write all the superlatives they were heaping on him.

With his staff rolling, Ralph Houk stepped into a time warp to fashion the team's attack: inside baseball from the days of John McGraw. The 1968 season would end up as the Year of the Pitcher, a season that saw batting averages plummet. Only six men in the American League would hit over .280. In 1930, thirteen teams hit over that figure. Thirty-eight years later the pitchers got their revenge.

This was great news for the Yankees. Their newly rejuvenated batch of pitching talent could play one-run baseball with almost anybody in the league except the Tigers. Detroit was a team that lacked the manners to play the same game as everybody else, an act of rudeness that resulted in their owning a whole bunch of home runs and a commanding hold on first place. They were, however, saved from the perils of complete boorishness by the performance of their right-handed pitching ace, Denny McLain. McLain was the league's pitcher of the year in the Year of the Pitcher. With his 31 victories, he became the first 30-game winner in the majors since Dizzy Dean in 1934.

The Yankees' bad start and lack of punch overruled any real chances of catching that talented squad, but in August they began to show that they were capable of playing with anyone else in the league. It started with a three-game sweep of the California Angels in Anaheim, a siege that was the beginning of a six-week campaign that would have the club win 29 of its next 39 games. This was a total team effort. Every day a different hero would emerge, among them:

ANDY KOSCO—A twenty-six-year-old first baseman–outfielder, he had spent seven years in the Minnesota Twins' farm system languishing behind the immovable object that was Harmon Killebrew. Alternating between first base and right field, he hit 15 homers and had 59 RBI. He gave the Yankees some of the right-handed power they needed.

CHARLEY SMITH—He had lost his third base job to rookie Bobby Cox, but he made himself useful by becoming the league's best pinch-hitter, getting 10 hits in 31 at-bats.

BOBBY COX—After taking Smith's job, he brought stability to the left side of the infield. He drove in 25 of his 41 RBI during those incredible six weeks.

BILL ROBINSON—He raised his batting average 60 points (to .240) after the All-Star break and started to live up to his advance notices.

JOE PEPITONE—After missing part of the season with an arm injury, he was reinstated into the lineup and became another source of runs for a power-starved team. He also established himself as an excellent center fielder.

JAKE GIBBS—Gibbs was the unsung hero. He batted only .213 but caught 121 games, and was the quarterback who led the Yankee pitching staff to a team ERA of 2.79. He also proved valuable as a second-place hitter—patient and adept at the hit-and-run.

HORACE CLARKE—He hit .230, but he managed to steal 20 bases. He provided a soft glove at second base despite a reluctance to hang in on the double play.

MICKEY MANTLE—An aging lion, but a lion still, he led the team in homers (18) and walks (106), and provided them with leadership. His fielding at first base had improved to the point where it was no longer a liability.

These men combined with Roy White, who had settled down to enjoy a merely excellent season, and the pitchers to grab win after win. Yet, even with their feats, it is conceivable that none of their labors would have been rewarded without the contribution of one man.

Rocky Colavito was a thirty-five-year-old outfielder who signed with the Yankees on June 15, having become a free agent after his release by the Los Angeles Dodgers. Another castoff. In his prime he had been one of baseball's most terrifying sluggers. But now his only value was thought to be as a pinch-hitter and outfield reserve. Who could know that he would turn out to be the team's new secret weapon?

On August 25, the Yankees were hosting the Detroit Tigers in a doubleheader. These were to be the final two games of a five-game set that had so far produced the most exciting baseball seen at the Stadium in years.

It started Friday evening with a twi-night twin bill. New York won the first game 2–1 behind Bahnsen. They were down 3–1 in the second game when they tied it with two runs in the eighth. Then John Hiller pitched eight innings of scoreless relief for the Tigers. That performance was actually surpassed by his opposite number on the Yankees, Lindy McDaniel. In seven innings pitched, the right-hander with the dancing forkball faced twenty-one Tigers. The result: no runs, no hits, no walks, and no errors. Perfect baseball. If curfew hadn't called the game at 1 A.M., he might still be out there. The Yankees won a single game on Saturday. This meant that if they could sweep the Tigers in Sunday's doubleheader, they would finally attain .500. The task would not be easy. Detroit was sending two pitchers to the mound, Pat Dobson and Mickey Lolich, who were always tough on the Bombers. The Yankee pitching staff was faced with the additional pressure of having to go up against the best team in baseball with an exhausted bullpen. This plight was made hazardous by a scheduling quirk that made this the first of three doubleheaders the Yankees would play in the next three days. The team was about to suffer a severe case of the pitching shorts.

Colavito was gifted with one of the great right arms in baseball history, a rally crippler. On balls hit to him in right field, enemy base runners realized that any thoughts of taking an extra base put them in a no-man's-land. Invariably they either stayed put or were thrown out. It was this majestic cannon that Houk turned to that Sunday afternoon, and its pitching performance provided the team with a lift that would last the season.

The Tigers took three and one-third innings to dispose of left-hander Steve Barber in the first game, scoring five runs on seven hits and three walks. When Houk strode in from the dugout to lift his battered starter, the stage had been set for Rocky's Moment: runners on first and second, one man out, and the Yankees on the wrong end of a 5–0 score. Not another

Tiger crossed the plate. Throwing nothing but overhand heat, Colavito pitched two and two-thirds innings of scoreless relief, giving up only one hit: a double by Al Kaline. He walked two and struck out one. The Yankees, meanwhile, obviously inspired by the sheer audacity and success of the gamble, cut and slashed their way to six runs and the ball game, Rocky getting the win. It was only the beginning. In the second game, with his team trailing 3–2, Colavito, now safely positioned back in right field, hit a game-tying home run off Mickey Lolich. Pandemonium. The shot left New York with no other options but to win that game, too, and sweep the doubleheader.

They finished that day at .500, but that was unimportant. What was important was the way they reached that mark: using a storybook performance to beat a powerful Tiger team. It was the sort of day that would rekindle the self-confidence that this club had once taken for granted. It gave them the motor to make their late-season charge, a run that would at one point have them as high as third place. Finally, as if the very effort of this push had exhausted all their reserves, they faded in the final two weeks of the season. They finished in fifth place with a record of 83–79. No one on the team could remember when so little had meant so much.

There were accomplishments that went beyond the gloss of a winning record. Stottlemyre reestablished himself as one of the game's great pitchers, winning 21 while losing 12. McDaniel looked to be the rock that would hold the bullpen together for several more seasons. Of greater importance were the performances of three players who represented the Yankees' future: Roy White, Bill Robinson, and Stan Bahnsen, the team's first Rookie of the Year Award winner since Tom Tresh in 1962.

Bahnsen had joined the Yankees, briefly, in 1966. He made his first big league appearance against the Boston Red Sox, a game he remembers because "it was my first game and I did well. I came in in relief and struck out the side. It was shortly after that that Carl Yastrzemski said something about my having the best fastball in the league, but that wasn't true. I was just well rested. I could throw hard, but I wasn't in the same class as a Sam McDowell or anyone like that. That game was a big thrill. Just joining the Yankees was a big thrill. Ellie Howard caught me in the few games I pitched that year, and he was terrific. I never shook him off. Of course, I didn't have much of a choice, being new to the league and not knowing the hitters. Ellie knew all the hitters, knew just what their weaknesses were.

"In 1968, when I came up for the whole year, I really felt good about the year I was having. People started talking about Rookie of the Year, but I tried not to think about it. You know you don't have a vote, so there's nothing you can do about it. You just go out and pitch your best. It was really gratifying to win it."

In late September an episode occurred in the Yankee clubhouse that few noticed. Yankee clubhouse man Pete Sheehey handed a player a new pair of spikes. As the player tried them on, he murmured to no one in particular, "This will be the last pair of spikes I will ever have to break in." Mickey Mantle had decided to leave baseball.

Dick Young broke the story in the *New York Daily News* in early January 1969, quoting Mantle as saying, "I can't hit anymore." The piece was categorically denied by the Yankee front office, but Young stuck by it. He had it right. After the column appeared, Mantle was approached by Mike Burke, who pleaded with the outfielder to wait at least until spring training before he made a decision. That request was born out of a sense of economics. Baseball was expanding to twelve teams in each league in 1969. Fans in Seattle and, especially, Kansas City, where Mantle had played minor league ball, would turn out in throngs to see the only reigning Yankee superstar. Mantle's name still meant big bucks at the box office. Rumors had the owners of both new franchises offering to pay part of Mantle's salary; his decision was postponed.

He reported to spring training on March 1, three days after the regulars. Mantle spoke with Houk and arranged to have breakfast with Burke. The decision became final. At a press conference later that day, Mantle spoke in words that seemed to be lifted almost verbatim from the disputed Young article: "I can't hit when I need to, I can't go from first to third when I need to. There's no use trying." Opposing players concurred. One catcher said, "Every time he misses a ball, he grunts in pain. You'd think he was going to fall down."

The retirement left the Yankees with a huge void to fill. He had been the team's fiber, and the leading player in its only remaining drama. Over the last two years he had dragged the infirm body once more to the plate, ready to wage battle with yet another young, hard thrower. All too frequently, he was overmatched, and the sight of this would make your heart ache as if it were impaled on a dull blade. You became angry watching him publicly mocked by time. Then some pitcher, sensing the kill, would try to whip a fastball by his ancient stroke. Mistake. The last sound the errant hurler would remember was the savage crack that sent the white sphere crashing upward on a parabola, so high it almost reached the top of the cheers that accompanied it. During those moments, rare and lovely, he was still Mickey Mantle. Wasn't that marvelous? Wasn't that baseball?

The Mick's exit put the next phase of the five-year plan into full swing. The team increased its commitment to go with a youth movement, correctly realizing the success of 1968 was no real indication of progress, but merely a testament to a team's heart and Houk's leadership. Veterans like Colavito, Barber, Bouton, Smith, and Dick Howser were released or sold. Tresh and Kosco were traded, Kosco for a young left-hander out of the Dodger organization named Mike Kekich. In their place came a group of youngsters headed by Bobby Murcer and Jerry Kenney, and a rookie right-hander expected to follow in the footsteps of Stan Bahnsen: Bill Burbach.

All three won starting jobs with the club in 1969: Murcer at third, Kenney in center field (where he combined with White and Robinson to give the once lily-white Yankees their first black outfield, only twenty-two years after Jackie Robinson broke baseball's color line), Burbach as the number four starter. The results were mixed. Burbach proved to be inconsistent in what would be his only full major league season. He was a classic example of a pitcher endowed with tremendous physical equipment, but humbled by the lack of one prime ingredient: control. Kenney and Murcer fared much better. They made their season debuts on April 7 against Washington in RFK Stadium, a game in which they reached Senator pitcher Camilo Pascual for back-to-back home runs in the third inning of a 7–4 Yankee victory.

Murcer got off to a swift start, leading the majors in runs batted in by the end of May, but showing no proclivity whatsoever for mastering the intricacies of infield play. It got so bad that fans on the first base side of the diamond took to yelling, "Look out, he's going to throw it again," and ducking for cover every time he got to a ball. He became too anxious at the plate and began to overswing, trying to kill every pitch. As this continued, his strikeouts climbed and his batting average tumbled.

Kenney did not make as spectacular an entrance as Murcer, but he had a steadier season, never straying far out of the .260 range. He showed little power, but possessed great speed, an element missing from recent Yankee game plans. Kenney also had good baseball instincts. He came up to the club as a shortstop, but was immediately converted to center field. Once there, he displayed the great range and soft hands that convinced Houk to make another shift. During the second week of May, Murcer was installed in right, Kenney went to third, and Bill Robinson moved from right to center.

They joined a defense that included only three holdovers from the previous season: left fielder Roy White, second baseman Horace Clarke, and catcher Jake Gibbs. Joe Pepitone was back at first after a two-year sabbatical in center field, and shortstop was manned by Gene Michael, picked up in a deal with the Los Angeles Dodgers.

It was not a terrible lineup. Once Murcer (.259, 26 homers, 82 RBI) overcame his midseason blues, he was a productive hitter. Clarke (.285, 33 stolen bases) and Kenney (.257, 25 stolen bases) set the table at the top of the order. Pepitone (27 homers, 70 RBI) provided power, and there was the added surprise of a heavy offensive contribution from the previously light-hitting Michael (.272). White continued to improve his all-around game, flirting with .300 for most of the season and finishing at .290. He won an All-Star berth. But Bill Robinson suffered a complete regression at the plate, batting .171. The only thing more disappointing than his showing was the performance of the pitching staff. Stottlemyre had his second straight 20-win season, and Peterson chipped in with 17 victories. But the rest of the staff was a disaster. Bahnsen fell from 17–12 to 9–16, and there was no bullpen.

Lindy McDaniel was forced to shoulder much of the blame. In 51 appearances he gathered only 5 wins and 5 saves, compared to 4 wins and 10 saves in only 24 games for New York the year before. Houk kept sending him out, hoping that each game would be the game when McDaniel came back. It didn't happen. In June, the club sent pitcher Fred Talbot to the Seattle Pilots for another former Fireman of the Year, Jack Aker. Aker labored admirably, almost equalling McDaniel's former heroics. The performance came too late.

It was too late because the team just didn't have enough of anything—speed, defense, power, or pitching—to play above their heads for two straight seasons. They finished fifth in a six-team division. Even the elements conspired against them, raining out their final game with the dreadful Cleveland Indians and depriving them of their last chance to finish at .500. Over in Flushing, the Miracle Mets were busy winning a world championship, electrifying a nation of baseball fans and turning Shea Stadium into the site of a baseball love-in. It was a depressing time to be a Yankee fan, unless you were really paying attention.

The Yankees followed the tradition of all noncontenders and brought up their prize minor league prospects for a September look at the major leagues. The group included two catchers. One was John Ellis, a big, strong right-handed hitter who did not look particularly agile behind the plate but was blessed with the ability to make a ball squeal every time he made contact, which was something he did frequently. The other was a squat, unlikely looking barrel of a ballplayer who greeted everyone with a grunt and displayed the cockiness and combativeness of a ten-year veteran. His name was Thurman Munson and, though no one knew it at the time, he was the light at the end of the tunnel.

Chapter
FOUR

I've been comparing our roster with the Mets and, to be honest, I think we have the better team.

—RALPH HOUK, spring training, 1970

IT should be noted, with no small sense of irony, that before Opening Day 1970, the Yankees chose to dispose of both Bill Robinson and Joe Pepitone. Neither had been able to extract the full measure of his physical prowess during his stay in New York—one because he tried too hard, the other because he tried hardly at all.

Bill Robinson was a victim of the Yankee decline. He was brought to New York in a trade for one of the team's most popular performers. Immediately he was hailed as a "new Willie Mays." This only occurred on those days that he wasn't being compared to Mickey Mantle. Pretty heady stuff for a twenty-three-year-old who had all of 11 major league at-bats.

Part of this hype could be attributed to the overall panic that permeated the club's executive chambers during the mid-sixties. Robinson wasn't going to be a star purely by reason of his ability. He *had* to be a star because the team would not have it any other way. Any time fans would grumble about the club's current position in the standings, Robinson could be trotted out as the hope for tomorrow. Had he been successful, the reflected glare of his celebrity would have masked many of the team's inequities: its failure to trade well, to sign better prospects, and so on. When he did not live up to expectations, there was no place left to hide.

Scouts could not be blamed for drooling whenever they saw the minor league Robinson perform. He was a delicately orchestrated symphony of power, speed, and coordination. Twice during spring training games with the Yankees he took an extra base. On a walk. He would leisurely drop his bat at the plate after taking ball four, stroll down to first, take a slight turn, and then...*whooooosh!* No throw. No play. He was that kind of ballplayer.

Had he been brought into a situation where he was just another member of the team, albeit an important one, he probably would have attained the stardom predicted for him. But he was cast as the guy who was going to carry the team on his shoulders. He just couldn't do that, not at this tender stage of his career. And especially not with Yankee Stadium's Death Valley reducing some of his best shots into harmless fly balls. Only one right-handed hitter had ever succeeded in carrying the Yankees, and that was the nonpareil DiMaggio. What did this team expect?

They certainly weren't insensitive to his needs. Mike Burke spoke about taking Robinson and his wife out for a night of theater and dinner, trying to loosen him up, but "even there he couldn't relax." Many found it exasperating to see talent that could not find a means of expression. Steve Hamilton recalled a conversation with Houk in which "Ralph and I were discussing the team. Bill's name came up, and Ralph turned to me and said, 'I don't know what it is but something's missing.'"

That was a bit inaccurate. The problem was what *wasn't* missing: constant pressure. After hitting .196 in his maiden year with the club and getting off to a bad start in 1968, Robinson should have been sent down to the minors, affording him the opportunity to adjust away from the fishbowl existence of New York City. It may be argued that, in not sending him down, the club was nurturing his confidence and proving they hadn't given up on him. Fine. That's valid, although the point begs to be made that a couple of months spent pulverizing minor league pitching may have been more beneficial to his ego than allowing his continued impotence on the major league level. Of course, to demote him, especially with Clete Boyer playing so well in Atlanta, may have been construed as an admission by the club that the trade had made a mistake. Mistakes were something that this team had had enough of; they didn't need any more. Errors in judgment didn't receive good press, instill confidence, win games, or fill ball parks. So Bill Robinson was allowed to fail and, in the spring of 1970, he was optioned to Syracuse. Shortly thereafter, the Yankees released him. Quietly.

Joe Pepitone may not have been the next Mantle, but, because of an obscene lack of discipline, he deprived his fans of the opportunity to discover if he was even the first Pepitone. He simply could not get out of his own way.

What he was was a gifted athlete who liked to let the good times roll. He and Jim Bouton joined the club in 1962, surely two of the most unusual rookies the club had ever encountered. Bouton read books and talked to reporters, for Christ's sake, and Pepitone showed no freshman shyness whatsoever when it came to telling veteran first baseman Moose Skowron that this would be his last year on the job because next year Pepitone was taking over. They were like a breath of fresh air. One reporter remembered being in the Yankee clubhouse after the third game of the 1964 World Series when "[Jim] Bouton was the winning pitcher and was being quizzed by a mob of reporters. All of a sudden Howard Cosell comes in, elbows his way through the crowd, and sticks his mike in Bouton's face. Jim didn't miss a beat. He launched right into his Cosell impersonation: 'Howahd! Howahd! Tell me, Howahd, where would you be right now if we had lost this game?' Howard goes right on asking questions. [Joe] Pepitone walks up behind him, from out of nowhere, and gives Cosell a big slap on the back and yells something like, 'Howard, you old cocksucker, how are you?' Howard goes into shock. I don't know if this was live or if he was taping, but he looked at Pepitone and said, in his most dramatic voice, 'Joe, how could you do this to me?' Pepitone grinned at him and said, 'Gee, Howard, I always wanted to screw up your show.'" When asked about this, Bouton did not recall the specific incident, but he did say, "That doesn't mean it didn't happen. It certainly could have. The anecdote is not out of character with the people involved." It certainly wasn't out of character for Pepi.

This was the ballplayer remembered by frequenters of the Improvisation, a showcase for comedic talent in Manhattan, as the guy who occasionally showed up at the club with a bow and arrow in tow, and who knew the location of all the best after-hours joints in town. His romantic escapades were well-documented in his amusing autobiography, co-authored with Barry Stainback. The title of this epic summed up the Pepitone career perfectly: *Joe, You Could Have Made Us Proud.*

The shame of it is that Pepitone could have owned New York. He was handsome. He was colorful. And, best of all, he could really play baseball. In his first four full years with the Yankees, he hit 104 home runs and averaged 84 RBI a season. Imagine what he could have done if he had gotten some sleep? Just as he should have been approaching his prime, he slid backward. It is demonstrably difficult to play ball in the major leagues. To do so under the shadow of multiple divorces, other various domestic problems, and debts in figures approaching the gross national product in miniature, is damn near impossible. Such distractions are not conducive to maintaining the level of concentration needed to perform well. By 1969, Pepitone, after two mediocre seasons, was at the crossroads of his Yankee career.

He almost pulled through. Pepitone always almost pulled through. He started off the '69 season looking like a Hall of Fame ballplayer, hitting homers in clusters, winning ball games with base hits and his always superb glove. In early May, one opposing pitcher complained, "This is the Pepitone we've always been afraid would show up someday." In two months the spell was broken, and the Pepitone who had finally arrived, disappeared. Literally. He pulled a Houdini.

Pepitone first went AWOL on August 12, and then again on

August 13. He missed two home games against the Minnesota Twins. He rejoined the club for the start of a road trip on August 14, explaining his absence as the result of "personal problems." Pepi had been in the midst of a soul-withering four-week batting slump that had caused his batting average to drop 40 points. Rumors of marital woes and money owed to loan sharks began to circulate. He termed the gossip ridiculous, telling onw reporter, "I'm only $4,800 in debt. Who doesn't owe that much?" The front office took no action. Instead, they took the avuncular view that Pepitone just needed a little time away from the office in order to put the scattered pieces of his life back together.

All was apparently forgiven. For about two weeks. On August 27, the Yankees hosted the Chicago White Sox. When the original lineup for the evening was listed it had Joe batting cleanup and playing first base. Just prior to game time, he extricated himself from the batting order, claiming a sore shoulder. Then he left the ball park without permission and without leaving any indication where he could be found.

This time the club was frantic. "Management had a lot of concern for his well-being," remembered one former Yankee official, "more so than with other players. Other players might show up late for a game—it doesn't happen much, but it happens. If a player is late for a game, you get angry and decide what you're going to fine him, and you can't wait for him to show up so you can chew him out. When Joe was late for a game, people would get very, very nervous about who he might have considered to be a friend of his and who has now deposited him on the bottom of the East River."

When Pepitone returned to the club the following evening, he was benched. For about five innings. In midgame, he excused himself, went to the clubhouse, and once again vanished.

He returned to the club on August 30, discovering he had been fined $500. The recalcitrant first baseman had a fit. He couldn't believe he was being punished for such an itsy-bitsy infraction. Once over his rage, he decided to protest the action. Pepitone, inspired by the teachings of Gandhi and Martin Luther King Jr., took the route of passive resistance. For some this method of defiance came in the form of sit-ins or fasts. Pepi did not have any experience with these options, but he did have one act that he had recently honed to perfection. It was with this that he found the ready-made vehicle to voice his dissatisfaction; he left the team. Again.

By morning, he was no longer simply fined; he was suspended. He met with Mike Burke that afternoon and explained he was not psychologically prepared to rejoin the club. Burke issued a statement: "He's been on a treadmill the last four or five years. Everything he's made has gone out again. He hasn't been able to live the way he wanted to. He couldn't walk around with money in his pocket and he was looking forward to meal money. He had an image for the public that he knew wasn't true."

The public image was that of a lovable rogue, a man-child whose life appeared to be a quest for the excessive. It would not be unfair to suppose that many of Pepitone's fans admired that trait about him, the live-for-today attitude that was so much *the* philosophy of the late sixties. To them he was a ball-playing Barrymore, a compelling figure whose prodigious talents lurked inside him like a demon, never bringing real joy and always threatening to exit.

He returned to the club on September 2, without fanfare, and did not miss a game for the rest of the season. It made no difference. The Yankees had decided to ring down the final curtain. On December 4, 1969, Pepitone was dispatched to the Houston Astros for first baseman—outfielder Curt Blefary. Lee MacPhail announced the deal, not without a trace of sadness. "In a way I feel relieved of a problem, but it will be hard to imagine the Yankee club without him. He's been a real good ballplayer, though not as good as everyone hoped he'd be. He was colorful and had the spirit of youth. And the problems that go with it."

In 1964, the Yankees had been a victim of the numbers game when they felt forced to leave Blefary outside the protection of the forty-man roster. He was snatched up by the Baltimore Orioles and, in 1965, was named American League Rookie of the Year. Blefary never missed an opportunity to remind New

York of their mistake. He bludgeoned Yankee pitching up to the time he left the American League during the winter of 1968. He had been the bait the Orioles had used to induce the Astros to part with left-handed screwballer Mike Cuellar. The trade to New York represented a homecoming.

It was also the first part of an attempt to seriously bolster the Yankee offense. The next day the club dealt Al Downing and catcher Frank Fernandez to the Oakland A's for Danny Cater.

Cater was the least known good hitter in the majors. In 1968, Carl Yastrzemski led the American League in batting with a .301 average. Students of baseball history are familiar with this statistic. What is not readily recalled is the name of the player who finished second to Yaz with .290. It was Cater. Despite this, and other hitting accomplishments of equal merit during his six-year career, Cater had failed to become a household name. Indeed, he frequently found his name misspelled as "Carter" in the morning box scores; it became his nickname. The reason for the anonymity could be traced to the things he could not do: run exceptionally well, hit home runs, or cut a colorful figure. What he *could* do was play an excellent first base, fill in well at several other positions, and hit wall-to-wall line drives from sunrise to sunset. For the Yankees this would be quite enough.

Houk and MacPhail made several other acquisitions, minor deals, in a sense, but designed to give the team the depth it had sorely lacked in recent seasons. To meet this end, they picked up two members of the Chicago White Sox: third baseman Pete Ward and shortstop Ron Hansen. The total price paid for both was minor league left-hander Mickey Scott (who went for Ward) and $20,000 (the price for Hansen). These deals did not cause very much excitement in the Bronx, because neither man had hit over .260 since 1964. Houk didn't mind. He did not expect them to be starters, only reserves. In 1969, Yankee pinch-hitters batted a combined .208. That same year, Hansen and Ward came up in emergency roles with the White Sox 71 times and delivered 23 base hits. It didn't take a pocket calculator to determine the .324 average those digits represented.

This sort of output could have made a decisive difference in the numerous one-run ball games New York threw away for want of a timely pinch-hit. Ward and Hansen represented late-inning offense and gave Houk the maneuverability he had craved for four seasons.

The new acquisitions were introduced to the press, and the scribes speculated just how much the Bombers had helped themselves. Blefary received particular attention; everybody loves a slugger. Blefary was a left-handed pull hitter, and it was felt that Yankee home cooking could help him produce as many as 35 home runs. Cater was figured to add consistency, and the two pinch-hitters were recognized as much-needed luxuries. Much of this speculation was forgotten by the second week of the exhibition season. The spotlight that had shone on this quartet turned out to be as brief as it was bright. It didn't take long for it to shift its fickle glance to the two rookies, John Ellis and Thurman Munson.

Ellis was having the sort of spring that gives managers problems—welcome problems. He was leading the team in RBI with 18 and batting a hefty .384 when the time came to go North. This stick work demanded that a place in the lineup be found for him. Houk started using him at first and third. Catching was out of the question; Munson had already staked his claim. From day one of camp it was obvious that he was something special.

It wasn't just the confident exterior that caught the eye. It was the quick release from behind the plate that enabled him to freeze or retire would-be base stealers. It was the lack of fear he evinced in dealing with his veteran pitchers; he never hesitated to chide them to bear down just a little bit harder. And it was the way he accepted victory. He never acted surprised by it. Munson always expected to come out on top. This was no small thing. It represented a winner's attitude, something that had been missing from the Yankee clubhouse for what felt like a millennium. Munson brought it with him and its effects were contagious. These attributes contributed to making the catcher a standout. They come under the heading of intangibles and are often hard to measure. Many lesser players had careers the length of an eyelash because they could not combine these intangibles with virtues of a more readily identifiable nature. Munson would not suffer their fate. He had one additional gift that was immediately recognizable: He could hit.

It was his hitting that had reporters mentioning him as a Rookie of the Year candidate before the exhibition season was half spent. It isn't often that a freshman batter comes along with no apparent weaknesses at the plate; Munson was one of the lucky few. He brought an intelligence to his hitting that went beyond the realm of experience. What especially impressed observers was his total lack of confusion in dealing with breaking pitches, and his patience. It was his extraordinary patience that enabled him to sting outside pitches hard to the opposite field. Fans watched the prodigy with the quick bat and powerful arm scurry to first, using his deceptive speed to beat out an infield roller, and murmured to one another, "He has it all."

His defense improved daily. Given his physical and mental aptitude, it would have been remarkable if it hadn't. Munson was under the tutelage of three of the catching school's most eminent professors: Ralph Houk, Ellie Howard, and Jim Hegan. By the time the Yankees broke camp, many touted Munson as the best catcher in the league, comparing him already to the All-Star catcher from Detroit, Bill Freehan.

Fortunately, those who were so quick to praise him were not as quick to spurn him when he got off to a bad start. And did he ever get off to a bad start.

The season opened at Yankee Stadium on April 7 with a 4–3 loss to the Boston Red Sox. Munson was able to scratch out a single off left-hander Gary Peters for his first hit of the season. For two weeks, it would be his only hit of the season.

Slumps are devious hybrids, part mental and part physical. They usually start with a few games in which the batter rips the ball for what should be several base hits. Nothing drops in. A couple of balls are caught at the fence. The opposing shortstop makes a brilliant stop and throw. The unplayable roller goes just foul. The hitter (unless he's Lou Piniella, who would have been ready to commit homicide by now) doesn't really mind. He cheerfully talks about "the breaks of the game." The next day he nails four line drives. All get caught. The batter still doesn't panic. Until the third day where he once again hits the ball hard but comes up empty. Now he starts to wonder if he will ever get a base hit again. The problem gets compounded as the public becomes aware of the slump-in-progress. Fans read, "Butterfingers Beradino hasn't had a hit in his last 13 trips to the plate." This news invites two responses from the team's loyal supporters. One faction sends good luck charms and Mass cards. The other faction boos. Soon the player starts to believe that there is something seriously wrong, when actually his original assessment about "the breaks of the game" was the correct one. If anything, he's hitting the ball too well. Right about this time the schedulemaker throws a Steve Carlton or a Fernando Valenzuela in his path—the type of pitcher who not only gets hitters out, but embarrasses them in the process. The batter strikes out. Five times. This is now a serious slump.

How serious it becomes depends on his ability to retain a semblance of sanity. He mustn't try to change the habits that have made him a successful hitter in the past, unless the switch is a concession to age or injury or an adjustment to new pitching patterns. He must have faith.

Munson was starting to lose his. On April 19, the team was 4–8 and Munson had gone 1 for 30.

Willie Mays was the National League Rookie of the Year in 1951. He began that season by gathering only 1 hit in his first 26 trips to the plate. Confused and frightened that he couldn't handle big league pitching, a tearful Mays begged Giant manager Leo Durocher to send him back down to the minors. Durocher refused. Mays was his center fielder. If he didn't get a hit for the rest of the year, he would still be the center fielder. Shortly thereafter, Mays went on a tear that lasted twenty-three years.

Munson had a similar conversation with Houk. The catcher did not tearfully request to be optioned to Syracuse, but it was obvious that his lack of offense troubled him. This was a delicate moment. The wrong choice of words, or no words at all, could seriously retard a young man's career. Perhaps destroy it. Houk was perfect. He told Munson that it didn't matter if he hit or not. The most important responsibility a catcher had was to contribute to the team's defense. Hitting was so much icing.

The Yankees played the Washington Senators on April 20 at RFK Stadium. In the first inning, Munson faced left-hander George Brunet. He hit a shot that caromed off third baseman Ken McMullen. Single. Munson later added another single and a double. He drove in two runs as the Yankees won 11–2. The next night he was on the bench. Sitting Munson down was a move based in logic and sensitivity. Houk had seen many players end a hitting drought only to go into another tailspin the next day. He gave the catcher the night off to relax and to reflect on those three base hits. The slump was over. Not just for Munson, but for the entire team.

When the catcher went on a hitting tear the lineup began to make some sense of itself. Munson's quickness and ability to make contact allowed him to frequently bat second behind Horace Clarke. Roy White, who had shown an uncanny ability to drive in clutch runs, batted third. Baltimore manager Earl Weaver made note of it when he cited White as a man "who has probably never made the last out of any game he's played in." The still streaky Bobby Murcer brought power to the cleanup spot, and Danny Cater was unspectacularly steady in the fifth spot. This was the best top five the club had had in years. Once Munson got in gear, he led the way for the entire attack. Pinstriped Blitzkrieg. They scored early and often, taking pressure off the formerly beleaguered pitching staff. After a 9–12 April, the team began to jell.

The club won seven of its first eight games in May, and continued its torrid pace right up to the last day of the season. The Yankees finished 93–69. Only three teams—the Baltimore Orioles, the Cincinnati Reds, and the Minnesota Twins—had better records. Unfortunately, the Orioles were in the same division as the Yankees.

Baltimore was a powerful club built along the lines of the great Yankee teams of the fifties. They had a surplus of everything. The best way to illustrate their depth is to cite the season of Merv Rettenmund. In 1968, Rettenmund had been *The Sporting News* Minor League Player of the Year. With the Orioles in 1970, he batted .322 with 18 homers and 58 RBI. No Yankee hit higher. Only two had more home runs. Three Yankees, and only three, had more runs batted in. Rettenmund was Baltimore's *fourth* outfielder. He only started when one of the regulars—Paul Blair, Frank Robinson, or Don Buford—was given the day off.

New York never seriously challenged the Orioles. But finishing second to such a sinewy team was a cause for real celebration, even if the gap between the two clubs was an imponderable 15 games. It didn't make the champagne taste any less sweet.

The Yankee improvement was a direct offshoot of the front-office planning negotiated during the off-season. The offense was greatly improved.

Munson (.302) did win the Rookie of the Year Award. He and Cater contributed in precisely the manner management had expected. Hansen (.297) and Ward (.260) delivered from the bench. Blefary was a major disappointment. The right fielder didn't hit his first home run of the season until early June. Blefary, who had been born in Brooklyn, felt enormous pressure playing before family and friends. After the season he remarked, "I was never as tight or nervous as I was on Opening Day in Yankee Stadium. I was worse than a rookie, and it was half a season before it wore off. By that time it was too late and I wasn't playing anymore."

Houk compensated for Blefary's shortcomings. In midseason, he turned right field over to a platoon of two youngsters: Jim Lyttle and Ron Woods. Both played splendidly, particularly the rookie Lyttle, who batted .310. They also provided an excellent defense that even an up-to-snuff Blefary couldn't hope to equal. Their performances were a tribute to Houk's managerial talents.

Houk's sixth sense was working overtime in 1970. Jake Gibbs had never batted higher than .258, or hit more than four home runs in any given season. He had lost his starting job to Thurman Munson. Yet his value to the club increased. He became the best backup catcher in baseball. With Houk picking his spots, Gibbs managed a .301 batting average of his own. He also surprised everybody with an unexpected show of power: 8 home runs in only 153 at-bats.

John Ellis was another Houk project. The wonder boy of spring had gotten off to a worse start than Munson. Houk brought him along. His final average (.248 after a 4- for-40 start) did not reflect the immediate value of his contribution. He provided enough right-handed power to negate some of the advantage left-handed pitchers held over the Yankees. By manipulating his offense, Houk was able to create an attack that scored 680 runs, the club's highest total since 1964.

All this scoring would have gone for naught if the pitching hadn't held up. Bahnsen (14–11) regained some of his former luster. He joined with Peterson (20–11) and Stottlemyre (15–13) to give New York a Big Three second only to Baltimore's. Steve Kline (6–6) was a Stottlemyre pitch-alike. He joined the club in mid-July, compiled a 3.42 ERA, and finally ended the team's six-year search for a fourth starter.

Every manager seems to have a particular strength. Earl Weaver ran his offense around the home run; Gene Mauch has had an unending romance with the squeeze play and the hit-and-run. Houk's specialty was his bullpen. He had once been quoted as saying that if he had Tom Seaver, who at the time was the best pitcher alive, he might not start him. If Seaver's arm was up to the strain he probably would have found himself in the bullpen. Houk didn't have Seaver. He did have Lindy McDaniel.

In May 1959, Lindy McDaniel had gotten off to a ghastly start as the St. Louis Cardinals' fourth starter. A similar slump the season before had winged him back to Omaha, the Cardinals' Triple-A farm club. Minor league baseball may seem romantic to fans, but to big leaguers it means long bus rides and short meal money.

McDaniel wanted to avoid that. He approached Cards' skipper Solly Hemus and offered to go to the pen. Hemus approved. Once there McDaniel came under the guidance of pitching coach Howie Pollet, who persuaded him to ditch the three-quarters style motion he had used as a starter. In its place, McDaniel came straight overhand. The substitution had an immediate effect: McDaniel's fast ball began to tail off. In his first appearance, he pitched five and two-thirds innings, giving up no runs on two hits and picking up the victory. A reliever was born.

His success did not dissuade Pollet from an opinion he had formed. Pollet felt McDaniel needed an off-speed pitch to complement his hard stuff. To that end, the right-hander spent the following winter adding a forkball to his repertoire: a pitch that was jammed between the index and middle fingers and thrown with the same motion as a fastball, but did not have the same rotation. This gave it the appearance of an extremely hittable heater—until it reached the plate. There it tended to react like a just-shot quail: It dropped. The pitch was as predictable as a five-year-old child, but McDaniel was its master. The following season, the results gave ample evidence of its effectiveness: 12–4, 26 saves, and a 2.09 ERA. McDaniel was designated the National League Fireman of the Year.

Lindy had been the goat in 1969; in 1970 he was Houk's best weapon. All the starters had to do was keep the opposition in check for six or seven innings and turn the game over to McD. He rarely failed, finishing the season with 9 wins and 29 saves. Those numbers, combined with Jack Aker's 4 wins and 16 saves, gave New York the best relief duo in baseball. With the additional help of Steve Hamilton and Ron Klimkowski, they enabled the Yanks to make the climb to second place. The bullpen was the team's MVP. It was also one of the primary reasons Fritz Peterson became a 20-game winner.

It is almost certain that Peterson would have also won 20 in 1969 if only the bullpen had been more efficient. It probably didn't bother him too greatly. Pitching better than his record indicated had become his way of life on the Yankees.

Today, Peterson lives in Chicago where he works for a metals company and is head of the Baseball Chapel. The milestone season of 1970 was a fitting reward for a talented pitcher who had the misfortune of joining the Bombers when they were no longer capable of exploding.

Thinking back to when he first signed with New York, he revealed, "I had really wanted to sign with the White Sox but when I went to work out at Comiskey Park with the Kansas City A's, my dad had wired the Sox that I was going to be throwing in their ball park. They didn't respond to the wire or our later telephone call. So the only two teams I really worked out with were Kansas City and the Yankees. The Yankees said, 'We'll give you more than they will no matter what they offer you.' So it was a choice between the Yankees and Kansas City, and the Yankee scouts did such a professional job that there was no question about who I would sign with. That was 1963, and the odd thing about it is that they told me that if a left-handed pitcher was going to make it, he just might as well do it with the Yankees because they always get you that World Series money. Of course, in my eight years plus with them we never did make it.

"In my first game with the Yankees in 1966, I was taking too long between pitches. Bobby Richardson came up to me and said, 'Hey, [Mickey] Mantle's out there in center, and he's yelling because you're not throwing the ball quickly enough. You're taking too much time.' You know, I thought each pitch was very important, so I took my time with each one. Not after that. From that day on I got the ball over as fast as I could.

"I won my first start in Baltimore. We had lost our first three games in New York. I was very nervous. I remember two things about that day. First I remember thinking I was going to be in the major league records. That spring was the first time I had seen big league ballplayers up close. To make the team was good enough, but when I realized I was joining them in *The Baseball Encyclopedia* or whatever, that was really amazing to me. I just couldn't believe I was really there. The other thing I remember was looking up at the stands. They were full. Must have been 42,000 people. That was something. The first guy I faced was Luis Aparicio, who had been an idol of mine from his days in Chicago. He got a base hit and scored, but I won 3–2. We were winning 3–1 in the ninth and Frank Robinson got a home run, but I finished the game anyway. I was really happy Frank got the home run. The writers couldn't believe that, but I didn't care. We won, so it didn't make a difference to me, and I figured it made the Oriole fans happy to see him hit one. I don't think the writers had ever heard anyone say anything like that before.

"Mantle was terrific. When I joined the team, he could see that I was shy, and he came up and introduced himself to me. As if I didn't know who he was. And [Roger] Maris was good to me. Just talking to those guys was a thrill. And, of course, Whitey [Ford] was great, and I became good friends with Jim [Bouton]. I found out early on that a lot of players didn't like Jim because he was always talking to writers.

"Mickey's retirement had an effect on me. I could never figure out why anyone would want to go and see the Mets when they had a chance to come to our ball park and see Mickey Mantle. Even if it was just to pinch-hit. When he left, we had a bad ball club. I felt the people shouldn't come out to see us for any reason. Not with the team we had. While he was with us, I figured that history was right there in that man. I think he could still hit today, right-handed, but his legs hurt him so much from the other side that he had to quit.

"You know in 1970 we finished second, but I really didn't think we were that good a club. I think everybody just sort of gave up because Baltimore was that good. In 1972, we were in the pennant race but I think we had a good club by then."

Peterson pitched as well in 1971 as he did in 1970. But he did not win 20 games; he was forced to settle for 15. Two other members of the 1971 staff—Stottlemyre and Kline—had ERAs under 3.00. Yet Stottlemyre won only 16 games, and Kline did not even finish at .500, winning 12 while losing 13. Bahnsen (14–12) fared only slightly better.

The low totals could be attributed to the old bugaboos: a lack of runs and a flaccid bullpen. McDaniel and Aker combined for eight saves. A year before, that would have represented a good two weeks' work for the duo. Their failure to come up to anything resembling their former effectiveness decimated the entire team. The Yankees fell back to fourth place, barely finishing over .500 at 82–80.

Munson started out the 1971 season with a huge slump (2

for 30). This time he did not recover as well as he had in his rookie season. His final .251 average represented a 51-point drop from his previous season's effort. He did manage to gain an All-Star berth, and he set a major league defensive record for catchers by appearing in 125 games and committing only 1 error.

Bobby Murcer arrived. He stopped trying to kill every pitch and started going to the opposite field. The result was a .331 batting average that brought him within six points of league-leader Tony Oliva of the Minnesota Twins.

None of this was headline news. That was because everything the team accomplished on the field was overshadowed by events off the field.

The Yankees were considering leaving town.

On January 12, 1971, New Jersey Governor William Cahill delivered his first annual message to the New Jersey legislature in Trenton. During the course of his speech, he casually mentioned that "negotiations are under way to bring the Yankees and [football] Giants to the proposed Meadowlands Complex." He termed talks with officials of both teams "productive and substantial."

The Yankees were considering the move because the Stadium was falling down around their ears. Literally. Chunks of cement were falling out of the ceiling. The lighting was bad. Parking was inadequate, as was the number and quality of the roads giving access to the Stadium itself. The place was in need of a complete overhaul.

A meeting had been scheduled between New York Mayor John Lindsay and Mike Burke. The date of the confab was January 13, 1971. It was purely coincidental that these two should be getting together the day following Cahill's pronouncement. It may not have been a coincidence, however, that this meeting was far more productive than four previous ones held during the last nine months had been. Burke left the conference telling reporters he was confident that the Yankees and the Giants would stay in New York.

Not everyone was as sure. The first inducement to stay offered by the City Planning Council was to build an eight-hundred-car parking facility adjacent to the stadium. This was supposed to be the city's reply to the challenge of the Meadowlands. A parking lot. Shrewd. The Yankees did not keel over in undying gratitude.

Neither did John Lindsay. He was determined to keep the team in New York. There was a psychological factor at play here. This was a period where any number of companies were pulling out of the city. Pepsi headed to Westchester; Chesebrough-Ponds to Stamford, Connecticut. A real exodus was beginning. People were not walking around humming "I Love New York." Quite the contrary. The Yankees were a comparatively small business. But they were a highly visible one. Keeping them in New York was a declaration of faith in the city's future. Had they left it might have seemed as if everyone was throwing in the towel on New York.

The mayor asked Burke to stay put. Burke was quick to reply. He told Lindsay that "he had to do something for us, and he said, 'Okay, we will do for you what we did for the Mets.' The books showed that the city had invested $24 million in Shea Stadium. I think it was something more than that, but that's what showed up on the books." On March 2, Lindsay announced his plan to renovate Yankee Stadium.

The city would acquire the Stadium either through purchase or condemnation proceedings (which was a nice way of letting the landlords of the edifice, Rice University and the Knights of Columbus, know that they had no choice in the matter). The city would then renovate the building and lease it back to the Yankees. The price tag placed on the project was $24 million.

This idea did not generate instant enthusiasm. The Stadium became a political football; everybody had an alternative plan. Some felt the Yankees should be allowed to leave, since they would still be part of what was fancifully referred to as the tri-state area. They pointed out that the money would be better spent improving the blighted neighborhoods lying in the Stadium's shadow. One group of feminists said the money shouldn't be spent on any sports that did not encourage the participation of women. Many pushed for the football Giants and Jets to share Shea Stadium with the Mets and the Yankees.

City Council President Sanford Garelik liked that idea. He proposed that the city invest $15 million and transform Shea into a sports complex a la the Meadowlands. This was the same man who once proposed the erection of a ski slope in the Bronx; it was to be built on a twenty-five-hundred-foot-high mountain of garbage and landfill. The idea of sharing Shea Stadium with the Yankees struck the Mets as being very much like that ski slope: a great pile of garbage.

The Mets had no intention of helping the Yankees. Nothing could have pleased them more than to have the team take their act elsewhere. Not only would it have left the city to the Mets, it would have also cut down on the possibility of any National League rival setting up shop in New Jersey in the near future. Mets president M. Donald Grant threatened to move the Mets to the Meadowlands if the Yankees came to Shea.

None of these protests stopped Burke and Lindsay. Their combined energies, in tandem with a little political back-scratching, pushed the Stadium bill through the City Council on June 4. The state legislature passed it four days later. The only hurdle left was the Board of Estimate.

No real opposition was anticipated. Then a slight complication arose. On August 26, the Giants dropped a bombshell; they had signed a lease to play their home games in the Meadowlands. The question now was whether it was economically prudent to spend all that money just to keep a single team in New York.

Opponents of the measure made a final desperate stand before the Board of Estimate in late November. They lost. On December 7, the board gave its blessing to a $225,000 engineering study, to be conducted by Praeger, Cavanaugh, and Waterbury. They estimated that a complete renovation of the Stadium would cost $36 million.

The projected expenditure did not prove to be an obstacle. The work was to begin at the end of the 1973 season, and would be completed in time for the home opener in 1976. During that period the Yankees would be the unwelcome guests of their National League counterparts at Shea. It was a courtesy extracted by numerous financial considerations, all to the advantage of the Mets.

Since the time of the final estimate, a small controversy has arisen over the actual cost of the architectural facelift. The figure has been blown out to the most unimaginable proportions. The actual price paid for the Stadium's top-to-bottom refurbishment is reportedly $54 million, though Burke claims a figure about $14 million lighter. There is an often-quoted figure that placed the cost over the $100-million mark. No one has produced a scintilla of hard evidence that the figure ever got that high.

But it could have.

When Burke looked over the proposed project, he told Lindsay, "Look, there is no point in just renewing and refurbishing the building. Create ten thousand parking spaces. Improve the access roads. And upgrade the environment so you'll have an attractive island in the Bronx." The city planners came up with an idea that would rejuvenate the area. The Farmer's Market was going to be torn down and replaced by middle-income housing, public parks, and tennis courts. An all-weather mall around the Stadium was plotted. Surrounding highways, streets, and buildings were to be upgraded. Landscaping was to be done in the area east of River Avenue. This was the plan that would have cost the city $120 million.

It never happened.

Why? Mike Burke may have had the simplest answer when he said, "The city went broke." What could you expect? They had just spent $54 million on a baseball stadium.

Chapter
FIVE

I have no intentions of getting involved in the day-to-day operations of the club. I have a shipbuilding business to run.

—GEORGE M. STEINBRENNER, on the occasion of his acquisition of the New York Yankees

"THE Yankees wish to announce they have traded Stan Bahnsen to the Chicago White Sox in exchange for Rich McKinney..." Picture a roomful of reporters, all anxiously waiting on the tips of their pens for the other shoe to drop. It did. It landed squarely on the head of the Yankee front office.

It was no secret that New York was looking to make several deals during the winter of 1971. Their top priority was landing an infielder. A relief pitcher would also be appreciated, and they would certainly not have looked askance at any power hitter that might come their way.

They were in an excellent position to deal because the team had finally had a surplus of a most valuable commodity: pitching. Mike Kekich had thrown well enough during the 1971 season to make at least one of the Big Four—Stottlemyre, Peterson, Bahnsen, or Kline—expendable. The Yankees had also been greatly impressed with young Ron Blomberg. The left-handed hitter had been the team's first pick in the 1967 draft, and was brought up during the second half of '71. In 64 games he batted .322 with power. The team would continue its commitment to youth by employing Blomberg at first base, platooning him with John Ellis. This would allow the Yankees to shop around Danny Cater.

It is a misconception to believe that New York happily stumbled into the McKinney deal with both eyes closed. He was not their first choice. Inquiries were originally made of the Orioles as to the availability of either second baseman Davy Johnson or shortstop Mark Belanger. At the time, neither could be had at any price. Baltimore was not in the habit of trading veteran stars unless they were absolutely confident that they had a younger, more accomplished player prepared to replace them. The greatness of the Oriole organization over the last twenty-five years is vested in their patience and their ability to maintain a continuity of personnel. George Kell gives way to Brooks Robinson, who gives way to Doug DeCinces, who gives way to Cal Ripken Jr., and so on. Johnson and Belanger weren't available because the Orioles weren't sure Bobby Grich could play major league ball yet. One year later, when Grich had proved himself, Johnson was gone.

Similar overtures were made to other clubs, most notably the California Angels. But infielders were at a premium, even more so than pitchers. The Yankee efforts to secure the services of Angel shortstop Jim Fregosi were shattered by the New York Mets. The Mets acquired Fregosi at the cost of three minor leaguers and a hard-throwing, frustratingly wild young right-hander they were convinced would never make it—Nolan Ryan.

After having other offers spurned (for Leo Cardenas, Sandy Alomar, and Richie Hebner, among others), the Yankees set their sights on McKinney.

The December 2 announcement of the deal—Bahnsen for McKinney—caught reporters flat-footed. They waited for several minutes before they realized that McKinney was all the Yankees were receiving. In order to understand their dismay, several things must be explained.

During that day rumors had floated around suggesting that the Yankees were on the precipice of a major deal. Names like Frank Robinson, Nate Colbert, and Richie Allen insinuated themselves into speculative conversations. Robinson and Allen were traded that day. Robby went from Baltimore to Los Angeles. Allen went from Los Angeles to the Chicago White Sox. Some gossip maintained that New York was about to be included in a four-corner swap. Perhaps a roundabout version of the often-rumored, never-consummated Fritz Peterson for Frank Robinson deal.

They were dreaming.

It became apparent that the deal was a case of "what you see is what you get." Once that was perceived, reporters, fans, and probably a few Yankee officials went about the business of finding out what, exactly, the club had received.

Rich McKinney was a twenty-five-year-old right-hand hitting infielder. The 1971 season had been his first full year in the majors. In 369 at-bats he hit .271 with 8 home runs. When the deal was announced the Yankees immediately designated him as the team's third baseman. There was one slight complication: The sum total of McKinney's exposure to the rigors of third consisted of 28 games. He had spent most of his playing time with the White Sox at second base. One New York official said, "He's played mostly at second base, but, from what we've seen, we think he can handle third." What he meant was that he hoped McKinney could handle third. New York had traded a healthy young pitcher, who had won 54 games over the last four seasons, on a guess.

The total volume of the criticism leveled against the transaction was so great it could not be measured on any known decibel meter. But not everyone thought it was a bad deal. One of those who understood it was Bahnsen. In discussing the trade he said, "Four days before I got traded I read an article that said that I was one of the guys on the club who was almost definitely *not* going to be dealt. A lot of people were surprised that all we got was McKinney, but they didn't realize how good he looked when he had played against us. We had a good pitching staff, but he would tear us up. The best way I could describe him would be to say that he looked a lot like Bob Horner— short stroke, good power. I could understand why they wanted to get him. Later on, I felt sorry for him because he had nothing to do with the trade, but he was hearing a lot of abuse."

If the deal had not been kissed by death from the very beginning, it had at least been casually embraced. McKinney was to have played third base during the winter season in Puerto Rico. He hurt his ankle and couldn't. Valuable time that could have been spent making the position his was lost.

The winter preview would have provided the Yankees with another piece of disheartening news: McKinney couldn't throw. Being able to throw is only as important to playing third as being able to breathe. New York first learned of his deficient wing in spring training.

X rays were immediately taken. They revealed a bone chip in his right shoulder. That was important. More important was the revelation of when the injury had occurred. It apparently was the result of an unplanned rendezvous with a fence while playing the outfield. In Baltimore. In August. In 1971.

This should have given the Yankee front office strong reason to suspect that they had been dealt damaged goods. But nothing was done about it. Certainly a protest would have had an excellent chance of getting the team some sort of compensation. None was filed. This club was desperate for a third baseman. Any third baseman.

It was decided that McKinney could play through the pain. Surgery was not deemed necessary until after the season. When asked if he was worried about McKinney's arm, Houk conceded that he was, but, "We have protection in Hal Lanier." Hal Lanier? Lanier was a utility infielder picked up from San Francisco during the off-season. He had a professional glove, but his lifetime batting average was .229, and he had no power to speak of.

There was some real third base protection in camp. His name was Celerino Sanchez. He had spent the previous season beating up Mexican League pitchers to the tune of .372. Sanchez's play at third was very much like that of Aurelio Rodriguez of the Tigers. At the time, Rodriguez was the best third baseman in baseball. Unlike McKinney, Sanchez had had a sensational spring. The only problem was, Sanchez was the wrong third baseman. McKinney, like Bill Robinson before him, had to succeed. The club had given up so much for him. Sanchez was sent down to Syracuse. His inability to communicate with the press and call attention to himself made the move an easy one for the Yankees. Sanchez spoke no English. His only fluency, besides that of his native tongue, was a physical one that celebrated itself on a ball field, where actions transcended the inadequacies of mere language.

The 1972 season started two weeks late. Eighty-six major league games were lost, the victims of a two-week strike by the Baseball Players Association over the pension plan. The whys and wherefores of that dispute do not need to be recapitulated. Let it be enough to say that shortly after the turmoil was ended, it is quite possible that Rich McKinney wished that the strike had lasted forever.

His bad start at the plate was in no way obscured by his fielding: ordinary. But it wasn't even that on April 22, the day that propelled McKinney into the record books. Only seventeen men in the game's recorded history had ever committed four errors at third base in a single game. On that date, McKinney became the eighteenth. The miscues allowed the Red Sox to score nine unearned runs in a game they won 11–7. When the debacle was over, reporters quizzed the third baseman in solemn tones usually reserved for the survivor of an awful car wreck. He answered all of them and displayed a touching candor when he admitted, "After a while, I was hoping that no one would hit the ball to me." With bitter irony, he had chosen this day to turn in his best hitting performance as a Yankee: three for four, with two singles and a home run. That would be his last good day at the plate.

His fielding did improve. After his catastrophic afternoon at Fenway, he went 20 consecutive games without making an error. Then, in late May, he made some key mistakes that cost the club a few games. The fans, who up to now had been tolerant of him, reacted as fans do: They booed.

They weren't booing McKinney. They were booing the trade that had brought him to the Yankees, and they were booing something more. It is baseball's great illusion that it is not a difficult game to play. When a player repeatedly fails to perform well, it destroys that facade of ease. It makes it painfully clear that the game of our youth, like normal life, is a hard and difficult business. There are too many daily reminders of that sort of thing. Booing implies many things, including: "Don't screw around with my dreams; don't take away my escape."

Houk was now finally forced to make a move. He pointed out how "the fans are really getting on him," and shipped McKinney out to Syracuse. It was a one-way ride. In 121 at-bats he had managed only 26 hits. Only three of those hits (two doubles, and that home run) went for extra bases. He had driven in seven runs. At the end of the year, he was dealt to the Oakland Athletics. McKinney's entire Yankee career consisted of 37 games. That same season, Bahnsen, en route to 21 wins with the White Sox, started 4 more games than McKinney played.

The Great Bullpen Collapse of '71 persuaded Houk that his relief staff was in need of an addition. Lindy McDaniel and Jack Aker were on the wrong side of thirty. A young, dominating short man was the prescription for what ailed the Yankees. Dave LaRoche, Lloyd Allen, Danny Frisella, and Ken Sanders were all supposed to be available. The Major was not interested. The only medicine he trusted was a full dose of Boston's Sparky Lyle.

The Red Sox were undergoing a process of realignment. They had decided to augment their powerful batting order with speed and defense. Such changing of skin was nothing new for Boston. It was something they did every six or seven years. That's about the time it took for the Boston front office to get sick of hearing how they never led the league in anything but runs scored.

Their latest attempts to diversify the team's gifts actually started in 1971. Tony Conigliaro, a right-handed slugger with a stroke born for Fenway, was traded to the California Angels at about the same time that Boston second baseman Mike Andrews was dispatched to the Chicago White Sox. In exchange, The Bosox received Luis Aparicio, Doug Griffin, and Ken Tatum—two nimble infielders and a right-handed reliever.

Griffin and Aparicio formed a dazzling double play combination, but Tatum was a disappointment. His arm seemed healthy, and the general impression was that he simply needed to be used more often. At the time, the Red Sox bullpen was occupied by a pride of lefties: Bill Lee, Sparky Lyle, and Roger Moret. Moret was slated to become a starter, and Lee was supposed to assume the role of long man. Since it was preferable to have a right-hander as the short reliever in Fenway Park, Lyle was seen as trade bait.

Determining what Boston wanted was simple. They had recently completed a swap, sending pitchers Jim Lonborg and Ken Brett, first baseman George Scott, and outfielders Billy Conigliaro and Joe LaHoud to the Milwaukee Brewers for outfielder Tommy Harper and pitchers Marty Pattin and Lew Krausse. They had been able to refill every spot left open by this dealing except Scott's. Yastrzemski was a possibility at first, but that would remove his Gold Glove from left. The Red Sox needed a first baseman, and the man they wanted was Danny Cater.

This is what is known as a common ground: two teams, each having what the other wants. Houk looked to Lyle to shore up his bullpen for the rest of the decade. Boston wanted Cater for the same reason that the Yanks wanted McKinney. Cater murdered them. Not only had he hit for an extraordinarily high average against them throughout his career, he also hit for power—the magic of Fenway.

You would think that the only thing that stood in the path of this deal's completion was a handshake. Wrong. After a possible trade was discussed at the winter conclave, it was put on hold. The Sox came back and asked that minor league infielder Mario Guerrero be included in a package with Cater. No problem. Then Boston gave New York a choice: They could have either Lyle or Lee. Some members of the Yankee front office were pushing for Lee. He was younger and had just come off an impressive season. Houk would not be dissuaded. As it turned out, any debate was moot. Boston manager Eddie Kasko had decided that he wouldn't trade Lee for Cater because "Cater will probably be a part-time player." The deal would have to be for Lyle. Well, as long as they insisted...

Former Yankee public relations director Marty Appel recalls,

"I don't believe I ever saw Ralph Houk happier than that March 22 when we got Sparky Lyle. He was beside himself with joy." He should have been. This was the deal that changed the balance of power in the American League East. Except for when they had Bill Campbell healthy in 1977, the Red Sox have always been desperately in need of an invincible short man. In at least two seasons, 1972 and 1978, Lyle could have meant a Boston pennant. It is not inconceivable that his absence cost Boston the World Series in 1975. The man who was not traded in that deal, Bill Lee, looked back on that black day in Red Sox history and concurred, "Yep, we would have won a lot more pennants if the team hadn't given up that slider-throwin', Dewars-drinkin' left-hander."

Lyle came to the Yankees and brought with him an aura of glamor the team had been lacking since the retirement of Mantle.

He was nicknamed the Count because, like a certain Transylvanian nobleman, he had the ability to draw the life's blood out of enemy rallies. The Stadium became his Paladium, and every appearance was a command performance.

Yankee fans reveled in this version of *The Perils of Pauline*. The scenario they witnessed several times each homestand usually started with New York somehow scoring just enough runs to lead in a close game. The starting pitcher would hold tight for about seven innings and then unravel, allowing a couple of loud base hits. The game would be perched precariously on the razor's edge. Up until now, all of its participants had been supporting players. Houk, the director in this epic, would stride to the mound, take the ball from his grateful starter, and signal to the bullpen with his left arm. A murmur would slither through the crowd as the pinstriped Datsun rolled onto the field. To the visiting team, this benign method of transportation had become a hearse. The door would open and Lyle would spring out to the opening strains of "Pomp and Circumstance." The Stadium would tremble with jubilant cries of "Defense, Defense." A tiny wave of applause would stretch itself out into a deafening crescendo until...*star time!* Sparky Lyle was warmed up and ready to face the enemy batsman. Most of the time the hitter had two chances: slim and none at all.

It was Ted Williams who explained to Lyle exactly how a slider rotated and broke. Using what can be described only as a form of visual imagery, Lyle figured out how to throw the pitch in order to duplicate those results. One evening his wife was awakened by what she thought was the sound of a small bulldozer intruding through her back door. A dash to the yard revealed it was her husband throwing his new toy against the wall at four in the morning. Shortly thereafter, the plaything became a deadly weapon: Sparky's Slider. Bill Robinson once described facing it, saying, "It's like trying to hit a sliding bowling ball with a toothpick." He was not the only player who felt that way. In the constant dialogue between batter and pitcher, Lyle invariably had the last word.

Lyle's feats lifted the Yankees to the status of contender. First place was a real possibility until the final ten days of the season. They settled for fourth, six and a half games behind the Detroit Tigers. It was the closest they had been to first place, at the end of a season, in eight years.

The left-hander wasn't the sole reason for the improvement. Houk had spent long hours during the season drilling Horace Clarke in the finer points of turning the double play. This maneuver had been the second baseman's Achilles' heel, but Houk's tutoring paid dividends. In 1972, no second baseman in the league participated in more twin-killings than Clarke, and the Yankees led the league in double plays with 179.

Bobby Murcer contributed a season that was even better than his last one. He finished in the top three in home runs, RBI, hits, and doubles, and he led the league in total bases and runs scored. Murcer's most dramatic improvement over his earlier playing days was underscored after the season was played out. He was named the American League Gold Glove center fielder. Now, when he got to a ball, nobody yelled, "Duck!"

In a season filled with heroes, one player joined Sparky Lyle on an elevated plateau: Celerino Sanchez.

The ignored man of spring training was brought up at the time of McKinney's demotion. He was the final piece to the jigsaw puzzle. Sanchez's exceptional glove fused the infield into a cohesive unit as he displayed an aerial repertoire reminiscent of Clete Boyer. The fans loved him. They seemed to sense that here was an honest craftsman who had labored patiently with a quiet fortitude, knowing his moment would come. He played in a country he did not know, in front of people whose language he did not speak. All he had was his will and his talent. And one more thing: that glove. It was a forlorn wreck of faded leather, until he slipped it on. Then it became a plumed quill able to rewrite the accepted meanings of grace and beauty. It was enough. He would not be denied.

Success for the Yankees that year was only partial. The Mets were never in their pennant race, finishing 13½ games behind the Pittsburgh Pirates. No matter. They outdrew the Yankees, 2,134,185 to 967,715. It was the first time since World War II that the Yankees had drawn less than a million. CBS had seen enough.

Pitcher George Medich hadn't. He had been up with the Yankees for the Mayor's Trophy Game, beating the Mets 7–4. His only other appearance with the club came at the end of the year. It was a disastrous outing against the Baltimore Orioles in which he failed to retire a single batter. That did not dull his appetite for the big leagues or New York. He couldn't wait for next season.

First memories of George Medich are of a big, rawboned right-handed pitcher who took a good fastball and a veteran's poise to the mound. He had studied medicine at the University of Pittsburgh. Of course, he was nicknamed Doc.

He retired at the end of the 1982 season after participating in the World Series with the Milwaukee Brewers. When he spoke for this book, it was at the beginning of his final season. He was then a Texas Ranger.

There was snow outside when Doc Medich sat in the Sheraton Plaza dining room. It was April, and the season opener against the Yankees in New York had been canceled. Medich sat wondering if the season would ever get started. Relaxed in the warmth of the hotel, Medich talked about his career as a Yankee.

"I was born in Pennsylvania, so I wasn't a Yankee fan. In

fact I was bored with them because they always won. In 1969, I was in New York to take some medical exams, and I stayed at a hotel on the Grand Concourse. First morning, I woke up, walked out onto the street, and the first thing I saw was the Stadium. Six months later I was drafted by the team. I had a feeling they might draft me because they had scouted a lot of my college games. I told all the clubs that I was going to go to medical school, and that made a lot of them back off. The Yankees were willing to take a gamble because of their experience with Dr. Bobby Brown. He played third base for them while he was going to medical school in the forties and fifties, and they didn't have any problems.

"I got a letter from Bobby right before I was drafted and, though he didn't come right out and say it, it pretty much was meant to discourage me from doing both things. Something about how it was more difficult to mix baseball with medicine today than it was when he played. He didn't say why. But I was in a position to do something I really wanted to do. As it turned out the two fields are not incompatible.

"My first appearance as a Yankee, not in Yankee Stadium, was at Shea in the Mayor's Trophy Game. I got the win but that was really an exhibition game. My first regular season appearance was in 1972 against Baltimore. I set a record that day. I'm the only pitcher in baseball to come to bat before throwing my first major league pitch. That's among players who were strictly pitchers. We batted around in the first inning, and I got up and walked. Then I pitched in the bottom of the inning and got knocked out before retiring a batter. It was my only appearance of the season, and it left me with an ERA for the year of infinity. It also gave me an on-base percentage of 1.000. Starting next season, the pitchers didn't hit. So I maintained a perfect career on-base percentage until I joined Pittsburgh in the National League in 1976. That move gave me a profound appreciation for the designated hitter rule.

"That first full year was great even though we didn't win a lot of ball games. We had a terrific bunch of guys. When I first joined the Yankees, I was something of a curiosity. I was the first rookie to make the team in a few years, and I came from out of nowhere. I had never been to spring training with these guys. But they looked out for me. Thurman [Munson], [Mel] Stottlemyre, [Sparky] Lyle, [Fritz] Peterson, and [Steve] Kline. They were like a bunch of big brothers. They were fun to be around.

"Bill Virdon was our manager in 1974, and I really liked him. He'd give me the ball every fourth day and say, 'Go get them.' He wasn't afraid to make decisions. Like moving Bobby Murcer from center field to right. That was a great move. Pissed Bobby off, but it was good for the club. He wasn't afraid to do what he had to do to make the club better, and that pissed a few guys off. He also knew he was the second or third choice as manager, and that it was only a matter of time before he got fired.

"Ralph Houk was a terrific manager. He never bothered anybody. He let everybody on the club know what their role was and then used them accordingly. If you didn't produce, he called you in and let you know he was making a change. Nobody ever talked back to him; Ralph was a man's man. I knew he was leaving the Yankees before anybody else did. After I pitched a game on the last Saturday of the 1973 season, I was supposed to leave for home. I was starting school on Monday. I went in to say good-bye to him. He shut the door and said, 'I won't be back next season. I'm quitting. I just can't take it here anymore.' I didn't have to ask what he meant, I had a pretty good idea."

Houk had almost left the club in 1972, though not voluntarily. The Yankees' languid crawl out of the starting gate had inspired a brace of rumors that Houk was about to be fired, leaving him free to become the skipper of either the Indians or the Red Sox, depending on which story you were reading. One speculation had New York already settled on a successor: Billy Martin. A group of reporters approached Mike Burke in the press box and asked him to confirm. Burke issued a vehement denial. He said no such change had been considered, and that he certainly wouldn't qualify Martin as a candidate for any Yankee job since Martin was currently employed. He was managing the Detroit Tigers. There is a rule in baseball against tampering with other clubs' employees, and Burke wasn't about to leave himself open to any charges. The fact is the gossip was based in truth. Eight years after the fact, Burke admitted, "We had a poor or mediocre start in '72. As a matter of fact, I wasn't so sure that we didn't need a change of managers. One always looks around, when a team is going bad, and wonders, 'What are we doing wrong? What can we do to improve the situation?' I even talked to Billy Martin, but we were friends and always talking. Then, the club had a good run, and we weren't really eliminated mathematically from the race until the first of October."

The team's success saved Houk's job and gave the organization the optimistic view that the five-year plan had not been far off.

Winter brought further evidence of this giddy outlook. The first move was made on November 25, when the team traded pitcher Rob Gardner and the forgotten Rich McKinney to the Oakland A's for outfielder—first baseman Matty Alou. At the time of the deal there were no more than a dozen lifetime .300 hitters in the majors. Alou was one of them. He had created a reputation while playing for the Pirates, Cardinals, and Athletics: a leadoff man who was always on base. This was very important to the Yankees. Horace Clarke's value in that role had diminished because he hardly ever walked. Neither did Matty. But Alou always got in the neighborhood of 200 hits. This was a high-rent district, and Clarke's batting average didn't even qualify him for the waiting list.

Within forty-eight hours of this transaction, the team made another pickup. New York had been after Indian third baseman Graig Nettles for three years; now they had him. The deal sent Cleveland four young ballplayers: outfielders Charlie Spikes (now there's a great baseball name) and Rusty Torres, infielder Jerry Kenney, and first baseman John Ellis. People who didn't know how really good Nettles was questioned the wisdom of surrendering so much youth. Houk made it clear what was on the club's mind when he fielded those critics' questions, and retorted, "I'm not worried about youth. I'm after the pennant this season." He didn't get it.

Missing the flag in 1973 was a big disappointment because the team was actually favored by the odds-makers to win it all. The addition of Matty Alou was a factor in this rating. But, essentially it was Nettles who was the larger influence on the forecast. The year before, the Yankees had seriously challenged the Big Boys with Sanchez, an excellent gloveman with little power, at third. Nettles was at least his equal defensively and had battered 71 homers in the last three seasons. That statistic opened up some eyes. What kept them open was the fact that Nettles was a left-handed hitter. Left-handed power and the Stadium's right field porch were a dangerous brew. There was no telling what Nettles might do in the Bronx over the course of a full season.

Well, he didn't do anything more than he had done in the past. He played a good third base, as expected. He also managed to hit 22 home runs. A disappointment. The total was good enough to tie Bobby Murcer for the team lead, but it hardly qualified Nettles as the second coming of Roger Maris. It did contribute to the revitalized scoring machine, but it wasn't enough. The team was starting-pitching poor after Medich and Stottlemyre. Once again, they finished fourth.

The Mets won another pennant that year and were the town's real noise. The only thing that seemed to get the Yankees ink was news that did not take place between the chalk lines.

One such item was the Peterson-Kekich "life-swap." The two lefties had decided to exchange families. News of this arrangement made the front pages and became *the* topic in most major sports columns. Baseball commissioner Bowie Kuhn called the two players in for a chat and, it is assumed, some sort of reprimand. Why? Who knows. Perhaps he thought it his duty, as did some journalists, to make a show of moral outrage. Really, it wasn't anybody's damned business.

The other headline grabber for the Yankees that year was, however, quite a few people's business. That was because it affected the lives of so many.

Back on January 3, 1920, the Yankees had announced the purchase of the contract of Babe Ruth from the Boston Red Sox. Fifty-three years later, to the day, the team called another press conference to herald another acquisition. No, they hadn't picked up another Ruth. They had acquired a new owner: George Steinbrenner.

When William S. Paley and the gray suits at CBS had decided to unload the ball club, Mike Burke was asked to handle the sale. The Yankee president got in touch with many of New York's most prominent citizens, but couldn't find a buyer. He attempted to put together a group of his own to make a purchase. Little progress had been made until the day he received a phone call from Gabe Paul. Paul had been the president of the Cleveland Indians. While in that position he had naturally been aware of shipping magnate Steinbrenner's unsuccessful attempt to purchase the Cleveland franchise. It was Paul who suggested to Steinbrenner that, if he wanted to acquire a ball club, the Yankees might be available. This phone call to Burke was the first move by Paul on Steinbrenner's behalf.

Burke, Steinbrenner, and Paul met for lunch at Manhattan's famous 21 Club in November 1972. The gist of what Burke told Steinbrenner was that the Yankees could be bought immediately, if two conditions were met. They were:

1. Cash must be paid.
2. The price was $10 million.

An arrangement was worked out. Steinbrenner would be the principal owner, heading up a syndicate of limited partners. Paul and Burke would be included in that group. Burke would receive 5 percent equity in the club as a finder's fee. With these terms worked out, a proposal was put together to take to Paley.

CBS got rid of the club in less time than it takes to sell a small home. Twenty-four hours after hearing the Steinbrenner-Burke team's offer, Paley called up and said it was a deal. The swiftness of the transaction shouldn't have been that surprising. The network was anxious to unload the team and, from a business standpoint, the Yankees were small potatoes. They represented less than 2 percent of the conglomerate's total holdings.

Burke brought Steinbrenner in with the impression that they

would be equal partners on the decision-making level. In fact, Burke expected something of a free hand in dealing with the club's actual day-to-day affairs. Steinbrenner was, after all, a novice in this business, and Paul was brought into the fold as a temporary consultant. The announced plan had it that Paul would stay around the club for a year or two and then gracefully retire.

That was not the way things turned out. There was a difference in styles between Burke and Steinbrenner that was irreconcilable. A picture remains fixed in the mind's eye: Steinbrenner and Burke posing for a publicity shot. Steinbrenner is in a conservative business suit, his hair the picture of Wall Street sobriety. Not a strand out of place. Burke is tastefully but casually attired in a work shirt. No tie. His hair is rockstar long and dancing in the wind. That picture should have been the tip-off. There was no way these two guys would ever get along. "Oh, yes, George [Steinbrenner] and I were worlds apart," remembered Burke. "We get along better at a distance than we did working together. There was this real conflict of sorts from the beginning—personal, chemical, style, whatever—so I said to him, 'You know we're really not compatible, and there's no point in our living together and fighting.'" Burke had decided to get a divorce. The announcement came on April 30, 1973.

He really had no choice. Gabe Paul was not just another consultant. It quickly became clear that Paul was there to run the show. Had Burke stayed, he would have been reduced to the role of figurehead.

When Burke took over the reins as team president, he qualified Yankee Stadium as "a grand old dame—but I don't mean that as a pejorative." Delighted journalists joked that they would look up the spelling of the word later. Upon his farewell, Burke chose to quote from Yeats's "An Irish Airman Foresees His Death." There was no public venting of hostility, no whining accusations. There wasn't any mention of his being forced out. Burke made an exit every bit as classy as his entrance. He didn't even bother to ask for a blindfold or a cigarette.

The Burke-Houk-MacPhail triumvirate was being dissolved.

By the end of the season, Houk announced his "retirement." No reasons were given, but one Yankee official confided, "I think Ralph [Houk] found it very difficult to live with George [Steinbrenner]. He hated leaving the Yankees. He always used to say, 'You're going to have to tear this uniform off me to get me out of here.' He had a strong emotional tie with the team. But, from what he told me at least, he found his relationship with George onerous, and he decided to go." MacPhail also left in October. As had happened to Burke, he found that his role in the club's activities would become greatly reduced with the arrival of Paul.

The last day of Houk's term as manager heard him soundly booed with his every appearance out of the dugout. Had the Stadium fans known about the decision he would not reveal until after the game, they might have been kinder. Then again, perhaps it wouldn't have made the slightest difference. Booing Houk was a way of exorcising the bile that had accumulated over the last nine years. The crowd saw the Major as the visible symbol of the troika that had failed to bring the Yankees back to what they had been.

The three had done the best they could, given the situation. MacPhail did make a few bad deals, McKinney for Bahnsen being the worst of them. But to castigate him for that would be to ignore the successful transactions he pulled off, deals that brought Lindy McDaniel, Jack Aker, Sparky Lyle, Felipe Alou, Fred Beene, Fred Stanley, and Graig Nettles. His scales are overloaded on the plus side.

Booing Houk was way out of line. His record as Yankee manager stands as proof of his ability to extract every last win out of his available talent. Nobody could have done a better job; many would have done much worse.

The Yankees were miserable when Mike Burke took over, and the rules had been manipulated to ensure that they would remain that way for a long time. The five-year plan vowed that the club would be a contender by 1971. It was only one year short. Burke kept the Yankees in New York, and he helped put their image in a better light. In 1966, the Yankees had the worst minor league system in baseball. Their Class-A team in Greensboro that summer usually sent out the following lineup:

	HR	RBI	Avg.
Tom Shopay	1	14	.267
Charlie Warmsby	4	34	.205
Chet Trail	19	57	.288
Jim Covington	7	35	.240
Herb Ferris	12	27	.169
John Montileone	4	25	.214
Al Otto	5	18	.151
Jerry McLemore	2	20	.173

And they didn't have much pitching, either. By the time Burke left, the minor league system was healthy again.

Burke also managed to keep the Yankee attendance above the million mark every year, except for the strike-shortened season of 1972. It was during his term in office that New York acquired Nettles and Lyle through trades and signed Thurman Munson. They were the beginning of the Yankee powerhouse to come. And, of course, he did one other thing.

He helped bring George Steinbrenner to New York.

Chapter

SIX

One man's shit is another man's ice cream.

—GABE PAUL

GABE Paul officially assumed the dual roles of Yankee president and general manager on November 1, 1973. At the time of his investiture, it was announced that this was:

1. A new beginning (yawn).
2. A move that would greatly revitalize the club (ho-hum).
3. The start of another five-year plan (*gasp!*).

While the press spent seconds trying to decipher these three clichés, Paul went about his business. He didn't believe the Yankees would be contenders in five years; he felt he could turn the club around a bit sooner. It took him the entire winter.

The Yankees were a mediocre club in 1973. Paul had spent the season observing that. He had also seen a team blessed with a good deal more than just average talent. Thurman Munson, Bobby Murcer, Roy White, and Mel Stottlemyre had all been recent All-Stars. Graig Nettles was a battler at third who could supply power and defense. Ron Blomberg added a quick, young bat to the lineup, although his fielding at first base was criminal and he seemed unable to hit left-handed pitching. Doc Medich could pitch, and so could Pat Dobson, the former Baltimore Oriole who had been acquired from the Atlanta Braves in the middle of the 1973 season. Sam McDowell had come over from the San Francisco Giants on the same day, and the left-hander with the host of personal problems and unclockable fastball was still on the roster, always a threat to live up to his immense talent. Fritz Peterson and Steve Kline were expected to rebound after off-years. And Sparky Lyle, one of the best relievers in the business, was ably assisted in the bullpen by Lindy McDaniel and Fred Beene. This was not a bad start. Surely it was a better bunch than the group Lee MacPhail had inherited in 1966.

Once the team's strengths were brought into focus, the new general manager concentrated on the weak links. The double play combination of Horace Clarke and Gene Michael was the first to come under his scrutiny. They were found lacking. Clarke's inability to turn the double play had resurfaced again and now was further mitigated by the perceptible deterioration of his baserunning game. He had stolen only 11 bases in 1973. The club could tolerate a second baseman who was timid on twin-killings as long as he was stealing bases, scoring runs, and helping to ignite the offense. Clarke had stopped doing those things. He had become too costly a liability. Michael had begun to lose a step at short. His problem was in direct contrast to Clarke's. Since Michael's glove carried his bat, his .225 batting average could go unnoticed in the glare of his defensive brilliance. As the gloss of his mitted performances began to fade, his offensive shortcomings could not be hidden. Both men would have to be replaced.

Matty Alou had already been sent away, sold to the Cardinals in September 1973. He had batted .296 during his stay in pinstripes, but it was a benign .296. Alou had driven in only 28 runs and scored just 59.

Besides a new double play pairing, Paul evaluated the present Yankee lineup as needing two things. One was a right-hand-hitting outfielder to replace the departed southpaw-swinging

Matty Alou, someone who could combine with Munson to keep the left-handed pitching wolves away from the Stadium gates. Designated hitter Jim Ray Hart had performed that function during the previous season. He had been bought from the Giants, got off to a quick start, and then faded. His final performance figures were only slightly better than adequate. The chief objection to his reprise in the role of DH was that it was the only job he could fill. He wasn't a gazelle in the field. In fact, he had no listed position. Even worse, he couldn't run worth a damn. His arrival on the base paths was an automatic signal for the start of another traffic jam.

The next item on Paul's list was a right-hand-hitting first baseman, someone who could platoon with Ron Blomberg. Paul's preference was for a long-ball threat. This had been Felipe Alou's job for the last three years. He had done it well until the previous season, when his birthday cake was ablaze with thirty-eight reasons for his bat to lose its sting.

No one could have expected Paul to satisfy all these needs. He had already made up his mind not to part with any member of the club's nucleus (Munson, Stottlemyre, Lyle, et al.) unless he was overwhelmed by another team's offer. Yankee minor league stars were similarly considered almost untouchable. When Paul left for the winter meetings in Hawaii, he was armed only with a credo. And a checkbook.

The credo belonged to Branch Rickey, and it was inscribed in indelible ink on baseball's Rushmore: "'Tis far better to trade a player one year too early, rather than one year too late."

Lindy McDaniel was thirty-eight years old. He had just come off a glittering season (12–6, 2.81 ERA, 10 saves) as the Yankees' primary long reliever. If ever a player fit into Rickey's "year too early, year too late" mold, it was McDaniel. As trade bait, he was at the height of his value, extremely attractive and expendable. His expendability was based on two things:

1. He was never going to replace Sparky Lyle as the team's main man out of the bullpen.
2. He could be replaced by Fred Beene.

Beene was a thirty-year-old right-hander the Yankees had acquired from the Baltimore Orioles in 1972. He had just spent the summer as New York's secondary long reliever, and had used his vast variety of curveballs to put up some numbers (6–0, 1.68 ERA) as dazzling as McDaniel's. This gave New York a surplus that enabled Gabe Paul to get the right-hand-hitting outfielder he coveted.

Lou Piniella was coming off his worst season as a Kansas City Royal. The thirty-year-old .285 lifetime hitter had only batted .250 in 1973. On a team overstocked with prospects, he, like McDaniel, would not be missed. Paul was drawn to Piniella. Scouting reports indicated that Piniella had hit a *hard* .250. Every other line drive he smacked was right at someone. Baseball, in its divine fairness, has a way of making up for that kind of season the following year. Piniella's hitting history, and his smooth but dismembering stroke at the plate, indicated that he was capable of making a lot of pitchers pay for his off-year. Despite his low average, he had still managed to deliver when he came up with men on base. Piniella had driven in 69 runs. The quantity of runs batted in was not as impressive as their quality. Most of his Royal teammates agreed that there was nobody on the club they would rather see coming up in a crucial situation than Piniella. Also, Piniella had an absolute and obvious hatred for losing. It was something he had in common with Paul.

The Royals were anxious to get a long reliever to team up with their own bullpen star, Doug Bird. They felt it would mean the pennant. When Paul offered McDaniel for Piniella, Kansas City was so excited that they even offered to throw in young right-handed pitcher Ken Wright to complete the deal. Paul, who would have been perfectly happy to walk away with just Piniella, allowed himself to be talked into it.

The Piniella-McDaniel swap presented a glimpse of Paul's future success as a Yankee trader. His next moves provided baseball historians with the first hard evidence that his boss George Steinbrenner was not afraid to follow capitalism's Golden Rule: "To make money, you have to spend money."

Paul tapped Steinbrenner's bankbook for about a quarter of

a million dollars. This amount was sent to the Texas Rangers in three separate deals. In return, the Yankees received Jim Mason, Elliott Maddox, and Bill Sudakis.

The light-hitting Mason was expected to replace Michael at short. Maddox, a genius in the outfield, was to provide the Yankees with late-inning defense. With Texas, Sudakis had been an all-purpose utilityman. He had put in time in the outfield, at first and third, and behind the plate. Sudakis was a switch-hitter, and had managed to hit 15 home runs in only 235 at-bats in 1973. Texas did not play in an easy park for power hitters. What made his stats especially compelling was the news that most of his homers had come against left-handed pitching. Sudakis was the early favorite to share first base with Blomberg.

Paul's sleight-of-hand act had succeeded in patching up most of the holes in the Yankee roster. Now all he needed was a second baseman. And a manager.

At the outset of Paul's Hawaiian excursion, it was generally agreed that the Yankees had already found a successor to Ralph Houk. They had—Dick Williams, the former skipper of the Oakland A's.

Williams had a résumé that made him an attractive candidate for any managerial position. He had been the architect of the Red Sox's Impossible Dream of 1967. In three years with the A's, his teams won three division titles, two league championships, and two world championships. There was one more thing. Williams was the only manager in western civilization who had ever lasted more than two consecutive years under the tyrannical Charles Finley, owner of the Oakland A's, who was not an easy man to work for. Finley was of the mind that the real star of the A's wasn't Reggie Jackson, Sal Bando, Catfish Hunter, or Vida Blue. It was Charles O. Finley. He had put the ball club together and considered it a tribute to his baseball genius.

As much of a character as Charlie O. may have seemed to be, it was a mistake to pass him off as just another know-nothing sports mogul with bank balances for brains. Finley was a baseball man. He had put together one of the greatest teams in the annals of baseball, and he did it on a shoestring budget. Finley immersed himself in every facet of the organization, trusting nothing to underlings. He was his own general manager, public relations director, head of ticket sales, chief cook, and bottle washer.

At times his philosophy of total involvement brought him, either physically or via telephone, into the manager's and players' domains: the clubhouse and dugout. He would harangue his manager with endless calls and meetings, suggesting new bits of strategy or lineup changes. He also had a penchant for humiliating his ballplayers. Finley was not above publicly insulting and demeaning them, both as professionals and as men. It was one such act that drove Williams beyond the limit.

Mike Andrews had been a decent ballplayer. He was Williams's second baseman on the Red Sox and had established a reputation as a steady hitter who could sting the ball at the plate. In 1971, he was traded to the Chicago White Sox for shortstop Luis Aparicio. Somewhere between Boston's Fenway Park and Chicago's Comiskey Park, he misplaced a good deal of the range he once had. By the time he came to Oakland in mid-1973, he was a second baseman in name only. On the A's this was of little consequence. They already had a fine second baseman in Dick Green. Andrews was expected to be used strictly as a utility man: a little pinch-hitting, a little DH, maybe an occasional turn at second or first, but only in an emergency.

In baseball, an emergency can be defined thusly: You are the manager. Your team is in the twelfth inning of the second game of the World Series. You have just pinch-hit for your second second baseman of the evening. Your choices for a replacement have narrowed down to five: three pitchers, a pinch-running outfielder who has worn a major league glove ten times in seven years, and Mike Andrews. Whom do you choose?

These were the circumstances that had placed Mike Andrews at second base just in time to make two errors, allowing the New York Mets to score four runs and win the game. Nobody suggested that Andrews be subjected to capital punishment. Such fumbles happen all the time in baseball, and the great teams are able to shrug it off and forget it by the next game.

Charlie Finley was not one to forget—or forgive. He forced Andrews to undergo a medical exam immediately after the conclusion of the four-hour contest. Citing the ambiguous results, he dropped the second baseman from the team.

With one despicable move, Finley had cast himself as the ultimate Bligh. So naturally his crew reacted with a threat of mutiny. It didn't matter that Andrews wasn't the player he once was. It didn't matter that the loss had allowed New York to tie the Series. No, none of that mattered. What did matter was that Andrews was one of them, a professional. His teammates would not allow him to be the victim of the owner's latest shabby impulse. Not without a fight. The Athletics threatened to sit out the rest of the Series.

Cooler heads prevailed. Bowie Kuhn disallowed Andrews's removal from the roster, and by the fourth game he was back in the dugout. Williams had decided to play Fletcher Christian. He called a meeting. In it, he let go of his pent-up abhorrence of Finley's behavior and its effects on the team. He finished his talk with an announcement: When the Series was over, win or lose, he was resigning. He had had enough.

The tormented and talented A's were victorious in the Series. And Williams did resign. Oakland threw a ticker-tape parade in homage to its hometown heroes. At the height of the celebration, Finley expressed his gratitude to Williams, saying, "Even if you're not going to be with us next year, I want to thank you for the great job you've done for the three years you've been with us." Pretty words. But what did they mean?

Williams took them to mean that his resignation had been accepted, and that he was now free to accept any job offers that came his way. The Yankees took the same reading. Therefore, imagine their surprise when they approached Charlie O. in Hawaii to seek his permission to talk to Williams. Finley gave them his best movie-star smile, cold as death, and said, "No way." Williams's contract had two more years to run. Finley had not formally accepted his resignation.

A few days later, Finley had a change of heart. Sure, the

Yankees could sign Williams. All it would cost them was a little bit of compensation. Say Munson, Murcer, or Lyle. The Yankees offered Horace Clarke. Not a chance. A couple more days passed. Again Finley took to the phone. This time he was willing to part with Dick Williams in exchange for two Yankee farmhands: Otto Velez and Scott McGregor. Gabe Paul balked. He was not going to surrender what he termed "the crown jewels of our minor league system." Finley was sorry Paul felt that way, but no jewels, no Williams.

After consulting with counsel, Paul and Steinbrenner decided to sign Williams without Finley's permission, and without giving him compensation. The announcement was made on the afternoon of December 13. That evening Finley filed a protest with American League president Joe Cronin.

The Yankees countered. First, they disputed Finley's claim that he had not released Williams from his contract. They introduced the owner's victory celebration statement as evidence. Then they challenged the contract Ralph Houk had signed to manage the Detroit Tigers. New York claimed that it too had not officially released Houk from his pact, an agreement that also had two more years to run. This last was just a piece of pre-courtroom maneuvering. The Yankee front office did not want Houk back. They were merely trying to establish a legal position in the event of a compromise. The compromise they hoped for would have the Tigers compensate the Yankees for Houk by sending Oakland compensation for Williams.

Cronin wasn't buying. When the imbroglio was over, the president ruled against the Yankees, right down the line. Houk's agreement with the Tigers was valid; the Yankee protest had come long after the fact. They had not objected to his signing when it was first announced, and that was construed as approval. Finley, on the other hand, had turned the Yankee request for Williams's services down flat from the onset. His words to Williams at the victory parade could have meant almost anything. As far as the American League was concerned, Williams's contract was the property of Charles O. Finley. The Yankees still did not have a manager. And then they did.

Bill Virdon had succeeded Danny Murtaugh as manager of

the Pittsburgh Pirates in 1972 and led them to the Eastern Division title that summer. The following season, he was dismissed. He was not the Yankees' first choice. No matter. On January 4, 1974, he was named manager of the New York Yankees.

The club he took over was a rollicking crew of privateers who would come within two games of Baltimore and the Eastern Division title. This was the Band on the Run.

Doc Medich remembered them as "a team, a real team of twenty-five guys. We played all right for the first four months of the season, but in August we just took off. It was a makeshift club with a lot of new people on it. We had great timing and chemistry that season. I remember beating the Red Sox 1–0 with a run in the ninth. The next day Dobber [Pat Dobson] beat them by striking out Rico Petrocelli in the bottom of the ninth with the bases loaded. That was great! Mike Wallace and Larry Gura, two guys nobody knew about, went 11 and 1 between them. Wallace pitched mostly in relief. He got one start all season, and he used it to beat Jim Palmer and the Orioles in a 3–0 game. Someone was always doing something. That was also the year that [Graig] Nettles became a great fielder. He was good in '73, but in '74 he was tremendous. Graig was the kind of guy who didn't care about publicity one way or the other, so it took time before people realized what they had here. I don't think the press started clamoring about his glove until just before I left. Maybe it was even a little bit after that. But we knew long before they wrote it. We just knew."

Nettles was the biggest news on the club during the first month of the season. The third baseman set a major league record with 11 home runs in the month of April. The following month, he tied another home run record for a month by hitting none. The drop-off didn't cripple the team. Others came along to provide punch, and the pitching was just good enough to keep the team aloft and in contention.

Gabe Paul continued to tinker. In late May, he used the underground railroad from New York to Arlington, Texas, and sent second-string catcher Duke Sims to the Texas Rangers for

Larry Gura. Gura was the epitome of the crafty left-hander: a control specialist who never overpowered anybody but still managed to get people out. His sinker and curve would be especially effective at Yankee Stadium. Afterward, Paul used Steinbrenner's ever-present checkbook to make two more valuable additions from the California Angels: Rudy May and Sandy Alomar.

May was a left-handed pitcher whose dapper appearance had gained him the nickname Dude. He was particularly fond of a nasty, emerald-hued suit which, when draped on his long, lean form, tended to remind his teammates of a giant green grasshopper. May could throw hard. He had found himself prematurely nudged out of the starting rotation and shunted off to bullpen duty in California. The reason for the demotion was an 0–1 record and an ERA over 7.00. The reason for the numbers was a lack of work. Paul and his scouts had properly assessed that there was nothing wrong with the southpaw's arm. They were also impressed with May's bulldog attitude; everything about it said, "Give me the ball!" After the Yankees acquired him on June 15, that is precisely what they did: They gave him the ball. He responded with an 8–4 record and an ERA of 2.25. His purchase price was $85,000. Cheap.

May had not been the only California Angel suffering from inactivity. For five years, Sandy Alomar had been the team's starting second baseman. Throughout that period, many observers felt that he was the finest fielder at his position in the league.

The problem was that he couldn't hit. Or at least he couldn't hit enough to satisfy the California Angels. Alomar had been their leadoff hitter since 1969, and had averaged 25 stolen bases a season. But, since 1971, he had been unable to raise his average as high as .240. The Angels had a fleet new center fielder in Mickey Rivers. His emergence as a base-stealing threat obviated the need for Alomar's presence in the lineup, and Denny Doyle, who had come over from the Philadelphia Phillies in an off-season swap, wore a glove that was as highly regarded as Alomar's. Doyle had just completed the previous season's work with a .273 batting average. The Angels didn't need a leadoff hitter, they didn't need a second baseman, and they didn't need Sandy Alomar.

The Yankees did.

They had finally ended Horace Clarke's tenure with the club, selling him to the San Diego Padres on June 1. The sale gave a sign that some of the coldness associated with the Yankees in their winning days had crept back into the organization. When Clarke left the team's hotel in Chicago to make his way to his new club, there wasn't a single member of the Yankee front office there to wish him luck. He had only been with the organization for seventeen years.

The Yankees spent the next six weeks auditioning replacements at second base. Gene Michael, Fred Stanley, and Fernando Gonzalez all gave readings. None of them had quite what the Yankees were looking for. Then the Yankees were struck by a piece of casting that was inspired. They turned their eyes westward, to the land of endless screen tests, and focused their sights on a rival studio in Anaheim. The Angels had not been boffo at the box office. They were paying a lot of moolah to a Latin character actor for whom they couldn't find a part. The Yankees alleviated the two problems with one check. By the evening of July 9, Sandy Alomar was back practicing his craft in a featured role: starting second baseman for the New York Yankees. He provided the team with performances that were always reliable and often spectacular. It was the strongest piece of second base work the club had seen since the retirement of Bobby Richardson. Alomar also took pains to demonstrate the versatility of his talents. He batted second, hit .269, and did all the little things necessary to become a valuable member of the team offense.

These acquisitions by Gabe Paul had a positive impact on the club's performance. None of them, however, had quite the explosive and far-reaching qualities of a deal he consummated on April 26. It was announced late that Friday evening, and the date has attained a hallowed position in the Yankee mythos. This was the evening of the Midnight Massacre.

"I seem to recall," said Fritz Peterson, "that it was as if the whole pitching staff was being called into Bill Virdon's office that night. First [Steve] Kline, then [Fred] Beene, then me, and finally Tom Buskey. It was like some sort of joke. I mean I just didn't expect a team that is in the pennant race to trade half its pitching staff." Neither did anyone else. Especially the ball-players. Kline and Peterson were two of the more popular members of the club, and Buskey was an excellent rookie prospect. The most criticized aspect of the deal was the inclusion of Fred Beene. Beene was supposed to be the best long reliever in base-ball. Munson couldn't believe Beene had been let go. He walked around the clubhouse in a Thurmanesque fit of perplexity, asking anyone who would listen, "How could we trade Fred Beene?"

Quite easily, really. Paul had a chance to make a deal with the Cleveland Indians for Chris Chambliss, Dick Tidrow, and Cecil Upshaw. Chambliss was a twenty-five-year-old first base-man who had been named the American League Rookie of the Year in 1971. He was an intelligent left-handed batsman who had improved with each succeeding season. Tidrow had been the AL Rookie Pitcher of the Year in 1972, and had won 14 games the following season with a bad ball club. He was twenty-seven. Upshaw was a thirty-one-year-old reliever whom Paul expected to do the same job that Beene had done. In order to get "a future batting champion, one of the best young pitchers in the league, and a veteran reliever with pennant race experience," he had given up two sore-armed pitchers, an untried rookie, and a relief pitcher he had already replaced. He had also succeeded in breaking up a dangerous status quo. Years later, after the Yankees had reestablished themselves as a force, Paul said, "That deal was the start of everything. It broke up the country club. There was a great camaraderie on those losing ball clubs."

Chambliss was in shock. "I had figured that I would be in Cleveland for a long time," recalled the first baseman. "I really didn't expect to get traded at that point. I was hitting .328. The night of the deal, I had driven in three runs to win the ball game for the Indians. After the excitement of the game they called us into the office—[Dick] Tidrow, [Cecil] Upshaw, and me—and told us we'd been traded. It was really a downer after being so high over the game. I didn't hit well for the Yankees that year. Part of the reason was because I was platooned. When I first got there, [Bill] Virdon told me that I would be the regular first baseman, against all kinds of pitching. I don't think a week went by before the first lefty came in and I was on the bench. I ended up being platooned most of the season. It really hurt my timing at the plate. Then, during the last month of the season, I got to play and I started to hit. And we kept on winning. I got my average back up, but I still finished at .255. That was my worst season in the majors. Moving from Cleveland to New York was a real adjustment, but I think my wife and I made it rather easily. The worst adjustment I had to make was not playing every day and not hitting. It really was the first time I had ever had a lot of trouble hitting the ball. The attitude toward me when I first got here wasn't overly friendly, but I could understand that. I was looked on as, 'Who is this guy we gave up our four friends for?' I think those four pitchers had been part of a strong clique on the club. They didn't know who I was."

When the team was at last assembled, they provided their fans with a summer of unexpected pleasures. The season was cluttered with small heroics. When strung together they formed a montage of the near-miraculous, and left the viewer's head crowded with vivid memories: Jim Mason bashing out five doubles in a 12–5 win over his former Texas teammates... Mason, an alert greyhound at short, enchanting fans with his daredevil acrobatics...Elliott Maddox catching everything... Munson hitting with the game, any game, on the line...Thurman agitating, keeping the team loose and playing on sheer guts through the pain of a damaged right hand...Sandy Alomar, at the height of the pennant race, making a diving stop and throw from short right field in Fenway Park, canceling a certain game-ending hit in an extra-inning contest against the Red Sox ...Alex Johnson, just bought from the Texas Rangers, and picked up only after Yankee efforts to get Frank Robinson from the Angels had failed, showing up in the middle of the same game and punctuating his first appearance as a Yankee by pumping a game-winning pinch-hit home run...Ron Blomberg torturing right-handed pitching...Mel Stottlemyre felled by a career-ending rotator cuff injury in a game against the California Angels...Doc Medich and Pat Dobson rising to the responsibility of replacing him by winning 19 games each...Rudy May striking out legions of batters...Sparky Lyle being Sparky Lyle... Bill Virdon spreading a meditative calm over the clubhouse... Roy White fighting his way off the bench ("Bill Virdon didn't know what kind of player I was at first. I'm the type who doesn't impress you on first glance. You have to see me play for a while") to help lead the Yankee attack...the Yankees fighting their way back after a late-September three-game sweep by the Orioles and a doubleheader loss to Boston, battling back to stay in the chase until the season's final days...the banners at Shea screaming, "Yes We Can!" Banners at Yankee games! It was incredible fun. None of this was marred by the imperfect ending, a climax bathed in irony.

The Implausible Dream came to a close on the next-to-last day of the season, in Milwaukee. The Brewers beat the Yankees 3–2. New York had led 2–1 going into the eighth. A long fly ball to right field was seemingly misplayed by Maddox and Piniella, and the game was tied. The Yankees lost it in ten. It wasn't the outfielders' fault. As Medich, who was going for his 20th win that night, later pointed out, "It was one of those plays that could have happened to anyone. I remember driving to the ball park that day with Mel [Stottlemyre]. It was snowing. The field was wet and almost unplayable, especially around third base where the tarp was. You know people forget how, in the third or fourth inning, Piniella was rounding third base, slipped in the mud, and was tagged out. That was the third run. That was the winning run. That's life. But that wasn't his fault either. It was like a marsh out there, really unplayable. People say Murcer would have caught that ball that tied up the game. Well, nobody can say for sure. Not with the shape that field was in."

Lou Piniella was in right field that night because Bobby Murcer was unable to play. He had been injured, the innocent bystander in a hotel scuffle between teammates Rick Dempsey and Bill Sudakis.

That Bobby Murcer couldn't play in the most crucial game of his career was the only possible capper to his nightmare of a season. If the Yankees were exiles, and Shea was their Elba, then Murcer was surely Napoleon in pinstripes. When the team first disclosed that they would spend the 1974 and 1975 seasons as hostages of the Mets, questions were immediately raised. What effect would the move have on the club's left-handed power, Murcer in particular? The speculation was that he would miss the cozy right field porch.

Murcer shrugged it off. But after really crushing a few balls, only to have them caught at the warning track, he obviously began to wonder. Months went by before he hit his first Flushing home run. Soon he wasn't hitting home runs anywhere. That he could handle; he still managed to drive in 88 runs that season. What he had a hard time accepting was his move out of center field.

Murcer was not a great center fielder, but he had worked hard to become a very good one. In order to maintain that status he had to be at the top of his game, mentally and physically. He wasn't. The psych job that was performed on him by Shea saw to that. His overall game suffered.

Elliott Maddox, meanwhile, was working his name into the box scores as an occasional starter and defensive replacement. His fielding excellence made a big impression on the defense-minded Virdon. Maddox made an even bigger impression on those rare occasions when he was allowed to hit. Shea Stadium didn't bother him at all. He sprayed enough singles and doubles over its terrain to hike his batting average over .300. In late May, Virdon decided to make a gutsy move. He replaced Murcer, the heir-apparent to Mickey Mantle in center field, with Maddox. Murcer went to right. It was the move to make. With the arguable exception of the Baltimore Orioles' Paul Blair, Maddox was the finest center fielder in baseball. Murcer had all the makings of an excellent right fielder. This singular act, more than any other, made the 1974 Yankees a contender.

"The first time I was traded," recalls Maddox, "it was as part of the Denny McLain deal. Detroit sent Denny, Don Wert, and me to the Washington Senators for Ed Brinkman, Aurelio Rodriguez, Joe Coleman, and Jim Hannan. I was crushed. Fortunately, I hadn't been with the Tigers for more than a year, otherwise I really would have been stunned.

"When I came up in '70, there was some confusion as to what position I was supposed to play. Detroit made a mistake. I should have stayed in the minors that year. I was ready to play major league ball, but they brought me up and I sat on the bench most of the time. I had jumped from A ball to the majors. Most of the games I played were at third, but I also worked in the outfield that year. I got a lot of instruction from [Al] Kaline and Mickey Stanley that was invaluable. To learn from those guys, two of the best, was fantastic.

"When I got to the Senators, the manager was Ted Williams. We had our first face-to-face confrontation—notice I used the word 'confrontation'—in spring training, 1971. I had already read how he was against the trade. Once we were playing in Baltimore, and I asked him how come I wasn't playing tomorrow. We were facing [Dave] McNally that night and he said, 'You're in the lineup tonight. If you get three hits off McNally tonight, maybe you'll play tomorrow. I said, "What do you mean maybe?' He answered, "Well, I don't know, I'd have to think about it.' So I said, "Fine. Take me out of the lineup tonight. I don't need this aggravation.' We were in Kansas one night, and we went at it again. I said, 'Gee, Ted, why don't you let me play.' He replied, 'If you would get some hits, then I'd let you play.' I laughed and said, 'You give me a bat one hundred feet long, so that I can reach the plate from this bench, and I'll get you some hits.' That's when they had to separate us. The best reason he gave for benching me came in early 1971. He told me he wanted to look at some of the younger players. I was twenty-one.

"When Billy [Martin] came [as manager] it was really odd. He was the one who traded me from Detroit. He didn't know me, but somewhere along the line, he had heard things about me. He made some comments to some of the Detroit reporters. That got back to me. He was asked what his plans for Maddox were. Billy was supposed to have said, 'I don't really know if I want him on the club because he's just a downtown nigger.'

Exactly what a downtown nigger is supposed to mean as opposed to an uptown one, I'm not sure. I did get the drift of the second part of the description, though. I had heard that one before. I told the writer who told me that it wasn't possible because Billy didn't know me. Then another reporter came up and told me the same thing. Two weeks after I was traded, I saw Billy at a luncheon. I was getting an award as the Tiger Rookie of the Year. He didn't say anything to me, so I just went about my business. I don't know what our problem was. When he got over to the Rangers, he called me into his office and said, 'You're going to be in the lineup every day. What happened in Detroit is over.' Right there I was suspicious. I figured what the reporters had said must be true.

"Naturally, the first night he was there I didn't start. He did call on me to pinch-hit in the ninth, runner on second, tie score with Oakland. He asked me, 'Can you hit this guy?' The pitcher was Paul Lindblad. I said, 'Sure.' Billy said, 'All right, go up and get a hit.' I replied, 'I don't know if a single will score the runner. Would you like a double?' He yelled, 'Just get a hit!' I go up and hit a line drive to left-center that Joe Rudi couldn't reach. Easy double. Actually I don't know if I got credit for a single or a double because it ended a ball game. I walked over to Billy and said, 'Nothing to it, anytime you need me just let me know.' I still didn't start after that, and three weeks later I was sold to the Yankees. That was a homecoming for me because I'm from New Jersey.

"I didn't start a lot of games at the beginning of the '74 season. I just went in for defense. I might have started two games in the first month. I did some pinch-hitting. I was hitting the ball well, hitting it hard even when it didn't drop in. Bobby [Murcer] wasn't hitting at Shea. It started after a few games there when he hit the ball fairly good, good enough, he thought, to be a home run. They probably would have been homers at Yankee Stadium. He'd hit them, and start into his home run trot, and guys would be catching them at the warning track. After three or four weeks of that, he would arrive at the ball park a little more solemn each day. By the latter part of May, he seemed really depressed. Four big things happen in '74: the [Chris]

Chambliss trade, getting Rudy May, getting Sandy Alomar, and the switch of Bobby with me. I honestly believe that helped the team more than anything.

"It didn't, however, help my relationship with Bobby. Murcer never spoke to me socially again. Ever. I felt really funny about it because I knew Bobby was upset. But I had always wanted to play regularly, and I had grown up a Yankee fan. Now I was playing center field with New York. It was great. But I did feel bad that, after the switch, Bobby never said as much as hello to me. Virdon told us seperately. He called me in and told me. He knew what I could do out there. He was hitting fungoes to the outfielders. He would hit them to left, hit them to right, one after the other. This would go on for about fifteen minutes. I loved it. I'd be talking to him the whole time, saying, 'Come on, try to hit one by me. I'm going to catch anything you hit.' He'd wear out the other guys, but I would still yell for more.

"[Mel] Stottlemyre was a great fielder. I was in center the day he hurt his arm. It was against the Angels. He threw a pitch and jumped. Grabbed his shoulder and rotated his arm a little bit, and kept pitching. I played shallow center, and I could tell immediately he wasn't throwing the same. He missed his next start, and then came back to pitch a game. He lasted a third of an inning. That was it. It probably cost us the pennant.

"[Bill] Sudakis and I started the Band on the Run thing. We used to play that song by Paul McCartney before and after each game. Sudakis and I would call each other bandits, and it caught on. We were just a lot of guys who knew what our strong points were, and knew how to compensate for our weaknesses. For example, if Roy White was in left, I would tell him to take care of the line. Anything hit into left-center, I would take care of it. Roy could catch anything he could get to, but he couldn't throw well. So anything in left-center I would get and throw. We would communicate [in the outfield] all the time. That was the only time Bobby and I would talk.

"You know at one point, Shea had gotten to Bobby so badly that it was obvious he was losing sleep over it. He would come to the ball park exhausted and would tell me, 'You got to help me out. You got to take everything I can't get to. Anything down the right field line, I can handle. Anywhere else, it's yours.' Of course this meant there were times when Bobby would tell me this, and I had already told Roy that I was taking everything in left-center. The guys used to kid me about it. They said somebody should pay for my cab fare out there because I was all over the place. But I loved it. The greatest thing in the world for me was running after a fly ball. Bobby turned out to be an excellent right fielder, and [Lou] Piniella worked hard to become a good outfielder. Virdon was super. He worked very hard with Lou, but, more importantly, Piniella was receptive to the instruction. Bill also worked with Ronnie Blomberg, but Ron just did not catch on like Lou did. I wonder how much Ronnie would have developed if he had worked as hard as Piniella. I don't think he had the fielding ability to begin with. Lou could catch a ball, but Ron did not have good hands.

"In late June, we realized we had a real shot at the pennant. We went out on the field, and every game was a big party. We went out and had fun. Attitude is so important in this game. In 1977, on the Orioles, we were in the pennant race, and a couple of guys were tight. Mark Belanger stood up at a team meeting, and said, 'Look, if you guys are so damned scared of balls hit your way, and you pitchers are bitching and moaning that no one is catching anything, just throw it so it gets hit to short. I want each one. Let them hit it to me.' That's what I used to tell our pitchers: 'Let them hit it to me, I'll find a way to get it.' You need that kind of confidence, especially in a pennant race."

One of the key contributors to the valiant season was Jim Mason. His inspired fielding and timely hitting were unexpected plusses. Mason was another feather in Gabe Paul's chapeau. It wasn't often that a team could come up with a shortstop of Mason's ability and youth without surrendering a player in return. The Yankees expected him to be their shortstop for the next ten years.

He barely made it through the following season. On the first day of spring training, 1975, Mason climbed into the batting cage to face Iron Mike. This was not a pitcher; it is a pitching machine. Its purpose is to give hitters a chance to hone their batting eye before they face live pitching. It can be programmed to throw at various speeds. It can even be set to toss breaking pitches. But it cannot duplicate the physical intricacies of Luis Tiant's motion or other flesh-and-blood acts of deception. Major league hitters generally find Iron Mike's offerings quite hittable.

That first day, Mason discovered it to be a bit of a puzzle. He didn't hit a pitch for ten minutes. Not even a foul tip.

Teammates recall that Mason seemed to start pressing a little bit more each day after that. He never did get straightened out at the plate, and it began to affect his efficiency in the field. One pitcher said simply, "When he lost his confidence, he lost everything. The fans started to get on him. Not just booing, either. He made an error one day that cost us a game, and as he left the players' parking lot at Shea, some nut threw a god-damned brick through his windshield. That kind of shit you don't need." Elliott Maddox observed the situation from center field. He stated, with some wonder, "It was remarkable. I remember a pop-up that he [Mason] went out for into short left field. He backed up maybe fifteen feet onto the grass, and started pounding his glove, calling for the ball. He never even touched it. It dropped five feet behind him. Sometimes you can lose a ball like that in the sun, but this was during a night game. His head shot down. He looked like he was trying to figure out what could possibly go wrong next. It was as though he wanted to dig a hole out there and jump into it. I mean, Jim never even chased after the ball. That was the end for him. It was late May, and he did not want to start a game after that. He'd do a good job as a late-inning replacement, but start a game? Uh-uh."

Mason's decline at short was just one of the unexpected factors that made 1975 one of the Yankees' most disappointing seasons—disappointing because it began with so much promise.

Gabe Paul and George Steinbrenner had pulled off two moves during the winter that hogged all the sports ink not only in New York, but in the nation as well. Maneuver number one was the first ever one-for-one trade of $100,000 ball players:

Bobby Murcer to San Francisco for Bobby Bonds.

Only a few weeks before, the Yankee front office had told Murcer that there were no plans to trade him. George Steinbrenner had assured Murcer that he would be with the club as long as the owner was. It must have come as quite a shock when Murcer received a phone call on the morning of October 22. It was Gabe Paul. He broke the news about the just-completed deal. According to one witness, the conversation "went on for about five minutes. Gabe [Paul] was telling Bobby [Murcer], 'Oh yes, it'll be great for you. You should fit right in over there, they really need you. Well, so long...What's that? Oh, Bobby Bonds.' It was as if Bonds were an afterthought."

The "afterthought" the Yankees had obtained in the swap was considered one of the five best ball players in the game. He appeared to be the only man in baseball capable of hitting 40 home runs and stealing 40 bases in the same season. Bonds was also one of the major league's finer defensive right fielders. The Giants traded him because they were desperate for Murcer's left-handed power. There were also whispers that Bonds had a drinking problem. The strength of these stories was reinforced by a couple of off-season arrests on drunk driving charges. No one had ever seen Bonds even slightly tipsy at the ball park. That's all Gabe Paul needed to know.

If the Bonds-Murcer deal had the rest of baseball reeling, the Yankees' next action set the game on its ear.

Catfish Hunter had spent the first ten years of his major league life pitching for the Athletics, first in Kansas City, then in Oakland. From 1970 to 1974, he won 106 games. Even Charlie Finley had to shell out some big bucks for that sort of performance. According to Hunter's contract for 1974, he was to receive a salary of $100,000. That was considered a lot of money in that pre–free-agent time. Half was to be paid during the regular season, and the rest was to be paid on a deferred basis to an insurance company chosen by the pitcher. This was fine with his employer, until Finley discovered that this method of payment was not in the payer's best interest when it came down to a little matter of taxes. Finley tried to have the language of the deferred monies clause changed. After being rebuffed, he reacted just like Charlie O. If they wouldn't change that section of the agreement, he would simply ignore it. The stipulated moment of payment came and passed. No check arrived. Hunter filed a grievance.

The expectation was that Finley would be chastised, forced to honor his debt, and be penalized some sort of interest. The grievance panel was made up of three men: Peter Seitz, an independent arbitrator; Marvin Miller, executive director of the Players Union; and John Gaherin, the owner's labor relations representative. Seitz and Miller overruled Gaherin in favor of Hunter. Finley was in breach of contract. The entire agreement was voided. Not only would Finley have to pay the money he owed, he would also have to relinquish title to his ace right-hander. Catfish Hunter was a free agent and could sell his services to the highest bidder.

Hunter's timing could not have been more opportune. He was coming off a 25-win season and had captured the American League Cy Young Award. There wasn't a team in the major leagues that didn't want him.

The Yankees hooked this Catfish with a five-year contract worth an estimated $3.5 million. The San Diego Padres had tendered a slightly higher offer. In fact, two days before the deal was revealed, Hunter's attorney had turned the Yankee offer down. It was Yankee scout Clyde Klutzz who changed the pitcher's mind. Klutzz had signed Hunter to his first professional contract for the A's. Klutzz was the reason the Yankees were able to call a press conference on New Year's Day, 1975, and introduce the Cat as their newest star. When he strode to the podium, Hunter made that clear. He pointed out that "Clyde never lied to me then and he wouldn't lie to me now. If it hadn't been for him, the Yankees would have had a little more trouble signing me."

The addition of Bonds and Hunter gave the club the appearance of a power. They had just missed the division title by a slim margin in 1974. Now they were the pre-season's overwhelming favorites to unseat the Orioles.

If they won, Mel Stottlemyre wouldn't be around to relish it. Stottlemyre had been the Yankee team leader. Through a decade of mediocre clubs, he had honored the Yankees with his presence. Stottlemyre was the last link with a glorious past. When he joined the club in Florida, it was obvious that he had not fully recovered from his injury of the previous season. The front office told him to take his time mending. The New York pitching staff was now strong enough to allow the right-hander that luxury. If need be, he could even stay behind when the team went North. All he had to concentrate on was getting his arm in shape. When camp broke, he did not go North. He didn't stay behind to pursue his rehabilitation either. Mel Stottlemyre was given his pink slip. It was a shabby way to treat one who had given so much, for so long, for so little.

If there was one word that described the 1975 Yankees it was "snakebit." Hunter held up his end of the contract by winning 23 games. Munson, Chambliss, Nettles, and White had excellent campaigns. But the rest of the lineup was devastated by injury. Piniella sustained a ruptured eardrum "while body-surfing in Puerto Rico. We were playing the Pirates three exhibition games there. An infection developed, and it robbed me of my balance." He was operated on in midseason and told to take the rest of the year off. At the time, his batting average was .196. Bobby Bonds tore up his knee while misplaying a fly ball on June 7. He missed two weeks. Before the injury, he looked like an MVP; he was not quite the same player when he came back. Six days after his mishap, the team suffered its worst loss: Elliott Maddox tore up *his* knee on the wet outfield of Shea Stadium. He recalls that "Shea had a terrible outfield. The players hated it. It's not enough to say it didn't drain well; it didn't drain at all. If it rained on Monday, and only on Monday, it would still be wet the following Saturday. We had to put our feet in Baggies before putting them in our spikes. Just to keep our feet dry. The outfielders used to go through one or two pairs of spikes each homestand. They would get ruined!"

On the evening Maddox was injured, the playing field resembled Romney Marsh. Maddox came in to corral a line drive to shallow center and slipped. As he went down, his spikes caught in the soggy turf and his knee collapsed under him. When Maddox was carried off the field, the Yankee season went with him. He was in the midst of his second consecutive .300 season, and his defense was even more eye-catching than it had been the summer before. It could truly be said that center field was no longer a patch of real estate located between right and left. It was wherever Maddox chose to roam. Maddox was the one player the Yankees could not replace.

The next player to wind up in the infirmary was Ron Blomberg. He ripped up his right shoulder and was lost for the season. Boomer had a tremendous following with the fans, and was a big favorite with members of the press. But he was not the most popular man in his own clubhouse. All Blomberg wanted to do was hit. He possessed astonishing reflexes, but was uninterested in using them to play any position. Blomberg was one of the fastest men in baseball, yet he had no idea how to run the bases properly. At least one player confided, "The guys thought Ronnie [Blomberg] was lazy. He did not like to do his work, unless it meant taking batting practice. He loved to do that. But he would always fuck up on the bases or in the field. He never saw a triple play on any level, and the one time he almost did, he was part of it. He dropped the ball. Still, he wouldn't work to improve himself out there. Now, I'm not saying that there weren't a few other guys on the team with the same outlook." To many of his teammates, Blomberg was not a ballplayer. He was a freak who could mash right-handed pitching.

The rash of injuries forced the Yankees to compete with a makeshift outfield. At times this trio consisted of Alex Johnson, Roy White, and Rick Dempsey. White was an excellent left fielder, but he was out of his element in center. Dempsey was a catcher, and, as an outfielder, Johnson was one of the league's best hitters. This defensive shuffling put pressure on the pitching staff. It didn't need it. It was already suffering due to the lack of a reliable reliever.

Sparky Lyle was ineffective. He had blown a couple of early games, and Bill Virdon seemed to lose all confidence in him, thinking the lefty was burned out. He began to use Lyle less and less often. This was one of the few wrong moves made by Virdon during his Yankee tenure. What Lyle needed was what he had always thrived on: work and lots of it. It was not forth-coming. Lyle had the worst season of his career, and the entire staff felt the negative effects.

During the pre-season manipulations and the strife-torn sum-mer, George Steinbrenner was uncharacteristically silent. It was not by choice. On August 23, 1974, Steinbrenner pleaded guilty to the following charges:

1. Making illegal contributions to the campaign of Richard Nixon.
2. Aiding and abetting obstruction of an investiga-tion of that and other charges.

He was fined $15,000.

Three months later, he was handed a two-year suspension by baseball commissioner Bowie Kuhn. Steinbrenner was to have nothing to do with the running of the Yankees for the length of his exile. Evidence suggests that he did not quite follow that ruling to the letter.

At least one action that had all the earmarks of a Stein-brenner operation was the firing of Bill Virdon. Steinbrenner had once explained, "New York is the Big Apple. The game is important, but so is the showmanship involved. You have to have a blend of talented players, but you also need to have another ingredient: color." Bill Virdon was a lot of things. Col-orful was not one of them.

Marty Appel was the Yankees' public relations director in 1975. He was bright and efficient, a superb PR director. But even he could make an error in judgment. Like neglecting to invite Billy Martin to Old-Timers' Day. "Actually," he con-fessed, "I really should have invited him as a matter of courtesy. But he was managing the Texas Rangers at the time, and it didn't seem like the practical thing to do. They were scheduled to play out on the West Coast that day. As it turned out, Billy [Martin] was very offended. He wore his Yankee heart on his sleeve. I heard how upset he was, and I made it a point to visit him in the clubhouse during the Rangers' next visit to Shea. I personally invited him. I apologized for the oversight, telling him he had to be there. I think I even said that we couldn't possibly have an Old-Timers' Day without him. He said, 'Fine, but what about Charlie Silvera here, he wasn't invited either.' Charlie was one of his coaches. So I said, 'Well, we couldn't have an Old-Timers' Day without Charlie Silvera either.' Billy knew I was throwing a little BS, and I knew that he was throwing it right back. But he got the invitation, and so did Charlie. A few days later Texas fired him."

It was around the time of Martin's firing that Gabe Paul decided to take a trip. He told Marty Appel that if anybody wanted to know where he was, to say that he was on a scouting trip in Puerto Rico. That was a fantasy, meant only for public consumption. In reality, Paul was on his way to Denver, Colorado, where Billy Martin was on a fishing expedition.

August 2, 1975. Yankee Old-Timers' Day at Shea. The displaced Bombers are 53–51, and in fourth place. They are several light-years behind the eventual American League champion Boston Red Sox. On this morning, Marty Appel is called into Gabe Paul's office and introduced to the new Yankee manager. Appel extends his hand to Billy Martin, chuckles, and says, "Well, I guess you got here for Old-Timers' Day after all."

The firing of Bill Virdon was one of the more honest dismissals in recent memory. It was made quite clear that he was not being blamed for the team's numerous injuries or its mediocre record. None of the excuses that were usually palmed off on the media after a removal of this sort were offered. There wasn't any need for any. It was simply explained that Virdon was being let go because Billy Martin had become available—just as Virdon had originally been hired because another "name" manager was not to be had.

After being told of the change in command, Virdon vanished into thin air. His now former players didn't see him until the following spring, when he reappeared as the manager of the Houston Astros. "I thought it was strange," mused Doc Medich, "the way Bill [Virdon] just suddenly disappeared. I mean, that was odd. But understandable. After all, he was a manager and had just been fired. What was much odder was the fact that Alex Johnson also disappeared, and he was a player. He had been with Martin in Texas. I saw him a bit later, after the season, and asked what happened to him. Alex said that after he heard that Billy Martin was the new manager, he was half-way across eastern Pennsylvania before the next pitch was thrown. He just knew that with Billy coming, he was gone."

Chapter
SEVEN

I ask only one thing of my players—hustle.

—BILLY MARTIN

THE Yankees became a championship ball club on December 11, 1975.

On that date a press conference was called in the midst of the winter meetings in Hollywood, Florida. At it, Gabe Paul announced that New York had acquired center fielder Mickey Rivers and starting pitcher Ed Figueroa from the California Angels. The price was Bobby Bonds. After baring the details of that transaction, Gabe Paul gave the assembled press another blockbuster: Doc Medich had been dealt to the Pittsburgh Pirates. The Yankees would receive two pitchers—Dock Ellis and Ken Brett—and a twenty-one-year-old minor league infielder named Willie Randolph. These trades were not met with the unanimous enthusiasm that had greeted the Bobby Bonds and Catfish Hunter deals of the previous winter. Frankly, many people thought Paul had been taken. When Billy Martin was asked if he knew he would end up leaving Florida without Bonds and Medich, he replied, "No, we gave up a lot. Only time will tell." That did not read like a vote of confidence.

145

Neither did Martin's response to the question of why Bonds and Medich had been dealt. "Ask the man who traded them," said Billy.

Thurman Munson was speaking for a great many teammates and Yankee watchers when he asked, "What are we going to do now for right-handed power? How can they trade Bobby Bonds?" You would have thought the Yankees had traded Freddy Beene again.

Paul never took a back step. He allowed that, after forty years of wheeling and dealing, he couldn't remember pulling off two trades of this magnitude on the same day. He even admitted some trepidation about the deals. Paul noted, "We didn't win last year, we had to do something. When you trade, you have to shoot craps a little. You always take a risk."

Not as much of a risk as it seemed. Unlike the nay-sayers around him, Gabe Paul knew exactly what he was doing.

The Yankees were returning to Yankee Stadium for the up-coming season. Paul wanted to field a team that could win at home and on the road. One of his requirements was to obtain an outfielder capable of reaching the right field seats. In his first deal of the off-season, he acquired that long-baller. On November 23, Paul traded Pat Dobson to the Cleveland Indians for Oscar Gamble. Dobson was coming off a poor (11–14) year, but Cleveland was famished for any kind of pitching. Gamble was precisely the commodity the Yankees were shopping for. He had hit 54 homers in fewer than 1,200 at-bats over the last three seasons. That was accomplished without any assistance from the friendly porch in the Bronx.

At the time, this was a relatively minor deal. It came first, and it did fulfill a need, but it was not at the top of Paul's list of priorities. What he desired most was a center fielder, some-one who could cover the vast uncharted territory of a Stadium outfield that was the size of a small duchy. The Yankees knew that Elliott Maddox would not be ready to open the season. The player Paul wanted to replace him with was Mickey Rivers.

Rivers had just led the league in stolen bases with 70. He could intimidate an entire team's defensive alignment with his raw speed, a quickness that would also enable him to do the job for the Yankees in center. He was available because the California Angels were sick of losing ball games with their relay squad disguised as a ball club.

California had spent the last two years trying to survive in the American League West with a popgun-and-run attack. Their lineup was so unimposing that Red Sox lefthander Bill Lee once observed, "The California Angels are the only team in the majors that can take batting practice in a hotel lobby without breaking a thing." The 1975 California Angels were the one club in the league with over 200 stolen bases. They finished last. As the ad says, "There's got to be a better way." The Angel front office concluded they had found it. California was prepared to become a team with less glide in their stride, but more crunch in their punch. Bonds, having the potential to hit 30 or more homers, looked mighty attractive. He would provide the lineup with power and speed.

The Bonds for Rivers part of the deal came together quickly. It was agreed upon when the Angels and Yankees initially met. The second piece of the transaction took some doing. California agreed that New York should receive an additional player. The Yankees preferred that that fellow be a pitcher. They asked for Frank Tanana, who was only the best left-hander alive. The laughter that greeted that request could be heard from Anaheim to the Bronx. The Angels decided they could be persuaded to part with either Bill Singer or Andy Hassler. The Yankees wouldn't even discuss the possibility.

After letting the Angels sulk for a few days, Gabe Paul came up with another proposal. New York would accept pitcher Ed Figueora as the other half of the package for Bonds. Figgy had won 16 games in 1975 and had registered the fifth lowest ERA in the league. He was probably the least-known good pitcher in baseball. Normally, the Angels wouldn't have parted with the right-hander. But they had a severe case of the big-eyes for Bonds. The swap was consummated one week after it appeared to be a corpse.

Thurman Munson was right. The Yankees had stripped themselves of a major portion of their right-handed power. But Bonds's muscle was wasted at the top of the batting order, and he had not shown an ability to perform in the crucial third or fourth position in the lineup. New York had come away with the fastest (though not the best) center fielder in both leagues and a first-rate starting pitcher. It was a transaction Paul could live with.

Sandy Alomar had proven to be an excellent stopgap at second base over the last season and a half. But it had become painfully obvious over the course of the previous summer that the elegant-fielding infielder no longer possessed the range he had once displayed. Evidence could be found in the numbers. Not in his fielding average. That generally deceptive statistic was a gaudy .985. More telling were his total chances accepted. They were a whopping 199 behind Gold Glove winner Bobby Grich. Alomar wasn't making a lot of errors, but he wasn't getting to a lot of balls, either.

For the umpteenth time, the front office was looking to alter its infield. They felt that Fred Stanley, having replaced Jim Mason in mid-1975, was competent enough to hold down short. Stanley had impressed Martin with the way he got the job done. He was an admirable player who made the most of his talents. If a better shortstop could be found, great. If not, Stanley would do. Alomar would not. The Yankees were determined to find a replacement.

Second basemen were in great demand that winter. Half the teams in the majors needed one. The other half weren't foolish enough to part with theirs. Only one club had a surplus at the position: the Pittsburgh Pirates. Rennie Stennett was twenty-four years old, an accomplished hitter, and one of the better fielding second baseman around. He was one of just three men ever to get seven hits in seven at-bats in a nine-inning major league game. On the day of that performance, he was removed in the ninth inning for a pinch runner: Willie Randolph.

If anyone was the jewel of the Pirate minor league system it was Randolph. He was a wunderkind, a young ballplayer with no discernible holes in his game. Randolph was a patient contact hitter with an excellent eye, a smooth stroke, and disarming speed. His range at second base knew no restrictions. The Pirates were going to be forced to come to a decision very shortly. Who was going to be their second baseman for the next decade, Randolph or Stennett?

The Yankees made the choice for them. Pittsburgh was known as the Lumber and Lightning Gang because of the potency of their offense. Hitters who come up in the Pirate organization believe they have a sacred duty to consume at least one pitcher every day of their major league life. It must have had something to do with a high protein—low carbohydrate diet. The 1976 Pirates also had a staff of efficient hurlers, but lacked a stopper, someone who could go to the mound every fourth or fifth day and take charge for nine innings. The Yankees did not have an overpowering club, yet Doc Medich had won 49 games over the last three seasons. How many would he have won with Pittsburgh scoring all those runs for him? That was a question that intrigued the Pirate front office.

Ten years before, the Atlanta Braves stole Clete Boyer from New York for another minor league phenom. Gabe Paul was not the general manager then. When Pittsburgh came sniffing around asking about Medich, the first player Paul asked for was Randolph. Then he reasoned he couldn't trade an almost-certain 20-game winner for just a minor leaguer. So the Pirates sweetened the pot. They tossed in left-hander Ken Brett, with his recurring sore elbow, and right-hander Dock Ellis. Ellis couldn't have an article written about him without the words "militant" or "outspoken" appearing in it. The Pirate front office viewed him as trouble and was glad to get rid of him. Paul couldn't care less about problem players. Ellis was a talent. He knew how to pitch, and, more importantly, how to win. That was all that mattered to Paul. Any trouble that Ellis brought with him could be dealt with. That's what Paul was getting paid to do.

When Billy Martin replaced Bill Virdon, he properly realized that the immediate impact he could have on the club was minimal. So he used the final 56 games of that season as a study period. His goals were to assess the team, help Paul strengthen it, and then use the following spring training to imbue the club with his fire. He was going to teach it how to acquire a killer instinct.

Reggie Jackson had made an observation about the Yankees in 1974, during the height of their ultimately unsuccessful pennant bid. The Oakland A's had just taken a hard-fought series from the Yankees on the West Coast. Jackson commented that the Yankees had improved and had "a lot of talent, but they don't know how to win yet."

If there was one thing Billy Martin had a firsthand knowledge of it was winning. He had been a sparkplug on the great Yankee teams of the early and mid-fifties, helping those clubs to five World Series. Martin was a marginally talented player. His play at second base was often excellent, but rarely remarkable. He never hit higher than .267 in a full season, and never had more than 15 home runs or 75 RBI in a season.

The numbers received little attention. They were obscured by the glow cast by Martin's competitiveness. Martin saved his best hitting for those games in which the Yankees found their backs shoved up against the Stadium wall. In a crucial contest, he could always be counted on to be in the middle of something: a flashy double play at second, a perfectly executed hit-and-run, a vicious slide to take out an opposing infielder, and, of course, an occasional brawl. Martin was the quintessential team player, and he was at his best in the World Series.

Long before Reggie Jackson was christened Mr. October, Billy Martin had also proved his worth in that month. In 28 Series games, he batted .333 with 5 home runs, 19 RBI, and 15 runs scored. These figures were far above his regular season norms. They speak volumes about exactly the kind of player Martin was.

Even more telling was a play he made in the 1952 World Series. It occurred during the seventh and final game against the Brooklyn Dodgers in Ebbets Field. The Yankees had a 4–2 lead. New York right-hander Allie Reynolds had dominated the Bums for three innings after starter Ed Lopat went three, but was obviously spent. Vic Raschi was brought in to relieve him. But Raschi had pitched seven and two-thirds innings the day before and was feeling the effects. He didn't have it. A walk. A pop out. A single and another walk. The bases were loaded. Stengel bounded from the visitors' dugout and signaled for left-hander Bob Kuzava. The dangerous Duke Snider was the batter. He struck out. It was left to Jackie Robinson to bring the runners home. There wasn't anybody the Dodgers would have rather seen carrying their hopes up to the batter's box.

Robinson worked the count to 3 and 2, fouled off four pitches, and popped the ball up, just to the first base side of the pitcher's mound. Catcher Yogi Berra called for first baseman Joe Collins to make the inning-ending catch. But Collins could not see the ball. He had lost it in the glare of a passionate afternoon sun. None of his teammates realized what had happened. Except Martin. He raced in from second base and caught the ball belt-high. The momentum of the catch carried him to his knees. The inning was over. So were the Dodgers. They went to their dugout convinced that "next year" was a cruel canard, a mythical time that they would never see.

It was this combativeness and hustle that Martin brought with him after his playing days were over. He had used it as a coach with the Minnesota Twins to cajole an MVP season out of Zoilo Versalles. That performance lifted the Twins to the pennant. Martin's fiery nature was the secret behind his success as a manager. It was also the reason he was constantly forced to change his business address. Martin got his first shot at managing in the big leagues in 1969 with the Twins. He directed them that year to a Western Division title, and was promptly fired. He took over the Tigers in 1971 and had them in first place the following season. By September 1973 he was cut loose again and picked up by the Texas Rangers. Martin didn't win a title with Texas, but he did turn them into the most improved team in baseball. In 1973, the Rangers had been the bad joke of the American League, winning 57 while losing 105. They finished last, 37 games behind the Oakland A's. One year later, they finished second.

Martin worked these marvels in a different fashion each time. With Minnesota, he had a balanced club whose only shortcoming was that they weren't the Baltimore Orioles. Detroit was more of a one-dimensional team. They were a group of slow (17 stolen bases in 1972), home run-hitting veterans (average age: thirty-two). Martin recognized this, so he shied away from the things they couldn't do, like stealing bases, and concentrated on what they were more adept at: playing defense and hitting the long ball. His manipulation of the Tiger pitching staff was faultless. At Texas he unveiled the forerunner of what would become known years later as Billyball. The situation with the Rangers was the reverse of what it had been with Detroit. Texas had a young club, and the only legitimate slugger in the lineup was Jeff Burroughs. Therefore, the Texas Rangers ran. They stole bases, pulled the hit-and-run, sacrificed, and drove the opposition nuts. And they won ball games.

Martin's firings were always the result of bickerings he had with his various bosses. It appeared that no matter who was in charge of his team's front office, Martin would manage to get embroiled in some sort of life-and-death struggle with them. Shortly after, he would get canned.

In the dugout, however, his ability was beyond query. He was one of two managers (the incomparable Earl Weaver being the other) who really made a difference.

Part of Martin's overall objective for the Yankees got set back when the owners locked out the players during spring training. This was part of a dispute over the reserve clause. Two pitchers, Dave McNally of the Montreal Expos and Andy Messersmith of the Los Angeles Dodgers, had played out the 1975 season without the protection of a signed contract. When the season was over, they declared that they were now at liberty to sign with whatever club they wished. The reserve clause was a section of the standard player's contract that allowed owners to renew that agreement ad infinitum. Or so they thought. It was Messersmith and McNally's contention that, based on the language of the clause, it applied only to the season following the one that the agreement had originally been drawn up for.

The owners didn't see it that way. The dispute was brought to arbitration. Peter Seitz, who had cast the deciding vote in the Catfish Hunter hearing, was once again in the role of Solomon. He sided with the players. The owners had only themselves to blame. The enlightened of their number (Bill Veeck) had warned them for years that the players would eventually win their freedom. Veeck thought it made sense for the owners to compromise on the reserve clause and come up with a palatable alternative that both sides could be happy with. Now there wasn't a reserve clause to compromise. Any talks on the subject between the Players Association and management had to commence with a new understanding. The owners would start with nothing. The players held all the cards.

It was in this atmosphere of labor unrest that the owners tried to force the players to accept a diluted version of the stricken clause by enforcing a lockout. It dragged on for four weeks. Eventually the camps were reopened at the insistence of Bowie Kuhn. The fracas over the new basic agreement, with its qualifications for free agency, was settled later.

The cutback in teaching time was a disappointment to Martin. But it may have worked to his and the Yankees' advantage. Martin came to Fort Lauderdale fully prepared. New York had the most organized spring training of any club in the major leagues. When the season opened, the Yanks burst out of the gate with 15 wins in their first 20 games.

Two games typified the type of season this club was to have. The Milwaukee Brewers played host to New York in an afternoon game on April 10. It was a game right out of *One Step Beyond*. In the ninth inning the Yankees had a 9–6 lead when the Brewers loaded the bases with nobody out. Third baseman Don Money faced Yankee right-hander Dave Pagan. On his second pitch, Pagan threw a fastball over the middle of the plate. Home run. The game was over. Milwaukee had won 10–9.

It was a victory that never found its way into the record books. Just prior to the pitch, Chris Chambliss had requested time out. Martin had been screaming instructions to Pagan, and Chambliss was certain that the pitcher hadn't heard them above the din of the crowd. Nobody had seen Chambliss call for time. Nobody except umpire Jim McKean who granted the request. Money's homer didn't count. The Brewers went berserk. After a lengthy debate and protest, play was resumed. The stage was reset. There would be no joy in Sudsville that day. Money, mighty Money, had struck out. The Yankees prevailed by a final score of 9–7.

Five days later, the Yankees reopened the Stadium in the Bronx. Their opponents were the Minnesota Twins. Rudy May started, but he was gone by the third inning, a victim of four Minnesota runs. Two of these came as the result of a home run by outfielder Dan Ford, a historic clout that was the first home run to be hit in the refurbished ball park. One year ago, such an early deficit usually had meant curtains for the hometown heroes. This was not one year ago. New York rallied for a run in the third, four in the fourth, and six in the eighth. The Yankees buried the Twins 11–4. On hand for the services were 52,613 fans, and not a tear was shed except in joy.

These two victories were produced with an alchemic mix of luck, talent, and persistence. Those elements were required staples for teams of destiny.

Fate had even been kind enough to allow George Steinbrenner to return from banishment a year early. Just in time for all the fun.

Steinbrenner had made a formal petition for reinstatement in November 1975. The "parole" was granted on March 2, 1976. Fifteen months of the original sentence had elapsed, and Bowie Kuhn took pains to point out that Steinbrenner had voluntarily disassociated himself from Yankee affairs in April 1974, several months before his conviction and suspension. This was one of three qualifying conditions that the commissioner used to justify the owner's early return. In his press release, Kuhn allowed that:

1. "The suspension had been handed down in an effort to assure public confidence in the integrity of the game. I think that has been achieved."
2. "Nearly two years have elapsed since April, 1974 when Mr. Steinbrenner voluntarily removed himself from the business of the New York Yankees."
3. "Managerial and financial problems of the Yankees asserted in support of Mr. Steinbrenner's reinstatement, will be significantly alleviated by his reinstatement. This will alternately benefit the team and its fans."

When asked if the reprieve meant that Steinbrenner had complied with the commissioner's original edict, a spokesman said, "If the commissioner didn't feel he had, I guess he wouldn't have lifted the suspension."

The exact language of the suspension had done more than expressly forbid Steinbrenner from being involved in the doings of his team. It stated that Steinbrenner was "ineligible and incompetent [to have] any association whatsoever with any major league team or its personnel." It went on to threaten that "any violation of this order will be grounds for further action against Mr. Steinbrenner or any individual who has knowledge of the order."

Steinbrenner had involved himself with the club during his spell in Kuhn's limbo. At the very least, he sent tape-recorded talks to be played for his players in the Yankee clubhouse. These were meant to fire up his team and, perhaps, were also meant to let them know that, suspension or not, he was never very far away. Perhaps the commissioner wasn't aware of this infraction. Or perhaps he was but chose to do nothing about it. It's possible that he recognized that Steinbrenner was following an old baseball tradition. Steinbrenner was like a manager who had been chucked from a game. He left the dugout, and directed his team from the shadows of the clubhouse tunnel, out of the umpire's sight. That had been going on since the days of Honus Wagner.

The amount of input Steinbrenner had in various decisions made by the Yankees during his vacation is conjecture. But in his autobiography, Billy Martin indicates that Steinbrenner played an active role in persuading him to replace Bill Virdon. Martin certainly wasn't Gabe Paul's choice. And you would think that Steinbrenner had something to say about the trading of Bobby Murcer (one imagines a scene in which Steinbrenner's phone rings at a pre-determined time. "George," whispers a familiar voice, "it's Gabe. I realize you can't discuss the Yankees, so I'm calling to talk about my baseball card collection. Horace Stoneham just dropped by and offered me a Bonds for a Murcer. What do you think?"), or the signing of Catfish Hunter

("George, Gabe again. I'm on my way to the market to take advantage of a great sale: Catfish at $17,000 a pound. Do you think that's too high?").

Whether or not these violations occurred is irrelevant. The mere possibility that they could have happened proves how utterly unenforceable the punishment was in the first place.

The reason for the suspension supposedly had something to do with the integrity of baseball, and the fans' perception of the game's honesty. Baseball fans, though, were not exactly losing sleep over Steinbrenner's conviction. After all, it had nothing to do with the Yankees. No one was walking around supposing that if Chris Chambliss struck out against Jim Palmer, it was because John Mitchell had put the fix in that day.

If Bowie Kuhn were really interested in guarding the game's integrity, he dropped the ball by commuting Steinbrenner's sentence. Kuhn's term of office was slated to come to an end in July 1976. His contract gave him the right to ask for a re-election vote one year before that time. That request was made. Four votes against him in either league would mean expulsion. On July 16, 1975, four American League owners—Charles O. Finley of Oakland, Brad Corbett of Texas, Jerry Hoffberger of Baltimore, and Pat Cunningham representing Steinbrenner and the Yankees—voted to unseat Bowie Kuhn. The National League was quick to respond. They tried to save Kuhn's hide by having that first counting designated as a straw vote. They tabled the final vote until the next day. On that afternoon of July 17, Kuhn escaped the gallows. The Yankees had switched their vote. Nine months later, George Steinbrenner got his early reprieve.

Was a deal made? There is no evidence to prove it, no photos or "smoking pistol" tapes to examine. Perhaps it was all coincidence. But certainly the image of the grand old game's integrity became a bit blurred just by the suggestion that a favor had been bought.

Steinbrenner was now able to visibly turn his attention to his team's fortunes. One of his first actions was to try to bring the recently liberated Andy Messersmith into the Yankee fold.

The right-hander did not have the same stature as Catfish Hunter, but he was a valuable property. Messersmith had been a 20-game winner twice. His numbers in 1975 (19–14, 2.29 ERA, 213 strikeouts) had been exceptional. It struck him as odd that, even with his attractive record, only six teams showed any interest in signing him. Messersmith and Players Union leader Marvin Miller smelled collusion, but the owners protested that there were honest concerns about the condition of the pitcher's arm. Rumors suggested that it was sore.

The Yankees crowed victory in this unexpectedly small sweepstakes on March 31. They claimed to have received a written agreement signed by Messersmith's agent, Herb Osmond. This was not so. What they actually had was an agreement to agree. Within twenty-four hours, that piece of paper was worthless.

Messersmith claimed that Osmond did not have the power of attorney. He could only listen to various offers and advise Messersmith on what course to follow. Osmond had been forbidden to sign anything. Messersmith went on to say that the terms spelled out in the agreement—calling for $1.5 million over four years—were acceptable. The tangle began when the actual contract was drawn up. Certain clauses pulled a Bill Virdon. They disappeared. Messersmith charged, "They agreed to certain things, and then they came back and those things were different. It's incredible. These are the people who run our country."

That last bit of overstatement could be excused. Messersmith was from California and wasn't used to the beat of the New York hustle. But his fury over the events could not be overstated. The "certain things" he alluded to pertained to a no-cut section of the agreement. Osmond had perused the Catfish Hunter covenant. It stipulated that Hunter was to get paid even if released, injured, or disabled mentally or physically. It also provided for payments to be made to Hunter's family in the event of the pitcher's demise. Osmond had requested that the Yankees make similar guarantees to his client. When the uniform player's contract was presented to them, it ensured

Messersmith payment only if he was released or injured. Osmond told Messersmith to forget it.

The Yankees raged that they had a deal and were fully prepared to let Bowie Kuhn decide who was right. Then, they had a change of heart. New York announced that it was withdrawing any claims they had on the pitcher. Steinbrenner explained, "It would be foolish for the Yankees to pursue a player who does not want to play for them." The Yankee front office also must have taken a good look at their situation. A preliminary hearing into the dispute turned up a letter of agreement, separate from the contract. One section of the letter dealt with the dress code. Also included was a clause calling for the Yankees to receive 40 percent of all fees Messersmith would receive from outside endorsements. In baseball, that sort of side agreement is illegal.

These irregularities, along with the fact that New York had nothing with Messersmith's signature on it, put the Yankees in a vulnerable position. If the commissioner had been impelled to render a decision, there is no way the Yankees could have won. As it was, they were lucky the episode didn't cost them a few dollars in fines.

Grant Jackson knew he wasn't long for the Baltimore Orioles. "I was a ten-and-five man," recalled the left-handed reliever, "or at least I would have been at the end of the season. Ten years in the big leagues and five with the same club. They [the Orioles] didn't want me to reach that. It would have given me the power to say whether or not they could deal me. So I knew I would be gone before I reached that level."

Rudy May also had a feeling that Yankee Stadium was no longer going to be his place of work. It had nothing to do with his contract status or longevity. He wasn't going to be around because "Billy [Martin] and I didn't see eye to eye on a lot of things. So I knew I would be traded. Either that or I wasn't going to pitch much here. Billy didn't like me, and he didn't want me on his team. He told me that. One day, he wanted to fight me. I had gone into his office to talk about a game I had pitched. I had a 2–1 lead against Cleveland with a man on and a man out in the seventh. He brought [Dick] Tidrow in, and [Rico] Carty hit a triple off of him to tie up the game. I went in when it was over and said, 'You know, skip, I don't feel real good about you taking me out of the game.' Billy lit right into me. He started cursing me out, saying, 'I don't give a fuck what you think, I'm the manager.' And so on. Then he said I wasn't going to pitch anymore, and that if I didn't get out of his office, he was going to punch my lights out. A few days later, Dave Pagan was scheduled to pitch against Detroit, but he came up sick. Billy came up to me and said, 'You're pitching today. All I want you to do is to throw the fucking ball, and I'll tell you when the fuck to come out of the game.' So I went out and beat Detroit. Didn't give up an earned run and pitched a complete game. After the game, he didn't say a word to me. Not even 'Nice game.' I didn't pitch a game after that."

On June 15, 1976, within hours of the interleague trading deadline, both pitchers saw their premonitions become fact. The Baltimore Orioles and the New York Yankees pulled off one of the largest trades of the decade. Ten players were involved. New York received pitchers Ken Holtzman, Doyle Alexander, and Grant Jackson, catcher Ellie Hendricks, and outfielder Jimmy Freeman. Going to the Orioles were pitchers Rudy May, Tippy Martinez, Dave Pagan, and Scott McGregor, and catcher Rick Dempsey.

It was a deal designed to ensure the pennant the Yankees seemed so capable of attaining. New York was in first place, four and a half games in front of the second-place Indians. The Bombers were the only team in the division playing over .500.

Holtzman was the key figure in the deal. Baltimore had obtained the left-hander and Reggie Jackson from the Oakland A's just prior to the start of the season. Both men were unsigned. In baseball's Brave New World, this meant they could declare free agency at the end of the season. The Orioles had decided to negotiate with Jackson but were anxious to unload Holtzman; a huge contract to him would have turned their pitching staff's salary scale inside out. An earlier attempt to send him to Kansas City was aborted. The Royals had been unable to come to financial terms with the pitcher. When the Yankees made their offer, the Orioles were ecstatic, especially since New York had agreed to part with one of the "crown jewels" of their farm system, the left-handed McGregor.

Holtzman came to the Bronx and was signed to a five-year contract. He went 9–7 the rest of the season. In 1977 and part of 1978, he won a total of three games. Holtzman was traded to the Chicago Cubs on June 10, 1978, for Ron Davis. Two years later, he had left the game.

The Orioles became the American League champions in 1979. McGregor, Dempsey, and Martinez had major roles in helping Baltimore win that flag. Two other valuable members of that club, reliever Don Stanhouse and outfielder Gary Roenicke, were obtained in a 1978 trade with the Montreal Expos. The Orioles gave up Rudy May. By the time Baltimore clinched the '79 pennant, New York had only Ron Davis to show for the deal. This has armed Yankee critics with ample ammunition to attack the trade as one of the worst in the team's history. To vilify the Yankee front office for wanting Ken Holtzman is to forget exactly who this pitcher had been.

Holtzman was one of the paladins of the Oakland A's pitching staff. He, Catfish Hunter, and Vida Blue had formed a triumvirate that was more proficient at providing insurance against lengthy losing streaks than Lloyds of London. In the past four seasons, Holtzman had won 77 games and registered an ERA of 2.94. He did not strike out a lot of batters. He did not throw particularly hard. What he did do was win. Holtzman had masterful control that enabled him to put a pitch anywhere he wanted. He was a pitcher who could sit on the top shelf. It would be convenient to say that his accomplishments were history, and that he was no longer the player he once was when the Yankees chose to acquire him. But at the time of his sendoff to the Bronx, Holtzman was pitching as well as he ever had. His record was only 5–4, but his ERA was 2.85. Many Baltimore writers pointed out that with some runs to work with Holtzman could easily have been 8–1. He was only thirty years old. There was no reason to suspect that he was going to be anything but a big winner for several years to come.

Holtzman's inability to perform up to the Yankees' expectations has been blamed on Billy Martin. Martin, it has been charged, did not like the type of pitcher Holtzman was, and ruined him by not allowing the lefty to work. That's not entirely fair to Martin. From the time Holtzman joined New York to the end of the season, he started 21 games. He completed 10 of these and pitched 149 innings. These stats were accumulated in half a summer, and are not the numbers of a pitcher starved for work.

Yet, while pitching for a pennant winner, in a park friendly to left-handers, he suddenly lost it. Whatever that mystical synchronization of substances that gives a man the ability to consistently get major league hitters out is, it deserted him. It would return only for interludes, just long enough to mock him, with only enough sweet fervor to be missed.

With the exception of Pagan, the players sacrificed for Holtzman have had splendid careers; when the deal was consummated, their worth to the Yankees was minimal. Rudy May had been a winning pitcher for New York. However, his record was not as impressive as Holtzman's. Dempsey was buried on the bench behind Munson and Fran Healy. Tippy Martinez was in a similar position behind Sparky Lyle.

The other players obtained by New York helped deliver a pennant. Alexander went 10–5 and flirted with a no-hitter on four separate occasions. Hendricks was a valuable left-handed pinch-hitter and gave Martin maneuverability at the catcher's spot. And Grant Jackson was the team's life saver. He went undefeated in six decisions, filling a breach near the end of the season when Lyle went into a slump.

The most nagging part of the deal was the deportation of Scott McGregor. Criticism along these lines is murder by hindsight. McGregor had arm trouble shortly before the deal was consummated. His future was far from certain. Besides, when the deal was made, Steinbrenner and company thought they were up to their money belts in left-handed pitching.

That misconception was created by another transaction. Its

announcement, which came shortly before the unveiling of the Yankee-Oriole exchange, sent Nagasakian tremors throughout the whole of the National Pastime.

Charles Finley was fearful that free agency would strip his team of most of its stars and leave him nothing in return. He was determined to prevent that. He sold outfielder Joe Rudi and reliever Rollie Fingers to the Boston Red Sox for $2 million. Just to prove he wasn't playing favorites in the league's Eastern Division race, he also sold Vida Blue. To the New York Yankees. For $1.5 million.

Blue ranked with Frank Tanana and Steve Carlton as one of the three premier left-handers in the major leagues. This sale would rejoin him with Hunter and Holtzman, and meant that the fabled Big Three of those invincible guerrillas from Oakland would be pitching for New York. Yankee fans were choking on delicious bits of greedy anticipation when Bowie Kuhn came along to spoil everyone's appetite.

The commissioner put an injunction on the two sales. Three days later he nullified them completely. He asserted that the huge sums involved were not in the best interests of baseball. They would have given two rich clubs (Boston and New York) an undeniable advantage over teams less financially blessed (Cleveland, Minnesota). Kuhn also claimed that it would be severely damaging to the Oakland franchise if it were to lose three of its brightest stars without receiving equitable talent in return. This ignored Finley's plight. He was going to lose six players at season's end anyway. When they walked the compensation Finley received would be zero.

Why this was in the game's best interest is anybody's guess. It was certainly in the other owners' best interests to squelch this gambit. The Frankenstein of free agency was staring them right in the wallet. And licking its lips. The owners were in no mood to entice the monster by allowing players to see how much their services were worth in an open market. Sales like these provided the players with a good indication of exactly that. It also had to be in the commissioner's best interests to rid baseball of Finley. Finley had been Kuhn's most vociferous critic.

When Finley argued that he needed the money to sign his other players and keep his franchise going, he was beating his head against a wall of best interests, none of them his. Blue, Rudi, and Fingers were returned to Oakland.

The Yankees suffered along without the services of Mr. Blue. Two weeks after the June 15 carnival, they widened their lead to 12 games. After that, it was never smaller than six. They clinched the division title on September 25. Baltimore finished second, 10½ games behind.

That title was won by a club that resembled a clear country night filled with stars of various sizes and brightnesses. It was a team.

Their infield was a quartet of contrasting styles and talents in harmony. Chambliss, the stoic and steady first baseman, quietly hitting, quietly driving in runs, quietly winning ball games. Randolph, the portrait of the veteran as a young rookie. Poised and silken, he covered more ground than his effortless strides promised and drove pitchers crazy with his base-stealing ability. Stanley was the blue-collar worker at short. His effervescent cheerleading masked a competitive nature that would never yield easily to defeat. He compensated for lack of great range with intelligent positioning and gutsy determination. He was not afraid to get his uniform dirty. Nettles was that rarest of infielders, a man who could dominate a game simply with his presence at a position. He had silently agonized through a three-month slump. It ended in July with a cannonade of shots that produced 32 home runs, enough to lead the league. He was the first Yankee to win that title since Roger Maris's herculean efforts in 1961.

Oscar Gamble and Lou Piniella masqueraded as a two-headed outfielder with 20 home runs and 95 runs batted in between them. Ed Figueroa won 19, and Dock Ellis was the comeback player of the year with 17 victories, a total matched by Catfish Hunter. These three pitchers' output, and the presence of Doyle Alexander and Ken Holtzman, freed Dick Tidrow for the bullpen and allowed him to become the team's long reliever. He responded with 10 saves and an ERA of 2.63. Sparky Lyle made up for the bummer of 1975 by resuming his role as the team's late-inning stopper. He led the league with 23 saves and made sure that none of his teammates took the pennant race too seriously.

The team's offense revolved around two men: Mickey Rivers and Thurman Munson. Rivers was the club's first method of assault. He would struggle up to the plate, obviously too beset by numerous infirmities to live past his next at-bat. Once a pitch was delivered, though, that guise was dropped. He was a dangerous, slashing hitter whose breakneck speed rendered any attempts to set up a defense against him useless.

Rivers led the team with a .312 batting average. His frail appearance kept hidden the power that enabled him to hammer 47 extra-base hits. Those blows were almost considered a blessing by his opponents. When Rivers merely singled, alarm bells went off. He stole 43 bases in 49 attempts. If the Quick made up his mind to commit larceny, he was impossible to throw out—not because of any Willsian guile; Rivers simply outran the ball. By the grace of this sheer speed, he turned the Stadium's center field into forbidden territory for enemy hitters, and he made up for a weak throwing arm with a quick, accurate release. Rivers was a one-man highlight film.

He might have been the American League MVP if he hadn't injured his shoulder and dogged it in September. But he did, and so he wasn't. That honor went to Munson.

There are no clear guidelines for determining an MVP. Munson spent the summer delivering runs in crucial situations. He finished the season batting .302 with 105 runs batted in. These are impressive figures, particularly for a catcher. No other backstop in the majors had over 100 ribbies or had hit over .300. Munson also managed to integrate himself into Billy Martin's running game, pilfering 14 bases. A chronic shoulder problem hampered his throwing, but he still possessed cobralike reflexes that enabled him to compensate for his weakened limb with a quick, accurate release. Munson's most potent resource behind the plate was located between his ears. That region stored a vast computer that broke enemy hitters down to a series of strengths and weaknesses. This same data base was equipped with a natural barometer that could readily detect what vital parts might be missing from his pitcher's usual assortment of weapons. Munson would take note, and make the necessary adjustments. Often this was done before the pitcher himself was aware of what he was lacking. Throughout Nettles's early slump, Rivers's erratic brilliance, Hunter's fluctuating performances, Randolph's season of nurturing, and other baseball mysteries, Munson was a constant. He was the man the entire team looked to to drive in runs, to win ball games, to be there. Others have had this sort of responsibility foisted upon them and had been found wanting. Munson reveled in the challenge, rose to its expectations, and outdistanced them. His were the unshakable hands that firmly gripped the ladder to the pennant. Munson's season tore away the ambiguity of the MVP award. With a dexterity worthy of Webster, he imposed a vivid definition on the prize. He communicated this without lifting a pen. All one had to do to get the message was to watch him play.

The American League playoffs opened in Kansas City on October 9. The Royals, like the Yankees, had pretty much had their own way of things in the American League West. Until late September. Then the Royals were forced to stave off a disarming charge by the Oakland A's. That late Oakland run was the dying gasp of a great ball club about to be dismembered by free agency. Larry Gura, having come to the Royals in a June trade with the Yankees for Fran Healy, had stopped the A's belated quest by shutting them out 4–0 on September 29. This was the third game of a three-game set in Oakland. The battle-tough A's had won the first two contests and had cut the Royals' lead to two and a half games. Any further slippage could have been fatal to this young Kansas City team, but Gura's win sealed Oakland's season of forlorn menace. Two evenings later, the Royals clinched the division. The A's were eliminated when they lost to the Angels in extra innings.

The drama of that finish gave Kansas City a prelude to the life-and-death struggle they were about to engage in against New York. Royals' manager Whitey Herzog named Gura to open the playoffs opposite Catfish Hunter. Gura had made some noise in the newspapers with a few less than complimentary remarks directed at Billy Martin. A 4–1 Yankee victory was Martin's sweet revenge. Hunter was magnificent, allowing only five hits. He received all the support he would need when the Yankees scored two in the first inning on a pair of singles and a pair of throwing errors by the Royal third baseman, batting champion George Brett. More injurious to the Royals' cause than the loss was a sprained ankle suffered by All-Star center fielder Amos Otis in the opening inning. The high-flying Otis had come down awkwardly on first base while running out a ground ball. He was shelved for the rest of the series.

Even without the services of a man who was a major part of their offense, the Royals refused to lie down. They returned the next day and splattered Ed Figueroa for a 7–3 victory.

Yankee Stadium was the scene of the third game. Dock Ellis surrendered three runs to the Royals in the first inning, then held them in check until the ninth. By that time five hurlers had allowed the Yankees five runs and the ball game. Lyle's entrance into the game in its final frame ensured the Yankee win.

Hunter and Gura went at each other again in game four. Both were gone by the fourth inning in a game won by Kansas City, 7–4. Nettles hit two home runs for three RBI. Diminutive Royal shortstop Freddie Patek also drove in three runs. But it was a Royals utilityman, Jamie Quirk, who provided the winning margin with a two-run triple, his lone hit of the playoffs. Quirk was usually a designated hitter and was starting in the outfield only because of the absence of Otis.

The fifth and final game has never ended. It lives forever, carried in the hearts of countless Yankee fans who had suffered through eleven years of watching other fans' teams play baseball in October. This was their moment of deliverance.

It did not start off well. The Stadium crowd held its breath as the Royals scored a pair in the first on a John Mayberry homer off Ed Figueroa. Rivers replied in the Yankee half of the inning with a leadoff triple against Dennis Leonard, and scored on a base hit by White. One out later, White came around to score on a sacrifice fly by Chris Chambliss. Kansas City went ahead on a run-scoring single by catcher Buck Martinez in the second. But New York tallied twice in both the third and sixth innings to take a 6–3 lead. Figueroa, meanwhile, had settled down and was confusing the Royals with an assortment of curves. He tired in the eighth and was removed after giving up a leadoff single to center fielder Al Cowens. The Stadium shook with the grateful chant: "Ed-die, Ed-die, Ed-die!" Grant Jackson came on in relief. He was waylaid by a Jim Wohlford single, and suddenly the crowd grew uneasy. George Brett was coming to the plate. He entered the batter's box with a single purpose: pull the ball into the right field seats. This goal was achieved on an 0–1 Jackson fastball. The Stadium was as silent as a crypt. The score was tied 6–6.

The Yankees failed to score in the bottom of the eighth. Only a phantom force play on Freddie Patek at second kept the Royals off the scoreboard in the top of the ninth.

The game was well over three hours old when Kansas City reliever Mark Littell prepared to face leadoff hitter Chris Chambliss in the bottom of the ninth. Swinging from the heels at the first pitch, Chambliss sent the ball on a high parabola, so lazy it seemed suspended against the night's dark curtains. As it descended, right fielder Hal McRae began to spring, screwing his body in a frantic attempt to defy the earth's jealous pull. For an instant, McRae seemed impaled against the right-center field wall, and the Stadium went quiet with anxious questioning. Then he came down. Empty-handed. Now it was Chambliss, still at the plate, and Munson, in the on-deck circle, who were no longer earthbound. They were leaping like frenzied Nijinskys in a dance of pure joy. Spectators poured onto the field in an atmosphere of freaky jubilation. The hallowed Stadium grounds were torn to shreds as Chambliss had to dodge through waves of well-wishers in order to circle the bases. It wasn't until much later, after first retreating to the safety of the clubhouse, that the first baseman finished his odyssey in the company of two security men. Almost lost in the celebration was the identity of the game's winning pitcher. It was Dick Tidrow. Chambliss and Tidrow, the two men whose acquisition had sparked so much resentment in 1974, had put their marks on an epic season with a finish that no Hollywood screenwriter could ever get away with. The Yankees were once again champions of the American League.

No one in the riotous, champagne-soaked clubhouse appreciated the victory more than Roy White. Without fanfare, as usual, he had had another strong season, leading the league in runs scored (104) and playing a flawless left field. He had been on this team during the era of its lost eminence. Now, finally, he was with a champion. "It was fabulous," White said later. "During that period, when the team was losing, it wasn't any fun to come to the ball park. We were really being ridiculed during those years. A lot of people were happy that the Yankees were losing. We always drew well on the road because people wanted to see us get beat. Those were some embarrassing years. The 1975 season had been a big letdown with all the injuries, because we really expected to win that year. We didn't, and [Bill] Virdon ended up getting fired. When Billy [Martin] was hired he made an immediate impression. A ball club usually takes on the personality of its manager, and Billy was fiery and smart. He wasn't afraid to be unorthodox. Everybody was rather excited when he joined us.

"Billy brought an excitement to the club; we all knew his reputation for winning. I know the first time I realized that something was different was when I was on second base in a game, and [Lou] Piniella was hitting. Billy gave the bunt sign to Lou, and Lou fouled the ball off. I went back to second, and I think we had a runner on first. I'm not sure. I am sure that I missed the next sign but I assumed Lou would be bunting again. The hit-and-run was on! Lou got a single, and I didn't score. Billy asked me later if I had missed the signs. I admitted I had. I knew from that day on that we would really have to keep on our toes because we had a manager who was capable of the unexpected. That tends to keep the players more alert. You don't want to be the one to miss a sign and mess up an inning or get fined.

"Mickey [Rivers] and I had signs between ourselves. Sometimes we would have the hit-and-run on, but the pitcher would throw a curveball. I'd take it because I knew there was no way any catcher was going to throw out Mickey on a breaking pitch. If it was a fastball where I wanted it, I could go the other way or, if I was batting left-handed, I could pull it. We'd have first and third with Thurman [Munson] coming up. That was really fun. It was like that all year.

"Our team had a confident personality. When we took the field for the final playoff game, we knew we were going to win. When we did, it was like taking the World Series. The Series against Cincinnati was almost a letdown by comparison; we were so high for the playoffs. The day after they were over, we were in Cincinnati to start the World Series. We didn't even have a chance to work out. I think we may have had a one-hour practice at Riverfront Stadium before the game. When the opener started, we were still thinking about our victory the night before. We were a little flat."

It didn't help that the team they were playing was the Cincinnati Reds. This was the legendary Big Red Machine of Pete Rose, Joe Morgan, Tony Perez, Johnny Bench, Ken Griffey, Dave Concepcion, George Foster, and Cesar Geronimo. As a team they had led the National League in runs, doubles, triples, home runs, batting average, slugging percentage, and stolen bases. They outscored their opposition by 224 runs. It is a common baseball adage that "a team must be strong up the middle in order to win." The Reds' middle defense—catcher, second baseman, shortstop, and center fielder—was manned by four Gold Gloves. Except for left-hander Don Gullett, most of their pitchers toiled in anonymity. But the staff's 3.51 ERA was the fifth lowest in the league. This was a team of men who had a casual obsession with winning and utter disdain for the slightest suggestion that victory would not be theirs. It was not a club one wanted to run into in a dark alley.

They were managed by Sparky Anderson. He and Cincy scout Ray Shore had devised a plan to handle the Bronx Bombers. Anderson was convinced that "the key to beating the Yankees was to stop Munson. We knew he was their best all-around hitter, so we wanted to keep him from hurting us. I didn't mind if he got singles. We decided to pitch him away, let him go to right field or up the middle. But we weren't going to give him anything to pull. He was just too great a hitter. He ended up having a great Series, but he never hurt us. He didn't drive in a lot of runs, and he didn't hit the long ball.

"The other thing we needed to do was keep Rivers off base. That's why we had Pete [Rose], at third, play all the way down the line. We wanted to take the bunt away from him, and we also wanted to challenge him to hit the ball past Pete. Meanwhile we were pitching him away, trying to confuse him. It was important for us to get him to think a little bit up there, and get him away from his usual game. He went for it. He hit a lot of pop-ups."

The Reds whipped the Yankees in four straight. New York was outplayed in every facet of the game, and was outscored in the four contests by a cumulative 22–8. Munson batted .529 with nine hits. All singles. A bewildered Rivers was held to .167, and blamed his showing on the cold weather. The lone Yankee home run came in the seventh inning of game three. It was hit by the forgotten shortstop, Jim Mason, in his only World Series appearance. It was his last at-bat as a Yankee.

Reds catcher Johnny Bench was named the Series MVP. It was an honor that caused Anderson to shower Bench with words of praise that were interpreted by Munson as a slur against his abilities. Anderson made no apologies, saying, "I knew Munson was in the room. He was directly in front of me when I said those things. In no way was I knocking Munson. I had too much respect for him; he was a tremendous ballplayer. But what I said then, I meant. And I would say the same thing today. What I said was I would not compare any player, not just any catcher, any *player*, to Johnny Bench, because it would not be fair to the other player. I think he [Munson] mistook what I said because his team had just lost four straight. When I realized how upset he was, I wrote him a long letter explaining what I meant. I don't know if he got it because he never acknowledged it."

Martin took his team's defeat badly. He refused to go to the

Cincinnati clubhouse to congratulate Anderson or the Reds. Steinbrenner did congratulate the National Leaguers and talked to the press about how "proud I am of my kids." Even as he made that statement, he was planning for next season, and for the next World Series. A World Series he had no intention of losing.

Chapter
EIGHT

*Mr. Paul, you've made a big mistake trad-
ing me. You know I'm a better ballplayer
than Reggie Jackson.*

—Oscar Gamble

"I played with Reggie [Jackson] for half a season in Baltimore
in 1976," recalled Rudy May. "The thing I remember most
about him was that he hit a lot of home runs and won a lot of
games for us. And talked about leaving the whole time he was
there. There wasn't any doubt about where he was headed.
Sometimes, after hitting a big home run or driving in a couple
of runs, he'd come into the dugout and look for me. He'd say,
'Hey man, how is it to play for the Yankees?' I told him he
couldn't go there because he'd never get along with Billy [Mar-
tin]. I knew both of them, and I could tell it wouldn't be a good
mix. You know what he said? He said, 'For the money they'll
pay me I can get along with anybody.'"

May wasn't alone in his opinion that Jackson should avoid
signing with the team in the Bronx. A former Yankee official
revealed, "He [Jackson] had a reputation for being a disruptive
force on a team. At least one of his Oakland teammates told
us how disruptive Reggie had been with the A's. Joe Iglehart,
a director with the Yankees at the time, had been involved

172

with the Orioles. He still lived in Baltimore and was aware of how Reggie had been with the O's. Joe made an impassioned plea at a Yankee owners' meeting in which he threatened to quit the organization if Jackson was signed. He said it was the worst thing the Yankees could do."

Reggie Jackson became a New York Yankee on November 29, 1976. That signing was the result of Steinbrenner's hustle, $3.5 million of his money, and the presence on the California Angels roster of a minor league shortstop named Tim Nordbrook.

One of the rules of the first free-agent re-entry draft was that clubs were limited to signing no more than two players each. There was only one way to circumvent this: If your club relinquished more than two players in the lottery, then it could sign as many as it lost. The Yankees, for instance, had lost only Doyle Alexander; they were restricted to two signings. The stripped-down Oakland A's could grab as many as eight.

The Angels could enter into contract with three. They had started the just-finished season lacking the autographs of only two players in their organization. Both were minor leaguers: outfielder-infielder Paul Dade, and infielder Billy Smith. In midsummer they procured Tim Nordbrook, a highly touted minor league shortstop with the Baltimore Orioles. He was also unsigned. The Angels did not tie up his phone with too many offers to change that status. When it came time for the re-entry draft, the Angels found themselves in a position to transform their pussycat of a franchise into a sinister panther. This metamorphosis could be accomplished with only a few strokes of the right pen.

California immediately signed Oakland outfielders Don Baylor and Joe Rudi. Baseball had come hurtling into the twentieth century. In a world soothed by instant coffee, instant oatmeal, and instant news, a ball club could now become an instant contender. The money for these signings came out of the saddlebags of Angel owner Gene Autry. Humorist Will Rogers had discovered Autry in the early thirties and helped launch him on a career in show business. As the Singing Cowboy, Autry followed Hollywood's plastic rainbow to his pot of gold. Shrewd business deals and investments parlayed that initial fortune into an empire. He could buy almost anything he wanted, and what he wanted more than anything was a pennant in Anaheim. With these two signings he demonstrated a willingness to spend whatever it took to field a champion. Plucking these two ripe plums from the tree of his West Coast rivals was just the start. After Baylor and Rudi came to terms, he shifted his gaze eastward: to Baltimore's Bobby Grich.

Autry couldn't ask for a finer fielding second baseman than Grich. He was unusually strong for his position and could hit for power as well as for average. His on-base percentage ranked among the league's finest, and he was a quick, intelligent base runner. Grich could play.

California was already blessed with an excellent second baseman, Jerry Remy, who was also their leadoff man. The Angels' interest in Grich was based on his background as a shortstop. He had come up to the majors at that position in 1972. It was where he played when he was named the International League's MVP. Grich had been switched to second base only because Baltimore already had Mark Belanger. God did not play shortstop as well as Belanger did. While Autry slept at night, he was entertained by visions of Grich playing alongside Remy in the Angels' infield. They never botched a play.

The Yankees had the same dream. Only in their version Grich was teamed up with Willie Randolph and had an NY on his chest. Steinbrenner and Paul weren't satisfied with Stanley at short. Stanley hadn't ingratiated himself with Steinbrenner when he made a costly error in the second game of the World Series. If the Yankees had any chance to win a game from the Reds it was that one. Cincinnati had led early, but New York clawed back to tie the game at 3–3. There it remained going into the ninth. Catfish Hunter was on the mound, clicking away with the lulling, deadly efficiency of Poe's pendulum. He retired the first two batters. Ken Griffey, the Reds' right fielder, hit a ground ball to Stanley that Stanley threw away for a two-base error. Hunter intentionally walked Joe Morgan. The next batter, Tony Perez, scored Griffey with a base hit as predictable as the dawn. Perez almost never failed in that sort of situation.

Six years later, Griffey maintained, "Stanley shouldn't have been charged with an error. He came up throwing off the wrong foot, but he had no choice. Not the way I was running." Griffey had gotten 38 infield hits during the summer of '76. He could get out of the batter's box faster than the speed of thought. That didn't matter. When the E6 went up on the scoreboard, it only confirmed Steinbrenner's suspicion that the Yankees could not win a world championship with Stanley at short.

The seeds of that belief had germinated long before that frigid October evening. The Yankees had made numerous attempts throughout the 1976 season to get shortstop Toby Harrah from Texas. The Rangers wanted too much. Charlie Finley had tried to sell them Bert Campaneris during his June fire sale. But Campy was thirty-four years old and had too high a price on his head. New York almost got Brewer third baseman Don Money. Like Grich, Money had started his major league life as a shortstop. That deal evaporated when Milwaukee asked for Oscar Gamble. The Yankees couldn't part with Gamble because they had just learned that Ron Blomberg, the oft-injured Blomberg, was going to be out for another summer.

This inability to come up with a better shortstop did not increase the front office's affection for Stanley. When the World Series was over, the Yankees, along with the eleven other American League clubs, were asked to submit a roll of unprotected players to be used to stock the league's newest franchises: the Toronto Blue Jays and the Seattle Mariners. New York left Stanley exposed on the list. There were no takers.

When George, Billy, and Gabe huddled to discuss the free agent situation, they came to a quick agreement: Cincy lefthander Don Gullett was their number one priority. Gullett had beaten them in the first game of the Series. Getting him was easy. The pitcher signed a Yankee contract on November 18. That pact represented a six-year deal worth about $2 million.

There was some risk in taking him. Gullett had been injured in each of the last two seasons. But he did have the highest winning percentage (.674) of any active pitcher with 100 or more decisions, was only twenty-six years old, and had a talent that his now former manager, Sparky Anderson, prognosticated "would take him straight to the Hall of Fame."

The other target of Steinbrenner's bankroll was not so easily agreed upon. He wanted Reggie Jackson. Martin opted for Joe Rudi; the Yankees didn't even draft him. Gabe Paul was interested in either Don Baylor or Bobby Grich. Paul won out. The Yankees pursued the second baseman with a ferocity. Too much ferocity, perhaps. At one point they tried to dissuade Grich from his initial leanings toward playing in the Sun State by inferring the Angels could be challenged on their right to sign him. Questions could be raised over the Nordbrook business. The Yankees could contend that California had abused the draft guidelines by dealing for a player they had no intention of signing. The implication was that Grich's contract would be disallowed. Canceling deals was one of the things Bowie Kuhn did best. Angel general manager Harry Dalton, a man Grich knew from their days with the Orioles, assured the infielder that this was so much bluster. Whatever chances the Yankees had of inking the second baseman had rapidly diminished.

But so had Steinbrenner's inclination to put Grich in a Yankee uniform. As soon as Grich pulled back, Steinbrenner began to seriously question if he wanted to spend $2 million to find out if Grich could still play shortstop. He hadn't been at the position in four years. Steinbrenner convinced himself that his original impulse was correct. He went after Reggie Jackson and got him.

With Jackson on the team, Steinbrenner felt he could now part with the unsigned Oscar Gamble in order to get the shortstop he felt he needed. He had a good idea who that man would be.

Bucky Dent of the Chicago White Sox knew who George Steinbrenner was. He had met the Yankee owner "at a basketball game in 1975. He was sitting in front of me. I introduced myself to him, and he said, 'Gee, our club has been trying to get you for quite some time.' I just kind of smiled and let him know that I had always wanted to be a Yankee. In 1976, the rumors got very strong that they were really trying to get me." Dent was available because he was unsigned and Chicago owner

Bill Veeck needed money. Veeck dickered with the Yankees and proposed a variety of deals, each revolving around Oscar Gamble and cash. Lots of cash. The Yankees were willing to let Gamble go. They could not agree with the White Sox boss on who would accompany the outfielder to the Windy City. Veeck requested Sparky Lyle or a minor league pitcher named Ron Guidry. Steinbrenner had no objections to parting with Guidry, but Paul wouldn't hear of it. Paul knew how hard it was to unearth a good arm. Guidry didn't have a good arm; he had a great one. Paul insisted that they turn down any deal involving the left-hander. He hadn't given up on getting Dent. He had a strategy.

Paul thought New York should wait Veeck out. He knew the White Sox were financially strapped and would eventually be forced to accept a lesser deal. The Yankees started talking up their minor league shortstop, Mickey Klutts. This young phenom had just driven in over 80 runs in Triple-A ball. They let it be known that they would be pleased to open the season with Klutts at short. Unfortunately, Klutts, though he had indeed played shortstop in the minors, was really a displaced third baseman—who broke his hand in spring training. The Yankee situation became almost as desperate as Veeck's.

But not quite. Veeck needed that money to open the season. He came up with an alternative proposition, one that the Yankees found agreeable. The White Sox sent Dent to New York for Gamble, minor league pitchers Bob Polinsky and LaMarr Hoyt, and $400,000.

There was a real outcry raised over this deal. Steinbrenner was accused of wanting to field an All-Star team, and the Yankees had to bear some bad press over their treatment of Stanley. Only days before the trade, with the deal apparently disintegrated, Stanley had signed a new three-year contract. He had counted on being the Yankees' regular shortstop. That was no longer a possibility.

Some critics pointed to a report by a Yankee scout asserting that Dent "had only slightly more range than Stanley and would hit only a little bit more." That assessment would have been a good indictment of Steinbrenner, the Yankee front office, and the deal. Except scouts aren't perfect, and in this case the scout goofed.

During the 1975 and 1976 seasons, in games he played at shortstop, Stanley managed to average 3.6 chances per game. Dent's average was around 5.1. This meant that, over the course of a full season, Dent would make over 200 plays on balls Stanley wouldn't touch. Dent had a better arm than Stanley and hit with more power. He was physically stronger than Stanley. (People tend to think of Dent as "little Bucky." Well, little Bucky is 5'10" and weighs about 175 pounds. Running into him at second base is about as enjoyable as sliding into a brick wall.) He was equipped to play 150 games every season. Most people doubted that Stanley had the stamina to endure the rigors of that sort of test. Finally, Dent possessed an amazing adroitness. He could catch anything he could get his glove on, no matter where it was thrown. Ever see a second baseman shovel a ball to his shortstop below the knees? How often does the shortstop drop that ball? Dent almost never did. He made that play better than anyone. Dent wasn't just a little bit better than Stanley; he was miles better.

There was another resentment directed toward Steinbrenner. It centered around what was perceived to be an arrogant use of his loaded checkbook. After signing Jackson and Gullett, he sent $100,000 to the Atlanta Braves for Jimmy Wynn, a right-handed power hitter with 290 career home runs. The $400,000 he gave Veeck was roughly equal to the amount he lavished on Dent in a three-year contract. Steinbrenner was being blamed for the spending mania that had gripped baseball.

The real culprits had been the always-innocent Boston Red Sox. They had been searching for a stopper in their bullpen ever since they had gotten rid of Lyle. After a season of watching dozens of ball games run away in the late innings, they were frantic to find one. Hadn't they offered Charley Finley $1 million for Rollie Fingers? Bill Campbell was a relief pitcher for the Minnesota Twins. He had just been given the Fireman of the Year Award for his previous season's work. At the start of the 1976 campaign, Campbell had tried to wangle a $30,000 annual wage out of Twins owner Cal Griffith. The best Griffith would offer was $22,000. So Campbell had toiled for that amount, only $3,000 above the major league minimum, without a signed agreement. Now he was ready to cash in. Big.

Just how big came as a shock to everyone. Most baseball people thought Campbell would get a contract calling for about $100,000 a year. The Red Sox weren't sure that would be enough. Rather than risk losing the right-hander to a higher bidder, they made Campbell a figure in history. He became the first member of the first re-entry draft to sign a contract. It was to run for four years, and its total worth was $1 million.

That was the signing that kicked off what was, up to then, baseball's wildest spending spree. But it was the other owners who went crazy, not George Steinbrenner. Steinbrenner merely picked the two best players on the market, and he got them at prices that looked cheap compared to some of the other funny-money figures that were being tossed around. Yes, it was obvious that Steinbrenner was trying to assemble his own All-Star team with these transactions. Isn't it an owner's duty to field the best team he can? And why did so many of the critics who indicted Steinbrenner for this also chastise the Mets' front office for refusing to sign anybody?

Steinbrenner needed every player he had acquired. The Yankees had won the '76 pennant because they were good. But they were also lucky. In Baltimore, Reggie Jackson had missed the first five weeks of the season while involved in a salary dispute. That had set the Oriole offense back for two months. Boston had been torn by dissension surrounding their unsigned trinity of stars: shortstop Rick Burleson, center fielder Fred Lynn, and catcher Carlton Fisk. Their bullpen had been in a shambles. These circumstances had helped New York get off to an early big lead that nobody could overcome. The Yankees couldn't count on that happening again. Boston had made peace with the three players and had added Campbell. New York had to make their moves just to keep pace.

When the new cast of Yankees reported to Fort Lauderdale, there were loud rumblings about the juggernaut Steinbrenner and Paul had assembled. The best summation of the attitude this group inspired was made during a meaningless exhibition game in mid-March. The opposition was the Chicago White Sox. Moments before the game, the home plate umpire looked into the Chicago dugout. Not a bad club. He then glanced at the Yankees who had just taken the field: Munson, Chambliss, Randolph, Dent, Nettles, Jackson, Rivers, and White. Catfish Hunter was throwing on the sidelines. In the Yankee dugout sat Jimmy Wynn, Lou Piniella, Carlos May, Fred Stanley, and center fielder Paul Blair, a recent addition who had come from Baltimore in exchange for Elliott Maddox. The umpire let go of a low whistle. Turning to the White Sox, he roared, "Play ball ... if you dare!"

These Yankees were an imposing army of killers. The hope around the league was that they would get tangled in a web of infighting and self-destruct. It was a possibility that Oriole pitcher Jim Palmer characterized as "wishful thinking." This hope faded when New York concluded their exhibition season without so much as one attempted murder.

On the surface, it seemed a placid enough spring session. Jackson hadn't received an enthusiastic welcome from his new comrades, but he hadn't been shunted off to a corner either. The camp was alive with the usual hijinks. On April 1, Lyle relieved Hunter in a game against the Orioles. He threw two pitches and collapsed to the mound, clutching his elbow. Trainer Gene Monahan raced to the stricken reliever. An obviously distraught Lyle told him, "Gene, I think I popped something." Monahan looked like he was contemplating the joys of suicide. He asked Lyle if he could straighten his elbow out. "Not much," rasped the left-hander. As the trainer started to walk Lyle back to the dugout, Lyle broke away and yelled, "April Fool!" Monahan should have checked his calendar.

Dock Ellis was still keeping things loose in the locker room, doing his impeccable impersonation of Muhammad Ali, and getting on everybody. Munson, Piniella, Nettles, Rivers, and Hunter still carried needles dipped in deadly mirth. But the laughter was a fragile veil of hilarity. Underneath it, a bomb hid. Ticking.

The players did not resent Jackson. They did not care for some of the remarks he had made ("I didn't come to New York to be a star, I brought my star with me"), but they had been prepared for that. They weren't terribly fazed by some of his insecure eccentricities like counting out his wad of hundred-dollar bills while sitting on the team bus. Or the way he always talked about his salary. A number of them did *not* care for the fact that he had received that small fortune. Not because of petty jealousy. They simply felt slighted by management. "Where was ours?" they wondered. Where was the reward for the guys who helped win the pennant? Lyle, Chambliss, Ellis, Gamble, and White had come to spring training unsigned. Gamble was traded. Nettles complained about the three-year deal he had signed the previous year. Nettles had made two mistakes: He signed before he got hot and won the home run title, and he hadn't realized the sort of numbers that would turn up on the contracts of those players who opted for freedom. What had looked like a great deal now made Nettles look underpaid. Munson was upset because he felt he had a verbal commitment from Steinbrenner, a promise that assured him that no member of the team would be paid more than the Yankee captain. After Jackson signed, Munson expected a raise. He got it. But he had since discovered that bonuses and other perks made Jackson's pact worth more. He felt lied to.

The team had other problems. Baseball problems. Jackson was nursing a sore left elbow. Nettles had had an ingrown wart sliced off his left hand, and it was slow to heal. These were relatively minor affairs. Of greater concern was the condition of the pitching staff. Ken Holtzman was getting shellacked in every outing, and so was Hunter. That was 40 percent of the starting rotation. Both pitchers appeared to have suffered serious losses of velocity. Ron Guidry, the rookie Gabe Paul had raved about, seemed unable to get anyone out. And Rivers was suffering from a severe case of the I-don't-feel-like-playing-today blues. Trade rumors had him and Dock Ellis going to Oakland for pitcher Mike Torrez and center fielder Billy North.

Ellis had orchestrated his own banishment by doing a couple of things. One was remaining unsigned going into the season; Lyle, White, and Chambliss had come to terms. Another was choosing to get into a shouting match with Steinbrenner. Ellis was fond of wearing an earring. He never went so far as to wear it on the field, but he wasn't shy about showing it off in the locker room. One day Steinbrenner opined that it wasn't exactly what he expected his Yankees to be seen in. The ever-demure Ellis told Steinbrenner, "Watch it, or I'll wear this fucking thing on the field. The only reason I don't is because I don't want to rock your little boat." Steinbrenner let Ellis know that if he did rock the boat, it would be the first and last time. Ellis retorted, "Motherfucker, get ready to trade me! We'll have a list of four teams you can send me to by tomorrow. We're going to get it on! Anything you have to say to me, you can do it in the papers. I'm going to kill you in the papers! This is war!" Ellis did not say any of this in a whisper.

When the Yankees opened the season in New York on April 7, they gave 43,785 fans a number of false signs. Hunter shut out the Brewers 3–0. Wynn, in his first official Yankee at-bat, hit a home run. Milwaukee is still waiting for it to drop. It was a 450-foot shot into the center field bleachers. Jackson went two for four, scored two runs, hustled his butt off, and was the object of universal love and affection. The one sour note occurred when Hunter was forced to leave the game after hurling seven tasty innings of three-hit ball. He had been KO'd by a line drive off the bat of Brewer center fielder Von Joshua that struck him in the left instep. The Yankees, having won their last seven exhibition games in a row, looked the All-Star team they were supposed to be.

Even the schedulemaker behaved like a loyal Steinbrenner employer. Ten of New York's first 12 games were against Milwaukee, a last-place club in 1976, and the Toronto Blue Jays, an expansion team. What could be easier? After 10 games with these cupcakes, the Yankees had 2 wins and 8 losses. They were in last place.

Martin looked to pull a winning rabbit out of his hat. Failing to do that, he went one better. He reached into his chapeau and discovered a lineup. Martin had done this at least once before in Detroit, as part of the Martin method for loosening up his troops. The magic cap spewed out the following batting order for game 11, an afternoon contest against the suddenly carnivorous Blue Jays:

> Randolph, 2b
> Munson, c
> Jackson, rf
> Nettles, 3b
> Rivers, cf
> White, lf
> May, dh
> Chambliss, 1b
> Dent, ss

That was not the most absurd lineup in the world. With the exceptions of Rivers and Chambliss, it was almost suspiciously perfect. The magic hat story was met with a lot of knowing winks.

Whether or not Martin, as he later claimed, had Jackson pick the lineup from Martin's cap is unimportant. The results saw to that. The Yankees won that afternoon's game and the next five by scores of 7–5, 8–6, 9–3, 10–1, 7–1, and 9–6. All with the enchanted lineup. When the streak ended, the order was scrapped. But, two weeks after its introduction into Yankee lore, New York was in first place.

They shouldn't have left that spot for the rest of the season. New York was the deepest and most powerful club in the league. Once they gained first place they should have pulled away and spent the remainder of the summer planning how they would spend their World Series shares. It did not turn out to be quite that easy.

It was Roy Campanella who said, "In order to play this game, you have to have a lot of little boy in you." It's true. Most of baseball's most incandescent deities—Babe Ruth, Willie Mays, and Pete Rose among them—were gifted with the touch of the man-child. This is not something to be dismissed lightly. For now the time has come to speak of Reggie Jackson, and the wonder he was to behold.

New York did not tender the highest bid for Jackson's services. Steinbrenner's offer had been bettered by both the Montreal Expos and the San Diego Padres. But Jackson had allowed himself to be seduced by the magic city and its whispered promises, promises held only by the flimsy lace of good intentions. It was Steinbrenner who made Jackson aware of what New York City could mean for him. And what Jackson could mean for it. When Reggie Jackson came to New York, he was handed a reputation as a guy who could put "the fannies in the seats." This proved to be true, but at the time it was purely speculation. If Jackson was a big draw before he came to New York, it wasn't obvious from the record. Nobody broke down doors to see him in Oakland. The A's attendance was atrocious throughout his tenure there. And they were a tremendous ball club. During Jackson's only season in Baltimore, average attendance actually dropped. When Jackson looked at New York, he saw a huge stage crying for him to make an entrance. People stopped him in the streets, telling how much the Yankees and the town needed him. That pleased Jackson. It was something that went beyond the cold dominion of dollar signs and decimal points.

One person who did not stop Jackson on the street to sing his praises was the Yankee skipper. Martin wasn't sure the club needed Jackson. Like most managers, Martin liked to have a certain sense of control over his team's fate. At times, this craving appeared so voracious it consumed him. He had won a pennant for Steinbrenner, a flag the owner had no right to expect. It should have won Martin a measure of respect.

But when the team was being made over, Martin's opinion wasn't taken into account. Martin felt the Yankees needed a strong right-handed hitter to balance his lineup. He had suggested Joe Rudi; the Yankees didn't even bother to draft the rights to him. Martin wanted to keep Gamble and play Stanley at short; Gamble was traded for Stanley's replacement. Dock Ellis was a player Martin valued highly on and off the field; he couldn't save the pitcher after that outburst against Steinbrenner. Ellis was traded on April 27, accompanying infielder Marty Perez and outfielder Larry Murray to Stalag Finley of Oakland. New York received Mike Torrez. Everywhere Martin looked he could see evidence that his power was being muted.

It upset him. Not with Reggie Jackson, but with the idea of Reggie Jackson. Things might have been different if Steinbrenner had considered Martin's feelings. Perhaps he should have called Martin in and explained why certain moves were made and others weren't. When Steinbrenner was romancing Jackson at 21, why wasn't Martin there? He was only a phone call away. Had Steinbrenner attempted to bring these two sensitive and talented egos together in the early stages, things might have gone differently than they eventually did. Perhaps not. No one will ever know.

Martin's response to having this superstar shoved down his psyche was predictable. He wrapped himself in a blanket of rhetoric and nearly smothered. Martin let anyone within earshot know that Jackson was just one of twenty-five players, and that he did not consider him a superstar. And so on.

It is one of the obligations of a manager to find the means to turn his players on. Sometimes that takes a little bending of the team concept cliché. Manager Chuck Tanner was able to work with Dick Allen on the White Sox, and Earl Weaver had handled Jackson in Baltimore in 1976. Martin had the same capability. He had proven that by prodding the delinquent Rivers into the role of team catalyst. Dock Ellis, a figure of controversy in Pittsburgh, had become a clubhouse leader under Martin. Yet Martin could not bridge the ravine between Jackson and himself. The clear inference is that he couldn't do it because he didn't choose to.

Jackson was not the little-lamb-lost in this fable, not by a long shot. He didn't make things easy for himself.

About the time Jackson was being wooed by the Expos, a picture of Montreal manager Dick Williams taking the outfielder on a tour of Olympic Stadium was circulated. It showed Williams with his left hand on Jackson's shoulder. The skipper's right hand is pointing to some distant area of the cosmos where Jackson was evidently expected to orbit several National League baseballs.

Jackson did not just like this sort of attention, he thrived on it. When the 1973 A's were preparing to play game six of the

World Series against the Mets, they knew they were on the brink of elimination. One more loss and they went home losers. Gene Tenace approached Jackson in the locker room and said, "Big man, I'd really like to be playing another ball game tomorrow." Big man. Jackson responded that afternoon with two RBI doubles and a single. After singling, he scored a run. The A's won 3–1. The next day Jackson homered. Oakland bagged the Mets, and Jackson walked off with the Series MVP Award. An Oakland teammate once commented, "What Reggie loves to be told is 'Buck, you're the strongest man in the history of the game.'" It was another way of saying Jackson wanted to be appreciated; he wanted to be loved.

It had to be dismaying, therefore, when he was the recipient of Martin's glacial treatment, and when his new teammates had more important things to do than tell him how glad they were to see him. The man in him could deal with this, new guy on the club and all that. He knew it would take time and performance to capture the club's minds and hearts. But the child in him must have rebelled. He felt mistreated. So he sulked. He counted out hundred-dollar bills in front of his teammates and talked endlessly about his wealth. And about "the magnitude of me."

Most of the Yankees found his behavior irritating. This was a relatively new experience for him. In Baltimore, he had been part of Earl Weaver's happy family. He had also known he would be gone at season's end. Most of the players on the Oakland club were guys he grew up with in baseball. They didn't always like his antics. But they were tolerant of them, and even found most of them amusing.

On the Yankees he was with a group of men who weren't interested in making the first moves to get behind Jackson's public face. They seemed unwilling to come close.

Finally it was Munson, the team captain, who broke the barriers and tried to bring Jackson into "the gang." He started to hang out with Jackson in the batting cage and included him in the locker room banter. The ice was just beginning to thaw when *the article* hit the streets. And everything else hit the fan.

The article was an interview Jackson had done for *Sport* magazine. In it Jackson was quoted as calling himself "the straw that stirs the drink. It all comes down to me. Maybe I should say [Thurman] Munson and me, but he really doesn't enter into it. Munson thinks he can be the straw that stirs the drink but he can only stir it bad." The entire Yankee clubhouse went into trauma. One player meekly suggested to Munson that perhaps Jackson had been misquoted. "For three fucking pages!" Munson demanded.

On the evening that the interview's contents were made public, Jackson hit a towering home run into the Stadium's right field bleachers, tying a game with the Red Sox at 2–2. After circling the bases, Jackson moved toward the dugout, apparently to receive the handshakes of his teammates gathered at the end of the dugout nearest home plate. He ignored them. In front of 35,000 people. Swerving to the left, he entered the dugout from the first base side. Later in the game, he overran a bloop single to right, allowing the batter to reach second unmolested. The misplay helped Boston build the winning run in a 4–3 victory.

Why did Jackson do it? The interview had been held during spring training when his opinion of his future with the team was not overly optimistic. He had come to New York proclaiming himself "the hunted on the team of the hunted." He was finding himself a stranger in a strange land.

The comments about Munson were made before Munson had begun his friendly overtures. The remarks obviously questioned Munson's leadership for failing to make the move sooner. Whatever the reason, Jackson picked the wrong forum to lay bare his hurt. It was a serious indiscretion.

The snubbing of his teammates was another faux pas. But Jackson had just re-made a lot of enemies that afternoon. When he approached that dugout and saw the sea of outstretched hands, he had to have been struck by the sheer hypocrisy of it all. In the clubhouse, no one wanted to speak to him. Now, he hits a home run, and everybody shows a glad hand.

All sports are filled with such facades. Jackson should have understood that. For his own sake, for the sake of the team, he should have made his stand in private. He should have accepted their congratulations. Now all the conflicts had been re-stirred, and threatened the team as a team. But it would pass. There would be a tense period of remission before it would slink back in more lethal form. In Boston.

The Yankees arrived in Boston on Friday, June 17. They were in first place. The Red Sox lurked one-half game behind.

Boston had fought their way into second place by implementing a policy of total annihilation of their opponents. They took no prisoners. Butch Hobson, their third baseman, was on his way to a 30-home run season. He batted eighth. The Red Sox strategy was to score enough runs to keep their starting pitchers around until the seventh inning. Then it was time for Bill Campbell. This method had been quite successful.

The Yankees did not have the same amount of punch, but they did have a more varied attack, combining speed with power. Their bullpen was deeper than Boston's. New York was still hounded by internal bickering, an inconsistent starting pitching staff, and a dearth of right-handed power.

After signing Gullett, the Bombers were purported to have the best pitching staff around. But Gullett was having another injury-plagued season. He won when he pitched, but he didn't pitch enough. Holtzman had been ineffective, and Hunter was getting rocked by ordinary teams. The Yankee doctors could not ascertain what was wrong with the right-hander; there were no outward signs of injury. Hunter provided the best diagnosis, remarking, "All my arm needs is a new screw."

Ed Figueroa had maintained his winning form, and so had Mike Torrez. Dick Tidrow again demonstrated the unique arm and temperament that made him the model swing man. And Sparky Lyle had never been better. Lyle was the best reliever in the league, the glue of this pitching staff.

But not its savior. That was Ron Guidry. The skinny left-hander had made the club by default after a rotten spring. He received his first start on April 29 against the Seattle Mariners. The only reason he got that chance was that Torrez was late in coming from Oakland. Martin had no one else to use. Guidry shut out the Mariners 3–0, with help from Sparky Lyle in the ninth. He spot-started a few games after that and was secure in the starting rotation by mid-June. He had become the team's best starting pitcher.

Right-handed power arrived on June 15, courtesy of the Houston Astros. Cliff Johnson remembered, "I found out that the Astros had traded me when I was about sixteen thousand feet airborne. We were coming in to play the Mets. Somebody told me that [manager] Bill Virdon wanted to talk to me. I was leading the club at the time in just about every offensive category, so I didn't think it had anything to do with my performance on the field. I went up to see him, and he told me I was a Yankee. The trade was not unexpected. I was upset with the Astros, and they were upset with me. I had bone chips in my ankle, that the club chose not to believe. I was surprised I went to the Yankees. When I got to the clubhouse, I was greeted by Reggie [Jackson]. He said, 'Hey, you're hitting over .300, you got 12 dingers, and 40 ribbies. How could Houston trade you?' I told him, 'Don't ask me.'" Johnson had arrived, it was hoped, just in time to put a hole in Fenway's Green Monster.

The Yankees lost the first game 9–4. The only holes in the Wall were put there by Boston batters at the expense of Catfish Hunter. He gave up four home runs in the first inning and was gone.

The next day the roof caved in. Jackson was sitting in the dugout before game time. Martin was also there, holding a seminar on an aborted squeeze play he had ordered the night before with Bucky Dent. During his discourse, the manager turned to Jackson and asked, "Don't you think that was a good play?" In a small way, Martin was reaching out. Jackson said, "No." It was an honest reply, just as his avoidance of those handshakes in New York had been an honest gesture. But, again, Jackson had goofed. He had shown his manager up.

The rage that had been dormant in Martin was ready to pour out. All he needed was one more excuse. Jackson accommodated him in the sixth inning of that afternoon's ball game.

The Yankees were behind 7–4 in the sixth inning. Boston's Jim Rice hit a pop-up into right field. Base hit. Jackson went after the ball hesitantly, and then made a halfhearted throw to the infield while Rice took second easily. Martin sent Paul Blair out to relieve Jackson. He was convinced that Jackson hadn't hustled on the play, and he was determined to make him pay a price.

The ugly scene that transpired in the dugout, Martin scrambling over his coaches to get at Jackson, and Reggie hurling invectives at his angry manager, was national news as it happened. Some 30 million people were watching on the NBC Game of the Week. Many who saw the Red Sox 10–4 victory thought that New York had lost more than just a ball game. They were convinced that the Yankees' entire season had just gone up in the flames of Martin's fury.

Martin was fortunate that Gabe Paul was not of the same mind as the television audience. It was Paul who saved Martin from Steinbrenner's guillotine. Steinbrenner, who had seen the event on the evening news, wanted to can Martin. But Paul realized that such an action would give the impression that Jackson was the manager. There was no choice but to stick with Martin for the time being.

Martin did receive a reprimand. He was made to realize just how close he had come to the abyss. One more gaffe, and he would slide right in.

The debacle in Boston ended the next day with an 11–1 Red Sox victory. After the game, Ed Figueroa said, "Nobody on this team gives a shit whether we win or lose." The Red Sox had hit 16 home runs in the three-game set. Even second baseman Denny Doyle hit one, and his home runs came about as often as Halley's Comet. Boston outscored the Yankees 30 to 9. New York had been totally outclassed. They left Boston in second place, two and a half games out. Two nights later the gulch widened to four and a half.

Somewhere amid all this gloom, a peace of sorts took hold. Steinbrenner and Paul used backup catcher Fran Healy as an intermediary between Munson and Jackson. Martin and Jackson were brought together next and had the facts of life explained to them. They would have to learn to live with each other, for the good of the team. The air wasn't cleared, but it was breathable. There were no suggestions made that the three start looking for wedding bands. But at least a working relationship had been established. It may have been a coincidence, but, shortly after, the club started to function the way it was supposed to.

Boston invaded the Stadium on Friday, June 29. They had hit 30 home runs in their last nine games. On this evening they would hit three more, all off Hunter. The Red Sox took a 5–3 lead into the ninth. The first two Yankee hitters were quietly retired. With Campbell on the mound, it looked as though the Bronx Bombers could kiss this night good-bye.

Willie Randolph could have been New York's last roll of the dice. He tripled off Yastrzemski's glove in left field. The game, and perhaps the season, was now perched on the shoulders of Roy White.

"I thought I was going to hit one out," admitted White, "because the previous time I had faced Bill [Campbell], I flied out. But I really felt good since I had just missed getting all of it. So the next time up I felt very comfortable. Sure enough, he hung a breaking ball over the plate, and I hit it. Perfectly. There was no doubt in my mind that it was gone. That was one of the most exciting moments of my career. The game, the opposition, the 54,000 screaming fans! It was something. And then Reggie [Jackson] won the game in the next inning with a pinch-hit double off Ramon Hernandez. We swept the next two games. When Boston left, we were only a game out, and we knew we could win it all."

Jackson was put back in the cleanup spot in August at Steinbrenner's request; Billy had batted Reggie as low as seventh during the season. That was a source of irritation for the proud slugger. Batting in the pressure position he loved, Jackson took off just as the team was jelling. Nettles, Munson, and Jackson ended up with over 100 ribbies each. Chambliss had 90. Johnson hit 12 home runs in 142 at-bats, and Piniella and Rivers batted over .325. Randolph and White found a way, any way, to get on base and win ball games. Even a last-minute pickup, Dave Kingman, was able to help the club with 4 homers in only 24 at-bats. The Yankees were a hitting machine.

They could pick it, too. Especially in the infield, where Dent and Randolph provided the club with its best double play combo since Richardson and Kubek. Nettles won a Gold Glove at third. And the beleaguered Fred Stanley was the best utility-man a team could ask for.

The pitching never got healthy enough to live up to pre-season expectations. But it was good enough. Guidry (16–7, 2.82 ERA), Figueroa (16–11), Gullett (14–4), Tidrow (11–4), and Torrez (14–12 as a Yankee) comprised a deep, if not over-whelming, pitching staff.

Lyle had his greatest season, winning 13, losing 5, and saving 26. He was the league's Cy Young Award winner, the first American League reliever to win the prize. These individual efforts helped the team win an astounding 40 of its final 50 games. That closing drive gave the Yankees their first 100-win season since 1963.

Neither Boston nor Baltimore, New York's only pursuers, was impressed enough to give up on their own chances. They stayed right behind the Yankees until the season's final week-end. On Friday night, September 30, the Red Sox eliminated the Orioles from the race. The next afternoon, Baltimore re-turned the favor. Boston hopes came to an end on a fly ball that was caught in center field. By Elliott Maddox.

When Maddox was sent by the Yankees to Baltimore, the parting had not been amicable. Maddox had been lied to by team officials about the severity of his knee injury, and later angered the Yankee front office by seeking a second opinion from a doctor of his own choice. Maddox's relationship with Billy Martin had been spiky. When the ball that would ensure New York the pennant drifted out to him, he recalled, "I almost let it drop. I'm serious. Jim Rice hit the ball. When he came up to the plate, I thought to myself, 'Don't hit it to me.' It was the first time in my life that I ever said anything like that on a ball field. I did not want to be the one to give Billy Martin the pennant, didn't want to have anything to do with it. If you ever see a film of the game, you'll notice that as soon as I caught the ball, I tossed it to Kiko [Garcia] at short. Immedi-ately. I doubt it was in my glove for more than half a second. I had even yelled to Andres [Mora] in left field, 'I may let it drop, don't count on me for this one!' It was a shallow fly, and the only way I could have flubbed it was to slip. But it was a close game, we were ahead by only a run, and we were playing for second place, so I caught it. But if it had been hit toward the wall, it would have fallen in. It's very easy to shy away from a wall. The thought was there. I hate to say it, but it was."

Once again, the Yankees would face the Royals in the American League playoffs. Once again, the series would go the full five games. Once again, there would be tears in the Kansas City clubhouse.

The playoffs were the Yankee season in microcosm. The Yankees lost two of the first three games, backing into a now-familiar corner. Only Ron Guidry, pitching a three-hitter in game two, kept the team from elimination. New York won game four with Lyle pitching five and one-third innings of impossible relief. He faced only 17 men in recording 16 outs.

Game five was Hollywood stuff. Paul Splittorff, having beaten the Yankees in game one, started for the Royals. A slumping Reggie was benched. He had looked helpless against Splittorff, prompting Martin to go with Paul Blair in right. It was a ballsy move, one that Steinbrenner objected to. But when Steinbrenner asked Catfish Hunter if Jackson could hit Splittorff, Hunter replied, "Not with a fucking paddle." That cinched it. Steinbrenner went along with the move. But, if the gamble failed, and the Yankees lost, Billy could hit the streets.

Guidry started for New York on two days' rest. He departed with the Royals leading 3–1 in the third inning. Mike Torrez entered the game as Kansas City fans started to lick their lips. Torrez had started game three and been smacked all over the ball park.

Pitching on only one day's rest, Torrez courageously held K.C. under wraps for five and one-third innings. The Yankees, however, couldn't do a thing with Splittorff.

Until the eighth. Randolph knocked the left-hander out of the game with a leadoff single. Kansas City skipper Whitey Herzog wanted right-hander Doug Bird to pitch to Munson. Thurman struck out, but Piniella followed with a base hit, moving Randolph to third. Cliff Johnson was due up next. He was a right-handed hitter, though, and Martin had a left-handed batter on the bench: a fellow by the name of Reggie Jackson. Jackson blooped a soft single into center field. New York trailed by one. The score remained frozen there going into the ninth. Herzog decided to go with his 20-game winner, right-hander Dennis Leonard, to grab the final three outs. Leonard didn't get any.

Paul Blair, the man who had started in place of Jackson, led off with a base hit. White walked. Larry Gura relieved and was greeted by a game-tying single off the bat of Mickey Rivers. Mark Littell, Chambliss's victim from last year, was raced in. Randolph took him to left for a sacrifice fly, scoring White. Another run scored on a wild throw by George Brett. The Yankees left the inning leading 5–3. Sparky Lyle was brought in to finish the Royals off. Lights out.

When the Los Angeles Dodgers prepared to face the Yankees in the World Series opener in New York, they were a very confident club. The Dodgers had four men—Steve Garvey, Ron Cey, Dusty Baker, and Reggie Smith—who had combined for 125 home runs and 398 RBI. Their second baseman, Davey Lopes, was one of baseball's most accomplished base thieves. The Los Angeles pitching staff had a quintet of reliable starters: Don Sutton, Tommy John, Burt Hooton, Doug Rau, and Rick Rhoden. No other club could match their front five. They had won their division by 10 games over the former Big Red Machine. They never had a chance. No team that had survived what the Yankees had gone through was going to lose the ultimate prize.

New York won the first game in twelve innings. Randolph, after homering in the first inning, doubled and scored the winning run on a base hit by Paul Blair. It was the second consecutive important game that Randolph had played a big part in putting away.

That was expected of the second baseman. From the time he had joined New York, Randolph had shown he knew how to do all the little things that add up to victory. If Jackson gave the Yankees their intimidating aura, and if Munson symbolized the team's heart and soul, it was Randolph who embodied its cool professionalism. Each day during the season, game after game, he would set up office on the plot of earth situated between first and second. Having him there gave Yankee fans and teammates the sense that all was right in this particular part of the world: Willie was on the job.

When he was traded to the Yankees he was "shocked." He recalled, "I was playing winter ball down in Venezuela when I first got the word. We got everything a day late down there. I called my mother to make sure it was true, and she said it was. She was very excited, and I was elated, being a New Yorker. The Pirates had me down in Venezuela to play a little second, a little short, and a little third. It looked like they were grooming me for a utility role. I didn't care much for that idea. I wanted to play! With the Yankees, I figured I'd get a chance to play every day. I knew they had Sandy Alomar, an excellent second baseman, but I also knew that he was a little bit older. I figured if I worked hard I might be able to beat him out. That's how much respect I had for Sandy. It never occurred to me that it was my job to lose, not to win. Gabe [Paul] had grabbed me right after the trade and said, 'We're only going to pay you the major league minimum this year because we're not sure you're going to make the club.' So he got me to sign for the minimum. I was so excited to be with the Yankees, I fell for it without consulting an agent or anybody. Dock Ellis really chewed me out for that. I told him what I signed for and he screamed, 'You little fool, they didn't want Ken Brett or me; they wanted you.' Dock thought I was crazy, and he was right. I was going to start for the New York Yankees! But it worked out all right.

"It was good to break in under Billy [Martin]. We got along extremely well, and he left me alone. He saw that I hustled, and I think he liked that. Billy never jumped on me when I booted one. Instead, he would take me aside and tell me what I had done wrong. That was constructive criticism. Maybe Billy saw a little bit of himself in me. We were both infielders, and we both played aggressively. I think he respected that.

"Billy had us running that first year. He had a steal sign. I didn't really know how to steal bases back then; I stole on pure speed. Mickey [Rivers] was the same way; he just flat out ran.

Mickey would make me run, too. He'd say, 'Let's go, bro, they're looking for us to run.' Mickey got everyone going. Occasionally, I would bat behind him. We had signs between us, but for some reason he kept missing them. He'd say, 'Yeah, I got you.' And I'd say, 'What do you mean you got me? Why didn't you go!' He's a beautiful man.

"That first World Series we were in [in 1976] was quite an experience. The reason Cincy beat us four straight is that we were emotionally drained from the playoffs. We were just happy to be there. We were also intimidated by the Big Red Machine. They were an awesome ball club back then. They just steamrolled us. But that was still a great experience for our ball club. It set the table for us for the next couple of years.

"When we beat the Dodgers [in 1977] there was nothing like it. I'll tell you a little story. I remember telling myself in the dugout not to get too excited when we won. I wanted to remember to grab my hat and get the hell off the field. The reason I thought of the hat was that I didn't want some fan to try to grab it off my head. You could lose your eye, and I remember how crazy the fans were when Chris [Chambliss] hit the home run last year. So I'm very cool, got everything planned. We get to the ninth inning. [Mike] Torrez is pitching, and he's got two outs. The ball goes up, and Thurman [Munson] is there. He catches it. We win. We're world champions, and I go nuts! I forgot everything I told myself. I started shouting, leaping in the air. All of a sudden, some kid creeps up behind me and *whap!* He's got my hat and some of my hair. I had to tackle him to get it back. When I got up I finally looked into our dugout. It was a mob scene; half of Yankee Stadium was in there. When I get to the dugout I see two cops have got my father by the neck and they're choking him! I yelled, 'What's going on, that's my father!' They finally realized what I was saying and released him. My father had gotten as excited as I did and had run out on the field. I took him inside the clubhouse, and we got soaked with champagne. It was great, especially after last year's mismatch. We were world champions. We had shown everybody."

They had shown everybody by beating Los Angeles in six

games. The final clash saw Reggie Jackson stamp his imprimatur on this turbulent season. Could it have ended any other way? Burt Hooton, Elias Sosa, and Charlie Hough. Three pitchers, three swings, three home runs. Rockets that illuminated a clear, dark October night in the Bronx and signaled the start of a love chant that shook the souls of those it reached: "Reggie! Reg-gie! Reg-gie!"

Randolph had a ringside seat for the pyrotechnics. He wasn't surprised by them. "No," he offered, "I really wasn't. Surprised is not the word. I sat there thinking how incredible this was. I couldn't believe that the man was coming out of his face the way he was. Bang! Bang! Bang! It was such a climactic game. You could see the confidence just beaming from the man every time he walked to the plate. And that typified what this team was all about. We had such a feeling that we could get the job done when we had to. Reggie really showed me a lot in that game. We all learned a lot from him about how to win and how the game is supposed to be played. He made us all a little bit better."

Jackson had homered in his last at-bat of the fifth game. In the second frame of the finale, he walked on four pitches. Reggie had homered in his last four swings of the 1977 season. He had also hit one in game four. Five home runs constituted a Series record, as did his 25 total bases and 10 runs scored. The total bases record broke a mark that had been held by Billy Martin. This exhibition of power earned Jackson the Series MVP award.

Rivers, Nettles, Figueroa, and Munson talked about wanting to be traded during the Series. Torrez, after winning two of the four Yankee victories, lamented that he would probably become a free agent. Published reports stated that Martin would be fired, win or lose, when baseball's Octoberfest concluded. That rumor was squelched on the morning of game six when the Yankees summoned the press to announce they were rewarding Martin with a bonus and a new car.

All of these things, and all that had gone on before them, were put aside in victory. Munson embraced Jackson in the jubilant clubhouse and repeatedly called him "Mr. October."

Jackson made his way into Martin's office and put his arm around the manager he had been at crossed sabers with all season. The outfielder proclaimed, "I love this man. I love Billy Martin. This man did a hell of a job. There's nobody else I'd rather play for. Next year we're gonna be tough. It'll be different next year. We'll win because we have a manager who's a tough bastard, and I'm a tough bastard. If you fuck with Billy Martin you're in trouble, and if you fuck with Reggie Jackson you're in trouble."

Oh, the camaraderie! Billy, Reggie, Thurman, George, and the rest of the Yankees had come through this year of fire and ice unscathed. As champions. What could possibly be better than that? What could possibly go wrong next year?

Chapter
NINE

Every time we play the Yankees, we suit up a little bit differently. It's like we throw on the armor and get ready to fight the Holy Wars.

—BILL LEE, left-handed pitcher and philosopher.

THE Yankees were about to conclude their spring training schedule. The reporter wanted to know if Billy Martin thought there was any possibility that New York would repeat as world champions in 1978. Martin never lacks confidence. He fixed his inquisitor with his most withering look and coolly replied, "I didn't come down here to get a suntan."

Despite this macho display, a lot of people had their doubts. The fear for the health of New York's pennant hopes could be summed up in one word: Boston.

The Red Sox had augmented their strength over the winter. They had revamped their one-dimensional offense, sending pitcher Don Aase and cash to the California Angels for second baseman Jerry Remy. Boston expected Remy to provide them with a Mickey Rivers–like ignitor at the top of the batting order. Funny, but at the time of the trade no one accused Boston of trying to field an All-Star team. Or of stepping on the toes of the poor incumbent second sacker Denny Doyle.

The Red Sox had also wearied of winning games 10–9. Actually, that's not quite accurate. They did not mind winning those games at all. They were a bit fed up, though, with losing games 10–9. They sought to rectify that situation by bringing over pitcher Dennis Eckersley in a trade with the Cleveland Indians. Eckersley was a right-hander with an overpowering fastball. He had the sort of stuff that justified fans' expectations of a shutout every time he pitched. He had already thrown a no-hitter against California and, at twenty-four, was about to embark on his best years. Eckersley's career won-lost record was a deceptive 40–32. He had pitched for a mediocre club. Pitching for a Boston powerhouse, Eckersley was expected to win 20.

The Red Sox had also made a purchase in an attempt to buttress their starting pitching corps. Aimed right at the heart of their primary antagonists in New York, this transaction was the signing of free agent Mike Torrez.

The Yankees would have watched the previous year's World Series on television if not for Torrez's outstanding relief stint in game five of the playoffs. The right-hander had started slowly after being acquired from Oakland. He finally began winning after being switched from four to three days' rest between starts. This was no coincidence. Torrez was one of those big, strong honchos who thrived on lots of work. He reeled off six consecutive complete-game wins after the All-Star break, victories the Yankees needed badly.

His last two triumphs for New York came in that World Series against the Dodgers. Torrez was the winning pitcher in the game that brought the world championship to the Bronx for the first time since 1962.

He had consented to cross over to the Red Sox because the Yankee front office did not appreciate his contribution to their fortunes. "I had a lot of pride in being a Yankee," he stated without rancor, "being a member of that team. I really hated to leave, but George [Steinbrenner] didn't want to pay me what I felt I should be getting. I felt unappreciated, especially after the job I did for them. I thought they would work something out to keep me. When the season was over, I later saw George in Vegas. Lou Piniella and I were at the dice table, shooting craps. We were down two or three grand. George came over and handed each of us an envelope, and said, 'Goddamnit, I sure wish you guys would get luckier.' He replenished what we had lost. Then he took me aside and said, 'Mike, we're going to stay with that figure we offered you. We just don't feel we can afford to give you much more than that. Now if you get a higher offer, I can't blame you for taking it. I suppose I'd do the same thing. I'd love for you to remain a Yankee. But, whatever you decide, I want you to know I enjoyed having you pitch for us.' So I really had no choice; I had to leave. I looked at the dollars and cents of it. I had never really made any big money in the game. George was fair in letting me know where I stood. But I still wondered why, if Boston was willing to offer me so much, the Yankees wouldn't at least match it. There was a big difference in the money, almost a million dollars over the length of the contract."

With Eckersley and Torrez joining the pitching staff, the Red Sox offensive giant took on an ominous demeanor.

The Yankees did not tremble in their shadow. They had pocketed a couple of right-handers of their own: relievers Rich Gossage and Rawley Eastwick. Eastwick had won the Fireman of the Year Award with the Cincinnati Reds in 1976. He had spurned the Reds' efforts to sign him and was traded in mid-1977 to the St. Louis Cardinals. Eastwick had suffered an off-year, but at twenty-seven was still young enough to attain his former glory.

Gossage had not had an off-year. His numbers, in fact, were downright frightening, particularly if you were a hitter: 11–9, 1.62 ERA, 26 saves, and 151 strikeouts in 133 innings. The Goose was a better closing act than Frank Sinatra.

In the late innings of a close ball game, Gossage would stride to the mound, his face contorted in a mask of contempt. He would grab the resin bag, squeeze it, and toss it to the ground as if he meant to cause it physical harm. He was ready. At 6' 3", weighing over 200 pounds, he resembled a mature bull. Taking the seemingly too-small white sphere in his hand, he would rock back and hurtle himself, and the baseball, forward with a motion that was smooth violence. The unleashed missile would streak in the general direction of home plate at a velocity of a hundred miles per hour. Or more. This was no longer an innocent object made for whacking. It was a sinister projectile that could maim or injure. Or kill. Batters meditated on these possibilities before they faced him. These options received further reflection from those same hitters as they toted their bats back to the dugout, the ring of "Strike three!" still strong in their ears.

It was a Yankee supposition that these two arms would join with last year's Cy Young Award winner, Sparky Lyle, to give New York the ultimate bullpen. This was expected to numb the impact of Torrez's defection.

But what could make up for the loss of Gabe Paul? He had resigned as president of the Yankees in December 1977. After constructing an American League power, he was returning to the more placid environment of the Cleveland Indians. His successor was former Indian third baseman Al Rosen. Rival executives had Rosen down as an astute baseball man, but had no idea if he possessed Paul's nose for a good deal. Only time would provide the answer. It was doubtful, however, that George Steinbrenner would hold Rosen in the same regard he had held Paul. No one believed that Rosen would be able to dissuade Steinbrenner from making the sort of disastrous moves (Guidry for Dent, Rivers for North, etc.) that Paul had been able to subvert. It was a situation that begged close watching.

After a docile spring, the team opened its season with a spate of losses, four in the club's first five games, all on the road. Gossage was charged with two of the setbacks. These losses were on the minds of a vast mob of fans when New York played its home opener. As the Goose was called out during the pre-game introduction ceremonies, he was met with a vociferous chorus of boos. Ken Holtzman, having been presented before him, had become an expert at identifying that particular tune. He turned to the reliever and said, "That's not 'Goose!' they're yelling." Gossage nodded. Inwardly he raged, "All right, all right, you motherfuckers. Go ahead and boo. By the time this season is over, I'll have all of you cheering."

He kept that vow. But not immediately. The Yankees won

that day, a 4–2 triumph over the White Sox that was the start of an infant winning streak. Gossage didn't have a hand in any of the glory. He dropped one more decision before finally gaining a win. During this drought, his teammates tried to relieve some of the pressure that was stymieing the costly free agent. Once, when the bullpen car was in the process of transporting the Goose into a ball game, "Mickey Rivers threw himself in front of the car," recalled Gossage, "and he started screaming, 'No, not him! Anybody but him!' I told him to get up off the car and get ready to catch this shit I was going to throw up there. I got out, threw the first pitch, and Mickey had to race back about sixty miles to get it. When we got to the dugout, he said, 'Hey, man. You weren't kidding, were you?' Thurman came out to the mound during another game and said, 'Goose, you've given up home runs to lose games, thrown wild pitches, you've lost on base hits, and you've gotten beat on errors. You've done it all!' Right after that, different game, Thurman came out and said, 'Look at your center fielder.' I had just gotten to the mound. I turned and saw Mickey, facing the center field wall, in a sprinting position. All I could see was his back with his number on it."

The problems ailing Gossage was short-lived. The moment the temperature shot up, so did the heat on his fastball. But there was still the little matter of Sparky Lyle to be dealt with.

Lyle was not crazy about the Yankees getting Gossage. He did not believe that there would be enough work for both of them, and he felt that one of them would suffer due to lack of opportunity. When the Yankees signed Eastwick, he became even more vocal in his criticism. No bullpen could ever be big enough for three such studs. How would they ever get in enough innings to be effective?

The Yankees said good-bye to April with a 10–9 record that left them three and a half games behind Detroit. Nothing alarming about that. "Detroit always gets off to a good start," Tiger fans were fond of saying. And everyone knew where they always ended up.

More nettlesome than the Yankees' current position in the standings was the impoverished condition of the starting pitching staff. Again. With Torrez off to a good start in Boston, Yankee followers were starting to wonder if he would have been a more prudent investment than the unnecessary East-wick or, at this point, Gossage. Gullett was taking his annual hospital tour, and Hunter and Holtzman were showing flashes of form. Unfortunately, it was last year's form. Only Figueroa and Guidry were doing the job, Figueroa by pitching well, Guidry by pitching spectacularly.

There are no adjectives to describe how Guidry pitched in that year of his Camelot. Let it be sufficient to say that no Yankee pitcher, not even the master Ford, had ever managed to look so totally incapable of losing.

Guidry was a lean bundle of nerveless energy, able to call on reserves of physical strength that belied his slight stature. The Cajun lefty had a wicked slider, taught to him by Professor Lyle, an overpowering fastball, and the mental toughness of a Confederate cavalryman. His appearance on the mound could lift an entire team. They were held by the conviction that, somehow, he would always win. It was a feeling he shared with them.

Guidry took pleasure in recalling a season that "started off kind of slow for me, at least as far as wins went. I had a couple of no-decisions in my first few games. But no losses. It seemed every time I went out there I just knew I was gonna blow people away. And I did. When I lost my first game, I figured, 'Hell, this is just a temporary setback, because I'm not going to lose again.' If I remember right, I won 13 in a row and then lost a game. Then I won two in a row and lost again. Then I won eight in a row, lost one more, and didn't lose a game for the rest of the year. I lost to Milwaukee with Mike Caldwell, to Baltimore with Mike Flanagan, and to Toronto with Mike Wil-lis. So, if your name was Mike, and you were pitching against me that year, you had a chance to beat me. But not much of one."

The left arm of Louisiana Lightning served as a life-support system for a ball club that was being left as a corpse in the wake of the Boston Blitzkrieg.

Eckersley and Torrez were pitching according to script. The

duo joined with veterans Luis Tiant and Bill Lee and rookie Jim Wright to give Boston their most formidable front-line pitching in thirty-five years. Their presence also allowed the Red Sox to patch up what could have been a crippling tear in the bullpen. Bill Campbell was hurt. He had been overworked during the 1977 campaign and was now paying a painful tariff. His once-mesmerizing collection of pitches had been reduced to ordinary and hittable. But Bob Stanley, a right-handed hurler who had split his time during the previous season between starting and relieving, was now free to bring his considerable talents to the bullpen. He and two veterans, right-hander Dick Drago and lefty Tom Burgmeier, were more than adequate replacements for the stricken Campbell.

These pitchers had the luxury of hurling in front of baseball's most virile lineup. Carlton Fisk, Rick Burleson, Butch Hobson, Carl Yastrzemski, and Dwight Evans were all pounding the ball as lustily as they had the year before. Fred Lynn, who had had a mediocre 1977, was once again displaying some of the brilliance that had marked his rookie season. Jerry Remy had brought much-needed speed to the Boston assault and manifested a taste for the extraordinary around second base. Only first baseman George Scott was having a sub-par season.

That was all right. The heroics of left fielder Jim Rice made up for Scott's drop in production.

Rice was having a year reminiscent of Yaz's Triple Crown season of 1967. Rice was the strongest man in baseball, with a sublime, compact batting stroke that struck with the swiftness of unexpected tragedy. He was the executioner on a team of executioners.

Yankee fans viewed the Red Sox with trepidation. New York had played satisfactorily during the month of May, winning 19 while losing only 8. But Boston had played ever better. They had taken over first place and led New York by three games. This was something to worry about. The Red Sox were not the paper Tigers, expected to fold after the season's first six weeks. They were for real. Already, vehement Sox watchers were comparing the club to the 1927 Yankees as the greatest team of all time.

Fear of Boston increased after June's games had been used up. The Yankees had played less than .500 for the month. The Boston lead had increased to nine.

New York was being decimated by injuries. In a brief four-week span, the club lost the services of Mickey Rivers (fractured wrist), Willie Randolph (wrenched knee), and Bucky Dent (severely pulled hamstring). Andy Messersmith had finally become a Yankee in December 1977. His contract had been purchased from the Atlanta Braves. Messersmith had pitched impressively in the spring, winning a spot in Martin's starting rotation. Then, a week before the season commenced, he hurt his shoulder while stumbling in an attempt to cover first base. Messersmith made his first start of the season on May 29. In five innings pitched, against the Indians, he allowed one hit and no runs. It was his only good outing of the season. Three weeks later, he was back on the disabled list, lost for the rest of the year.

Thurman Munson and Catfish Hunter weren't on the disabled list, but they should have been. Munson's knees ached terribly, making it almost impossible for him to drive off his legs while hitting, and robbing him of much of his extra-base power.

Hunter's arm continued to be a dead weight, while Don Gullett's wing was being held together by paste and old tape. Nobody knew when it would fall off again.

This was the casualty roll as the team prepared to clash with the Red Sox, in Fenway Park, on June 18. It was their first get-together of the season.

A week prior to the visit, speculation was rampant on the subject of whom the Yankees would start in the first game. It had already been determined that it would not be Guidry. He would start the night before the series began. The rotation's order also ruled out Ed Figueroa. Two nominees for the spot were wild guesses: Rawley Eastwick and Ken Holtzman. Holtzman had not pitched well and had a terrible career record in Fenway. Choosing him would engender another problem that became apparent on June 10: one of distance. Holtzman would have had a hard time getting his fastball over home plate in

Fenway Park while pitching from a mound in Wrigley Field. The left-hander had finally been dealt to the Chicago Cubs for minor league reliever Ron Davis.

Eastwick seemed a more logical option. He was a right-hander—a plus at Fenway—had shown good stuff in the bullpen, and, wonder of wonders, was healthy.

But Eastwick was traded also. Surprisingly. He was shipped to the Philadelphia Phillies for Jay Johnstone, a left-handed outfielder–first baseman. The next day, New York sent Del Alston and Mickey Klutts to Oakland for Gary Thomasson, a left-handed outfielder–first baseman. During the off-season, they had purchased Jim Spencer, a left-handed first baseman–DH. One look at the Yankee roster was enough to cause anybody to shout. "What's going on here?"

Rosen and Steinbrenner hadn't lost their minds. They also didn't view left-hand-hitting first basemen the way the Hunt brothers viewed silver. The deal for Thomasson was originally to include Roy White. New York would have received Gary Alexander, a catcher who hit the ball from the right side. Alexander was a power hitter, having already accumulated 10 home runs in 174 at-bats. He was supposed to be this season's Cliff Johnson, who was in a horrendous slump.

White was a ten-and-five man and had no interest in joining that Fellini movie of a ball club in Oakland. He vetoed the deal. New York went ahead and completed the portion for Thomasson, who was to play center field in the absence of Rivers. The Yankees already had Paul Blair, but his hitting was as suspect as his fielding was magnificent. With the team batting average in its current depressed state, New York could use all the hitting help it could get. Thomasson had hit 17 homers in 1977.

The deal for Eastwick seemed most bizarre. Why would a team starved for pitching trade an able-bodied hurler for a commodity they already had to excess? Because they had no intention of keeping that commodity. Popular conjecture ran to the theory that Rosen had another deal not just cooking, but made. Or so he thought. He had been talking to the Giants about obtaining Jim Barr. Barr had been pitching well for the Giants, but San Francisco was getting plenty of pitching. They were looking to get an outfielder but couldn't satisfy the Phillies' demands. So they told Rosen, "Look, if you can get Johnstone from Philadelphia, we'll send you Barr in exchange for him." So that's what happened. Only New York never got Barr from Frisco, and Frisco never got Johnstone from New York. While the Yankees were busy dealing with Philadelphia, the Cubs made the Giants a better offer; they sent Hector Cruz to the Giants for Lynn McGlothen. Cruz was also an outfielder, and he could play third base. The Giants certainly preferred losing McGlothen instead of Barr, so they made the deal. They got the outfielder they needed, kept Barr, whom they weren't anxious to part with, and got rid of McGlothen, a pitcher they really didn't need. They were happy, the Cubs were happy, and Rosen and the Yankees were screwed.

Ken Clay, a second-year man, was forced to start for the Yankees on June 18. The Sox belted him for four runs in less than three innings. Then New York tied the score, 4–4. In the bottom of the eighth, six Boston runs off a tired Gossage sealed the game.

The Yankees beat Torrez the next evening, 10–4. This made the third game critical, so critical that when rookie Jim Beattie absorbed a 9–2 beating, Steinbrenner overreacted. He sautéed the youngster, publicly questioning his courage, and sent him packing to Tacoma. Hunter had pitched in the ninth and given up two long home runs to Scott and Lynn. Catfish finished the evening on the disabled list. The Yankees left Boston eight games out.

One week later, the Red Sox landed on the Bronx shore and split two games with the Bombers. New York was grateful when June came to an end. What they could not foresee was that, as bad as things had been, they were destined to get worse.

The first time the Yankees fell behind the division leader by as many as 10 games was on July 5. That loss was the beginning. New York won only twice in their next 10 outings.

During that string, several things of note happened. Munson was forced by pain to give up catching and was placed in right field. Lyle, 6–1 with 7 saves, grew markedly inconsistent. He started complaining about a lack of work. And Reggie Jackson tried to bunt.

The problems between manager and star had resurfaced. Jackson wasn't hitting and looked especially inept against left-handed pitching. Martin responded by batting him sixth or seventh against southpaws. Billy also removed Reggie from right field, making him the designated hitter. Jackson hated that. It was another indication that Martin did not consider him a complete ball player. Equally galling, it was Munson who had usurped Jackson's position. It may have been more palatable if it had been another outfielder. But to be supplanted by a catcher?

Jackson took his frustrations with him as he approached home plate on July 17. It was the tenth inning of a home game against Kansas City. Munson had led off with a single. Jackson was due up next. On the first pitch, he surprised everybody by attempting to bunt. Strike one. Jackson gave it another try. Foul ball, strike two. After that call, third base coach Dick Howser ran down to home to tell Jackson that Martin wanted him to swing away. This wasn't a scoop. Martin had wanted him to swing away from the time he had gotten up to bat. Jackson listened to the coach and then did an amazing thing: He bunted with two strikes on him and fouled off another pitch. That meant an automatic strike three. The Yankees failed to score, and Kansas City won the game 9–7, in eleven. The loss put New York 14 games behind the Red Sox.

After the game, Martin was livid. He had ordered his slugger to swing away and had been ignored. Jackson's attempted sacrifice wasn't the action of a ballplayer giving himself up to win a ball game. It was the work of a man telling his manager, "Go screw yourself." A price would have to be extracted for this defiance. Jackson was suspended for five games.

In his absence, New York went undefeated. And Martin went down the tubes.

Jackson rejoined the club in Chicago on July 23, ostensibly to work out for his return that evening to the Yankee lineup. The swarm of reporters covering the event prevented this. Instead, his arrival signaled the start of an impromptu news conference during which he defended the bunt. Jackson claimed he was not swinging the bat well (true), and he felt bunting was the only way he could move the runner over. But nobody could remember Jackson ever bunting successfully. Sacrificing was not exactly Jackson's trump card. And nobody *ever* bunts at the potential third strike. Not even a great bunter like Paul Blair. It's just not good baseball. When asked if he planned to apologize, Jackson said, "No...I don't know." He also didn't know if he and Martin could ever kiss and make up, and coexist.

The time spent answering reporters' queries caused Jackson to miss batting practice, giving Martin a reason to inform him, through Howser, that he would not be playing that night. The Yankees won again without his services.

Martin was in Chicago's pressroom/bar after the game, hoisting a few with White Sox owner Bill Veeck. It was there that Billy read a newsman's copy of the not exactly remorseful remarks uttered by Jackson that afternoon. Martin could not restrain himself from passing a few comments of his own. The gist of his outburst was that if Reggie didn't keep his mouth shut he wouldn't play. Ever.

Martin was fuming over more than just Jackson's refusal to say mea culpa. While drinking with Veeck he had learned of a proposed trade between New York and Chicago, a trade he had not been consulted on. The reason his opinion hadn't been sought was that he was to be part of the deal. About a month and a half before, the Yankees had proposed trading Martin to the White Sox for then Chicago manager Bob Lemon. Veeck turned them down. Martin couldn't believe it. He felt Steinbrenner had betrayed him. When he reached O'Hare International Airport for the team flight to Kansas City, Martin was an accident waiting to happen.

Martin had spied Murray Chass, a baseball reporter for the *New York Times*, on the team bus. He asked Chass to see him in private as soon as they reached the airport. Once there, Martin repeated his declaration that Jackson had better shut up or else. Then he went further, stating, "And I don't care what George [Steinbrenner] has to say. He can replace me right now if he doesn't like it...It's like a guy getting out of jail and saying, 'I'm innocent' after he killed somebody. He [Reggie Jackson] and every one of the players know he defied me."

By the finish of the monologue, Chass had been joined by two colleagues: Henry Hecht and Frank Brown. Chass made sure to ask Martin if this was for the record. Martin assured him that it was. Chass filed the story with his paper. When he finished, he encountered Martin again.

"Did you get that in the paper?" Martin wondered.

Chass told him that he had. Martin smiled and started toward the departure gate. Chass and Hecht tagged along. During the next few minutes, the feisty manager delivered a crunching right hook to his own temple. "He's a liar," Martin said, referring to the Jackson charge that Jackson and Martin hadn't spoken in a year and a half. "He's a born liar. The two of them deserve each other. One's a born liar; the other's convicted." That last was an obvious allusion to Steinbrenner's 1974 conviction. The quote was headline news by the next morning.

Steinbrenner struck back quickly. Martin was forced to resign on July 25. His replacement was Bob Lemon, who had been fired by Veeck on June 30. The "resignation" of Martin did not sit well with his fans. They lit up the Stadium switchboard with a flood of protests. Rumors proliferated that Martin was considering an offer to manage the crosstown rival Mets. The team in Flushing was no longer the toast of the town. Steinbrenner and the Yankees' success had turned them into an afterthought. They were taking a worse beating in the turnstile wars than they had ever inflicted on the Yankees. Signing Martin could give their awful attendance a tremendous boost. Letting Martin go had suddenly become as much of a problem as having him around.

Old-Timers' Day was scheduled for July 29. People wondered whether or not Martin, having received an invitation, would attend. It was one of his favorite events, affording him a chance to see his old comrades and relive days of his past glory.

Mickey Mantle and Joe DiMaggio are, traditionally, the last two Yankees to be introduced on that day. After they were brought out, people assumed that Martin had decided not to come. But an odd thing happened. PA announcer Bob Shepard quieted the crowd and declared that the Yankees wished to say that "the manager of the Yankees for the 1980 season, and hopefully for many seasons after that, [as] Number One..." He didn't have to identify whom that digit belonged to. And if he had, no one would have heard him. An overwhelming din of love and affection had drowned out the name of Billy Martin.

When the post-announcement press conference ended, the shocked Yankees still had a season to attend to. Maybe Martin would be back in 1980 (and then again, many thought, maybe he wouldn't). But this was 1978, and the manager of the moment was Bob Lemon. And Boston was still eight games away.

No matter what the media suggested, most of the Yankee players had not given up on snaring the Red Sox. Mike Heath, the rookie catcher, couldn't help "thinking that there was no way to catch the Sox. I figured we were playing for second place. At least that's what I thought at first. But all the veterans thought we would still pass them. Lou Piniella told me, 'You just wait, Boston won't stay there. This club knows how to win. We've got a veteran ball club, and we're a great second-half team. We're going to catch them.' After I heard it enough times, I started to believe it."

The new manager was also of the opinion that the pennant wasn't quite out of reach. His first moves said as much. Lemon returned Jackson to right field, Munson behind the plate, and White and Piniella to the everyday lineup. When asked why, the skipper replied, "That's the lineup that won the World Series last year; why mess with something that worked so well?"

Bob Lemon had been a Hall of Fame pitcher for the Cleveland Indians (1946–58). His first crack as a major league manager was with the Kansas City Royals in 1970. In his second year at the helm, he piloted the young Royals to a surprising second-place finish. This achievement won him recognition as the league's Manager of the Year. One year later the Royal front office decided he was "too old to communicate with his players," and he was told to take a hike.

Lemon resurfaced as the Yankee pitching coach in 1976. He left that job next season to take over the managerial reins of the White Sox. Lemon once again took a ball club with a bad record (64–97 in 1976) and made them a contender, earning himself a second Manager of the Year prize. After what had happened the last time he won the award, this should have been a warning. Sure enough, by mid-'78, the faltering Sox replaced him with Larry Doby.

Al Rosen, a friend and former teammate, had told Lemon that he wanted him in the Yankee organization as soon as a spot could be found. Martin's throat-slitting had provided that spot.

Only Gandhi could possibly have been more the opposite in temperament to Billy the Kid than Bob Lemon. Martin was an intense competitor who took losses as a personal affront and seemed lost if not operating in a bubbling cauldron. Lemon was also a competitor, with 207 career wins as a pitcher to prove it. But he also had a different perspective on the game than his predecessor. It wasn't a life-and-death struggle. Upon his induction into the Hall of Fame, he had mused, "I never took a game home with me. I always left it in some bar along the way." He was a soft-spoken gentleman who, in an age of computerized charts and stats, summed up his managerial philosophy simply: "All I do is let the players play."

This easygoing nature did not mean the new manager was a marshmallow. As the Yankees quickly found out, Lem was not a man to be trifled with.

Ed Figueroa was the first to get the message. He had stormed off the mound in the midst of a game, just as Lemon was coming out of the dugout to remove him. This was a breach of protocol, and the manager reacted swiftly. He confronted his pitcher in the clubhouse, read him the riot act, and dropped it. Figueroa never did it again. For the rest of the season, he pitched the best ball of his life, becoming the first native-born Puerto Rican to win 20 games in a single major league season.

Lemon handled other such incidents in a similar fashion: the iron bat in the velvet glove. The club relaxed for the first time in two years; laughter was no longer a foreign sound in the Yankee locker room. As the tensions dropped below the boiling point, the Yankees started to get hot.

They opened August with Dent, Rivers, and Randolph back in the lineup, still seven games behind the suddenly slumping Red Sox. On August 1, they beat the Texas Rangers 8–1. The score and the opposition were not the story of the day. The most important news to come out of that game was the name of the pitcher who got the win with a masterful three-hitter: Catfish Hunter. The Cat was back. And God help anybody who thought this club was finished.

For eight seasons, Hunter had been the workhorse of the Athletics pitching staff. He threw over 230 innings in each of those years (1967–74). Hunter assumed the same role in New York, pitching 328 innings in 1975 and completing several extra-inning affairs. The last of these was a thirteen-frame marathon against Frank Tanana and the California Angels. A Yankee scout later commented, "He was never really the same pitcher after that game. Maybe it was a coincidence, but it's as if all the life got drained out of his arm after that. He sure pitched a lot of innings before he was thirty. I think it wore his arm out."

Hunter first showed signs of deterioration in 1976 when he won 17 but lost 15. He was in and out of the rotation in 1977 and was lucky to finish at .500 (9–9). The 1978 season had been pure hell until the Yankee orthopedist, Dr. Maurice Cowan, used a series of arm manipulations to break down adhesions that were causing the pitcher's pain. When he finished, Hunter could throw hard again. He rolled off six consecutive victories in August, finishing the season at 12–6.

His return gave the club a much-needed psychological lift. Despite losing two games to Boston on August 3, they refused to give up on themselves. They finished August exactly as they started it, six and a half games behind Boston.

It could have been frustrating. New York had gone 19–8 that month and had gained nothing. But the players took a positive outlook, figuring they hadn't lost any ground to the leaders, either.

Lou Piniella admitted, "We expected to win. Even after the bad start, the finger-pointing, and all the squabbles, we never lost sight of the fact that we were a championship team. If we could put things together we knew we had the ability to get back into the pennant race. Sure enough, we started to win, Boston started to slide. When it got to September we were looking at those seven games we had left with Boston. We figured if we could just cut their lead down to four by the time we played them, we would have a real good shot. That became the most exciting thing I've ever been involved with. I'd come to the park every day, knowing we had to win, and later leave the park having won."

New York took four of their first six games in September. This trimmed the gap down to Piniella's magic number. On September 7, they roared into Boston for a four-game set.

The Red Sox had been beset with injuries that betrayed their one real weakness: a lack of bench strength. Dwight Evans had been beaned and was suffering debilitating dizzy spells. Jerry Remy had a fractured wrist. Butch Hobson's right elbow was so sore he had to dash halfway across the diamond to make a throw. Carl Yastrzemski had a bad back. And Carlton Fisk was playing with a collection of nagging hurts. In their place played Garry Hancock, Bob Bailey, Frank Duffy, and others who were not up to the task. When New York had suffered similar losses, their reserves had risen to the occasion. Mike Heath, Fred Stanley, and Brian Doyle were more than just adequate replacements for Munson, Randolph, and Dent. Thomasson hit over .300 in Rivers's stead. They didn't transform the Yankees into a powerhouse. But they did enable the team to keep its head above water. Now the club was healthy. Now they were coming on.

There was a point in the Ali-Foreman "Rumble in the Jungle" when George Foreman was pummeling the rope-perched Muhammad Ali with fierce-looking but ineffective blows. Near the end of the exchange, Ali twisted Foreman around and initiated his own attack. Its malevolent suddenness suggested to Norman Mailer a vengeful declaration: "Now it's my turn!" Boston was about to find out how Foreman felt.

For the tables had been reversed. It was the Red Sox who were hurting, and the Yankees who were on the charge. New York showed up at Fenway with bats that were clandestine stilettos, nostrils filled with the fresh scent of warm blood, and hearts overcrowded with dead mercy.

The Yankees humiliated Boston, sweeping all four games.

Boston came into Yankee Stadium on September 15, trailing New York by one and a half games. The bloodletting continued as New York took two of three.

During the final two weeks, the Red Sox corpse stood up, opened its eyes, said, "Hi!" and simply refused to die. Both teams played superior ball, but, by the final day of the season, the Yankee lead was down to the wafer-thin margin of one game. Boston defeated Toronto that afternoon, 5–0. Meanwhile, the Cleveland Indians ganged up on Catfish Hunter and four relievers. Indian left-hander Rick Waits tossed a four-hitter, beating New York 9–3. The season had ended in a deadlock.

A one-game playoff was scheduled the following day, Monday, October 2. Fenway Park had already been chosen by coin toss as the site of the tie-breaker.

Torrez and Guidry were the starters. Torrez was seeking revenge against his former teammates, having been beaten by them three times during the season. Guidry was going for his 25th win. He had lost only three times. Oddly, in each loss the winning pitcher was named Mike (Caldwell, Flanagan, and Willis). Guidry was pitching on only three days' rest, instead of the four he preferred. Sox fans pondered these two variables and found reason to hope.

That hope intensified when local landmark Carl Yastrzemski rifled a Guidry fastball into the right field stands, giving Boston a 1–0 lead.

They scored again in the sixth. Rick Burleson doubled, and Jim Rice singled to give Boston a 2–0 advantage. Torrez worked in a passionately efficient manner. He allowed his former teammates only two hits in the first six innings.

The seventh began uneventfully. Graig Nettles led off with a fly-out to right. But then, White and Chambliss singled, as Boston fans clutched at their throats, feeling for a pulse. They detected a tremble when Spencer flew out. Two down, and the next batter was Bucky Dent.

Dent went to the plate "looking for something to drive."

Torrez peered in, got his sign, and wound up. The pitcher was feeling "very comfortable. I had tremendous concentration that day. Bucky took my first pitch for strike one. Then he banged strike two off his foot and limped around for what seemed like five minutes. That time spent limping robbed me of that extra snap of concentration. When he got into the box, Carlton called for a fastball inside. We were going to jam him. But I didn't get the ball in far enough and..."

Don Zimmer, the Red Sox manager, was crouched on the dugout steps as Dent lofted a fly ball to left. From his vantage point, Zimmer thought, "The inning's over. Really. When Dent hit the ball I figured, 'Good, that's an out.' Then I saw Carl back up and I said, 'Wait a minute, the damned thing's off the wall.' But Yaz kept looking up, and the ball never came down. I realized, 'Oh my, it's in the net.' And that was it."

Dent never saw the home run. The moment he hit the pitch he "took off running. I thought it was off the wall because of the shadows. I didn't find out it was a home run until I passed first base and saw the umpire's signal. People ask me if I got excited about that. To tell the truth, I didn't realize the magnitude of what I did until it was all over. In a moment like that, you're just thinking about winning. You're more concerned with the outcome of the game than with being a hero. The whole thing didn't hit me until after the World Series."

That shot gave the Yankees a 3–2 lead. Torrez, laboring now, walked Rivers and was replaced by Bob Stanley. Rivers swiped second and scored the fourth run of the inning on a double by Munson. The Yankees led 4–2; it was Goose time.

Gossage came on in the bottom of the seventh. In his last 30 appearances, the right-hander had saved 15 games and won 6. He protected the Yankees' lead through the inning. That two-run margin grew to three when Jackson homered into the center field bleachers in the eighth.

Boston chipped into that lead in the bottom of the inning. Jerry Remy, leading off, doubled. Jim Rice flied out. Yaz singled to left, sending Remy home. The Red Sox captain took third on a base hit by Fisk and scored on Lynn's single. The score was 5–4. Gossage escaped further damage by retiring Butch

Hobson on a fly ball to right and striking out George Scott.

New York went quietly in the ninth. Boston was down to its last swipes. The first batter, Dwight Evans, flew out to left. Burleson walked.

Jerry Remy rammed a line drive to Piniella in right. Piniella had gone out there thinking, "I hope they don't hit the ball to me because it was almost impossible to see out there. It was really bad. The sun was right in my eyes, especially down the line. I had even mentioned it to some of the guys. I was playing shallow for Remy; he didn't have a great deal of power. When he hit that ball, I never saw it so I had to play on instinct. I had noticed the trajectory of his swing and figured the ball had to be hit on the line. I took a few steps over and never let the base runner know I had lost sight of the ball. If you let the runner know you're having problems out there, he'll take off on you. So I stayed as calm as I could and decoyed that I was going to make the catch. All of a sudden, the ball drops out of the sun and hits in front of me. It bounced to my left, and I grabbed it and made a good throw to third. That kept Burleson from advancing."

It became the crucial play of the game when Jim Rice hit a deep fly to Piniella for the second out. Had Burleson been able to advance to third on Remy's hit, the game would have been tied. Instead, Burleson merely moved up to third.

For months these two teams had scraped and clawed at each other. Now the season came down to Gossage and Yastrzemski at sixty feet six inches.

Gossage delivered ball one. He set, took a deep breath for everyone, and fired again. Yaz swung and lifted a lazy pop-up near the left field stands. It hung for an eternal moment, then gently plummeted into the comfort of Nettles's outstretched glove. It was over. The Yankees had won.

It was fitting that, finally, a lone run provided the measure of difference between these two noble adversaries. They had given too much of themselves over the space of a season. When the final clash of Olympians was over, one felt proud. Proud of the tenacious defending champions, proud of their unyielding foes, proud of the baseball so valiantly played. One could not help but be seized by the merriment of the victorious Yankees while being gripped by the heartbreak of the fallen army from Boston. There were no winners or losers, one wanted to cry, they were all champions.

For the third straight year, New York met the Royals for the league championship. This time there were no fifth-game heart-attack comebacks. The Yankees took them in four.

The playoffs were brief but memorable. The two youngsters of the pitching staff, Jim Beattie and Ken Clay, combined for a 7−1 opening game victory. K.C. rebounded behind Larry Gura to square things the next day, 10−4.

Game three was played at the Stadium. Three home runs by George Brett, all off Hunter, were not enough to defeat New York. The Royals took a 5−4 lead into the bottom of the eighth. Splittorff retired leadoff batter Mickey Rivers. Roy White singled and, with the right-hand-hitting Thurman Munson due up, Splittorff was removed in favor of Doug Bird. Munson rapped Bird's fourth delivery into the Yankee bullpen, some 430 feet from home plate. It turned out to be the winning hit in a 6−5 New York victory.

Kansas City was in a must-win situation. All they had to do to prolong the series was beat Guidry. When asked if this was possible, Brett replied, "Ron Guidry isn't God."

On the evening of that fourth game, a note was delivered to the Royal locker room. It was addressed to Brett. It read, "George, maybe I'm not God but, right now, I'm the closest thing to it."

Brett tried to repudiate this minor blasphemy with a triple off the lefty in the first inning. He scored on a base hit by Hal McRae. It was the last time a Royal would touch home plate in 1978. Nettles knotted the score with a home run in the second, and White put the game and the pennant away with a solo shot in the sixth. It was all Guidry needed.

The World Series against Los Angeles was being billed as a grudge fight, a Texas-style death match between the retribution-seeking Dodgers and their tormentors of the previous October.

Things did not look good for New York. They were forced to play the Series without the services of Randolph, who had pulled a hamstring before the season ended. Rivers was bothered by a pulled leg muscle, and Chambliss had also come up lame. Guidry would be unable to start until the third game. When the Dodgers took the first two games in their park, it began to look as if the Yankees had run out of miracles.

But the Dodgers made two grave errors. The first was a continuation of what had become a garish display of public mourning for their deceased coach, Jim Gilliam. This tasteless exhibition just barely stopped short of their propping Junior up and having him throw out the first ball. Aroused to a frenzy, the kids from L.A. began to talk about winning it for Gilliam. They felt like a team of destiny, and behaved in a manner they imagined a chosen team should.

This attitude was best exemplified by Dodger second baseman Davey Lopes who, after hitting the second of two first-game homers, insisted on flashing the "We're number one" sign as he rounded the bases. Lopes had been exceptionally close to Gilliam. Unfortunately, someone forgot to tell Davey that this was a best-of-seven series. His actions piqued a Yankee team that was best left unperturbed.

The second error was a bit more important than the first. The Dodgers failed to beat Ron Guidry in the third game, on a night the Amazin' Cajun was extremely beatable.

Boston's Jim Rice won the MVP award in 1978, yet it is hard to see how he could have possibly meant more to the Red Sox than Ron Guidry meant to the Yankees. Guidry finished the regular season as the major league leader in wins (25), ERA (1.74), shutouts (9), and winning percentage (.893). He lost just three times. Only J. R. Richard of the Houston Astros and Nolan Ryan of the California Angels had more strikeouts than his 248. His winning percentage was the highest ever posted by a 20-game winner, and the 9 shutouts tied the league record for most blankings by a left-hander. That record, shared by Babe Ruth, had stood since 1917. The Yankees won 30 of his 35 starts. Guidry allowed three runs or fewer in all but four of those games. Fifteen of his 25 victories came after a Yankee loss. In every sense of the word, Guidry was the Yankee stopper.

Guidry recalled, "It kind of pissed us off, really, the way

Lopes was acting, and the things the Dodgers were saying. I felt we were a team with a lot of class. Even when we were beating them the year before, we didn't say anything about it, we just beat them. We figured, 'Hey, if you want to talk, let's do it out there, between the lines.'

"There were a bunch of us in the clubhouse on the day I was scheduled to pitch, and Thurman came in and said, 'If it were any other team but the Dodgers, I might say let's just forget it. But the way these guys have been carrying on, I would like nothing better than to beat them four straight.' So he turned to me and said, 'If you got enough to win this game, let's take the following three, forget about it, and go home.' I didn't have my best stuff, but Graig was incredible. He made four plays that have to be among the best ever made. He saved me at least six runs, catching balls from out of nowhere. We won that game. The next day, we won again. Now we had the advantage because we had one more game here [at Yankee Stadium], and the Dodgers were looking kind of stiff.

"We beat them bad the next game, got 17 or 18 hits, all singles. Brian Doyle filled in for Willie [Randolph] and had a great Series, hit over .400. He had three hits that day, and so did Bucky. Jim Beattie pitched a hell of a game. He had one complete game all year and that was it. We beat them 12–2.

"That game was something. It was just hit after hit after hit. Then the Dodgers started to make errors, and they looked like they were saying, 'Don't hit the ball to me!' You know the good players are always saying, 'Hit it to me.' But with them it was more like, 'Hit it over there!'

"When we beat them in that fifth game, it really ticked us off because we realized we were just going to fly out West for one game and come home."

Catfish Hunter certainly thought so. He was scheduled to pitch the sixth game, and he had already reserved a flight back to North Carolina for that evening. He knew there wasn't going to be a seventh game. When the Yankees took the lead, early in the evening, they took the champagne off ice. New York buried the Dodgers 7–2. Doyle and Dent once again got three hits apiece. Hunter held the Dodgers until the eighth, and

Gossage nailed it down. When the Series ended, Dent (.417, 7 RBI) was chosen as Series MVP. He won out over a wide field of worthy candidates: Doyle (.438), White (.333), Munson (.320, 7 RBI), Jackson (.391, 8 RBI), and the magic-gloved Nettles.

In the celebrants' clubhouse, a reflective Thurman Munson, speaking for himself and the team, paused to say, "Maybe now they'll stop questioning us. Maybe now all the talk will stop, and people will just realize what we are—a great ball club."

When a reporter asked him about the talk of his seeking to be traded to Cleveland, the Yankee captain replied, "I don't want to talk about that now. I'm not going anywhere."

Chapter
TEN

Show me a hero and I will write you a tragedy.

—F. Scott Fitzgerald

THE schedulemaker lied. If you were to grab a 1979 American League Red Book and flip to the back to that great easy-to-read schedule, you would see that the Yankee season was supposed to end on September 30 in New York. Didn't happen. Summer in that town came to a stop on August 2. Don McLean can sing all he wants of Buddy Holly and coats borrowed from James Dean, but as far as Yankee fans were concerned, that August afternoon that couldn't have happened was the day the music died.

Life abandoned Thurman Munson that afternoon. He had been practicing takeoffs and landings at the Akron-Canton Airport in his twin-engine jet, a Cessna Citation. The catcher was about to make his fourth and final approach when the plane crashed some 870 feet from the runway.

The impact sent the jet careening through a mob of trees like a drunken comet. It hit an unyielding stump and stopped. In less time than one could count, the plane was engulfed by flames. Munson's only two passengers tried to lift him from the pilot's seat, but he was pinned. As the cabin became black with smoke the survivors were forced to flee. Munson never had a chance. Firefighters arrived within minutes of the accident; it was too late. The plane Munson loved had only helped him keep an appointment with death.

At the news of the crash, fans were stunned. Munson had always embodied those mythic qualities that elevated an athlete from mere celebrity to god. With his physical frailties (those aching knees and chronically sore shoulder), unbridled talent, childlike moodiness, and heroic stoicism, Munson seemed infinitely vulnerable and utterly indestructible. His sudden death forced a fan away from the game's promise of eternal youth and made him give a knowing nod and pleading wink to his own omnipresent mortality.

Guidry felt the finality of his battery mate's passing, remembering Munson's death as "the final shot for that season. When he died it just put us under. It truly would have been a miracle if we could have come back and won again. Bigger than '78. But there was just no way. Thurman was one of the catalysts who made the team go. He spoiled the pitchers because he did almost everything. All you had to do was throw the ball; you didn't have to do anything else. When you took him away it was like taking a cylinder out of our car. It's hard to run on seven."

The accident left the entire team numb. It occurred when the team had just gotten past the point of asking, "What can happen next?" It took place in a season that should have been locked in an asylum.

That summer was heavy with the nightmare of twisted metal. Before the first pitch of spring was thrown, in the winter following his team's greatest triumph, Bob Lemon had a piece of his world shattered when a car accident took the life of his twenty-six-year-old son Jerry. It left Lemon with a broken heart and a dulled competitive edge. The team played languidly under him and, in late June, he was replaced by Billy Martin. Lem was asked if his attitude toward the game had changed. He admitted, "It's not that I don't want to win, but when I lost it didn't bother me as much." No one had to ask why.

Lemon's personal hardships had nothing to do with the club's failure to contend; the manager was too much the professional to allow that to happen. The Yankees started the season as overwhelming favorites. They had acquired left-handed pitcher Tommy John, the ace of the Dodger pitching staff, and Luis Tiant of the Boston Red Sox in the free-agent draft. They had also accommodated Sparky Lyle's request for a trade, sending him to Texas along with Mike Heath, infielder Domingo Ramos, and pitchers Dave Rajsich and Larry McCall. New York received outfielder Juan Beniquez and pitchers Dave Righetti, Paul Mirabella, and Mike Griffin, and minor league outfielder Greg Jemison. Beniquez was a Gold Glove center fielder, and Mirabella was a highly touted prospect. But the trade wouldn't have been made without the inclusion of Righetti, a left-hander with the potential to become, to use Al Rosen's words, "another Guidry."

In *Street and Smith's Official 1979 Baseball Yearbook*, Richard Dozer picked the Yankees to win their fourth consecutive Eastern Division title. New York was portrayed as a team without weaknesses. With one qualification: "If there is a hole anywhere in the Yankee structure," Dozer wrote, "it could surface in the bullpen. Bob Lemon's club is no better off in stoppers now than a number of clubs around the circuit. They have that ONE big star of the bullpen, as many do. Last year they had two, but Sparky Lyle got away to Texas, leaving Rich Gossage to do a job that wasn't big enough for both of them apparently." Dozer must have had a crystal ball.

The season was only a week and a half old when the chink in the New York armor was exposed.

It started with some teasing banter. Gossage, very wild of late, had tossed a rolled-up sock in Cliff Johnson's direction. It missed. Johnson hadn't bothered to duck, joking, "I don't have much to worry about the way you're throwing." It was a typical piece of repartee that broke up everybody, including Goose. Reggie Jackson, picking up on Johnson's comment, asked Johnson how he had fared against Gossage when they were both in the National League. Johnson replied he hit Goose "pretty decently." Gossage good-naturedly countered, "He swung at what he heard."

Actually, Johnson had faced Gossage all of three times in the other league. The result: two strikeouts and a ground ball force out. Three at bats.

Gossage's rejoinder should have been the end of it, but Johnson confronted the reliever in the clubhouse bathroom. Words were exchanged, at first kiddingly. Then a playful shoving match started. It did not end playfully. It ended with both of these huge specimens wrestling on the floor.

The next day, Gossage reported to work with a swollen right thumb. X rays revealed torn ligaments. The general prognosis had the right-hander out for as long as three months. The Yankees were in a whole lot of trouble.

Yankee relievers had experienced a very healthy run for the last three years. Alarm bells hadn't sounded from the bullpen since 1975, the season Bill Virdon convinced himself that Lyle was suffering first-degree burnout. It wasn't until the middle of that season that the manager had turned to Dick Tidrow to pick up Lyle's reins. Tidrow did an excellent job, combining with Tippy Martinez to give the team some late-inning stability.

If the greening of Reggie Jackson stands as the best free-agent deal ever made, then the fattening of the Goose is a close second. The awesome work he turned in during his first season was merely a warmup for the spectacle to follow. Rollie Fingers has been the model of consistency, and Bruce Sutter, when his split-fingered fastball is on, may be unhittable. But from 1980 to 1982, Gossage was the premier relief pitcher in the game. This was the era of Gossage Maximus, throwing his fastball at a speed that had no place in time. For those peak years he was the Franchise; the one player New York could least afford to lose.

When he did come up lame, it was expected that Tidrow would be the bullpen's top gun. There was no doubt among his teammates that he could do the job, though even he admitted, "All I can do is take it day to day. Nobody told me I have the job. All I know is that if they let me pitch, I'll do a decent job. I might not strike out the side like Goose, but I'll get guys out."

The Yankees never gave him the chance to prove himself right. Gossage was injured on April 20. Tidrow made his first appearance as the short man one week later. He got bombed and took a loss. Three days passed until he was out there again. He faced one batter, gave up one hit, and was gone.

Over the next four weeks, Tidrow appeared in five games. Five. He pitched a total of eleven and two-thirds innings and gave up 14 runs. How anybody could have expected him to do much better than that on the poverty rations of work he was receiving is a wonder.

Once the Yankee brass concluded Tidrow was not the answer (a conclusion they reached in about four and a half seconds), they made a series of hilarious moves to fill what they perceived as a serious breach in the bullpen.

First, Ron Davis and Paul Mirabella were moved ahead of Tidrow. After a couple of shaky appearances by each, New York summoned Jim Beattie from the minors.

Beattie had been working on the farm, a victim of the numbers game. He had lost any chance of starting for the Yankees when New York insisted on signing Luis Tiant. This was a mistake. In taking on Tiant management was sending a message to Beattie and every other young player in their system: "What you did in September and October last year isn't enough. As long as there is a proven veteran around, and our checkbook holds up, you'll never get a chance to star on this team."

It was easy to shunt Beattie aside when it looked as though he wouldn't be needed. All the fine work he had done in the previous season's pennant drive was quickly forgotten. Until now. Now, Beattie was being hailed as the new ace of the bullpen before he even threw a pitch. This designation lasted all of twenty-four hours. In his first relief appearance of the year, Beattie pitched one inning, gave up two runs, and lost a ball game. It was the seventh Yankee loss in eight games.

Ron Guidry stepped forward and volunteered to be Goose's bullpen stand-in. By now, the Yankees had worked themselves up to such a robust state of panic that they were willing to try anything.

The left-hander performed like a thoroughbred. But it was obvious that New York couldn't spare him from the starting rotation; they had to make a deal.

Tidrow was traded to the Chicago Cubs for Ray Burris at the end of May. At the time of the deal, Burris's season was distinguished by the fact that Tidrow was the only pitcher in the majors to have an ERA (7.83) that was higher than his (6.14). Burris had been a Cub for seven years and had proven himself to be a pitcher who could do a lot of things. Unfortunately, none of them included pitching relief. He didn't last out the season.

Given Tidrow's history, it was obvious what the team should have done. They should have given Tidrow the ball and said, "You're the man," and then let him pitch. Really pitch. If it took him a little while to find his stride, fine. He was a proven veteran and had earned that right.

Nobody on the Yankees ever told him anything. They were content to band a bunch of guys together and hope that one of them would emerge as a bullpen stopper via the process of elimination. The front office didn't make a bad decision. They didn't make a good decision. They did something far worse: They didn't make a decision at all.

Tidrow reported to the Cubs and was told exactly what was expected of him: hold the fort in the middle innings until it was time for Bruce Sutter. Tidrow responded with a season (11–5, 2.71 ERA, 4 saves) that was exactly what New York had been looking for. It was too late.

New York finally found its ace reliever. It turned out to be Ron Davis. They had to demote him to the minors and bring him back up before they realized it. That demotion came "after I gave up a broken-bat single to Willie Horton. I only threw that one pitch. Then Tidrow came in, gave up a double, and we lost the game. After that they sent me down. I knew I could pitch in the major leagues, I just hadn't had the opportunity yet. When you throw one pitch and get sent down, well, that's not what I would call an opportunity."

The stint in the minors helped Davis acquire the good sense to pitch well in his first appearance back in the big leagues. He ended up pitching well enough (14–2, 2.86 ERA, 9 saves) to receive strong support as a Rookie of the Year candidate. Davis held the bullpen together until Goose's return. The shame of it was that Davis could have been doing this a lot sooner than he did. Like Tidrow, all he needed was someone to give him the baseball.

Cliff Johnson, having shouldered a large portion of the blame for this upheaval, was exiled to Cleveland on June 15, traded for left-hander Don Hood. This was obviously the Yankee version of capital punishment for the Gossage injury. Having divested themselves of one of the few right-handed power hitters on the club, New York spent the rest of the season searching for his replacement. They didn't find him.

When Billy Martin replaced Bob Lemon in June, he was able to revive the club somewhat. They had been 34–30 under Lemon and went 55–41 under Martin. It was too little too late. By the time the Yankees got around to playing good baseball, the Orioles had all but wrapped up the division.

Guidry (18–8, 2.78 ERA) and John (21–9, 2.97 ERA) led the pitching staff. If not for a leg injury that forced him to miss 29 games, Jackson (.297, 29 home runs, 89 RBI) would have had his finest year as a Yankee. The tension between Jackson and Martin had dissipated. Though they weren't buddy-buddy, they did manage to treat each other with mutual respect. Willie Randolph had a quietly outstanding season (.270, 13 triples, 61 RBI, 95 walks, and 98 runs scored) and Lou Piniella (.297, 69 RBI) was still master of the line drive. Their performances couldn't lift the club higher than fourth. Like many fallen champions, New York started breaking up the club before the season ended.

The club had tired of the same old melodies found on the album "The Many Swinging Moods of Mickey Rivers." They dispatched the center fielder to Texas in July. The deal brought Oscar Gamble back to New York.

Gamble wasn't the only returning former Yankee. Bobby Murcer had come from the Chicago Cubs in June. He performed

well as a part-time player and ended up as the star of an unwelcome drama in August.

Few members of the team had been as close to Munson as
Murcer was. Both had graduated from the Yankee farm system
and had been two of the team's legitimate stars during the bad
old days of the early seventies. It was Murcer who had flown
to the side of Diane Munson, bringing immediate support to
his fallen friend's widow. Piniella and Murcer had helped with
the funeral arrangements, and both delivered stirring eulogies
at the August 6 service held at the Civic Center in Canton.

There was a ball game that evening against the Orioles. Yankee Stadium was packed. A ceremony honoring Munson was
held before the game. When the Yankees took the field, each
player went to his position and faced the vacant catcher's spot.
All of them, on the field and in the dugout, were visibly moved.
Many wept openly. The Stadium shook beneath the weight of
an emotional outpour as the crowd shared in the team's loss
and made it their own. For an evening Manhattan lost its luster;
the heart of New York was in the Bronx.

The Yankees were behind 4–0 in the seventh when Murcer
stepped to the plate with two men on and hit a line drive home
run into the right field seats. The score was now 4–3. It stayed
there into the bottom of the ninth when Murcer again came
up with runners on second and third. He fouled off the first
two pitches. The crowd, recognizing the moment, was on its
feet joining with his teammates, that band of brothers, in ex-
horting him to bring the runners home. Murcer slashed the
next pitch, a low breaking ball, over the left field wall for the
ball game. The Stadium rocked with celebration. The most
tragic four days of any summer had given birth to the season's
most memorable moment.

George Steinbrenner had no appreciation for the team's eventual fourth-place finish. As soon as the schedule was played
out, the Yankee management started to engineer the team's
return to prominence.

Billy Martin was not involved in this latest facelift. He had
been fired. Again. Martin had found himself in the midst of an
incident in a hotel bar in Bloomington, Minnesota, on October

26. It ended with a marshmallow salesman out cold on the hotel lobby floor. Martin protested his innocence, claiming self-defense. But as far as Steinbrenner was concerned, Billy the Kid had pulled his six-gun once too often. This was the second time in eleven months that the feisty manager had used his fists in public. Steinbrenner fired him on October 28, saying, "I did it to save his [Martin's] life. The next time he hits someone, the guy might pull a knife."

Al Rosen also had no part in the restructuring, having left before the 1979 season was over. His resignation as president and general manager had come within a month of Lemon's firing.

Martin's and Rosen's replacements were handpicked by Steinbrenner: Dick Howser, who succeeded Martin, and Gene Michael, who inherited Rosen's general manager's duties. Upon taking these positions, the duo's first order of business was to fill in the fissures that had developed in the Yankee empire. The necessary caulk to accomplish this task would be composed of the following ingredients: a center fielder to replace Rivers, a catcher to make up for the loss of Munson, a right-handed power hitter, and pitching reinforcements.

Pitching had played a large part in the Yankees' poor season. Catfish Hunter's lame right arm was finally beyond the help of Dr. Cowan's manipulations; it had run out of innings. The hurler retired before the season came to an end. Ed Figueroa, the club's other 20-game winner in 1978, was laid up with painful bone chips in his pitching elbow. He had won only four games in 1979 and was never effective again. Tiant (13–8) had to overcome a woeful start, and high-priced free agent Don Gullett had spent the season on his Kentucky farm, finished by a torn rotator cuff at age twenty-eight. In their place came veterans Jim Kaat and Don Hood, who were not the answer, and youngsters Jim Beattie and Ken Clay, who were never really given a chance.

Steinbrenner made his now-mandatory dip into the free-agent pool, picking up pitcher Rudy May (10–3) from Montreal and Bob Watson (.337) from Boston. Watson was a first baseman with a lifetime batting average over .300. He and another off-season acquisition, Texas Ranger infielder Eric Soderholm, were supposed to supply the right-handed power the club had lacked all summer. It was hoped that Rudy May would prove to be another Tidrow: the Yankee version of Everypitcher. May would be used as a starter or reliever depending on the pitching staff's needs. The left-hander had left the Expos and returned to New York for several reasons, only one of which involved money.

"I had a lot of problems in Montreal," May recalled, "problems that I hadn't figured on when I got traded there. My wife and I couldn't speak French. That turned out to be a hassle, especially for her. When we were together it was fine because then she was Mrs. Rudy May. But on her own she was just another American trying to get over in Quebec.... The other thing was [manager] Dick [Williams] wouldn't pitch me. The first year I was there [1978] I was 8–10, but I had broken my ankle in the middle of the season and really didn't have a complete year. I thought I pitched better than my record indicated. The next season I was 10–3 but I only pitched 90 innings or so. The Expos kept putting me in ball games they thought they had no chance of winning; I was a mop-up man. But I'd hold the other team, and we'd come back and win. I was lucky. When we got to spring training that year we had just traded for Bill Lee and we already had Ross Grimsley. I sized everything up, saw we had three lefties, and two of them— Ross and Bill—couldn't pitch relief. So I went to Dick and said, 'I guess I'll be in the bullpen,' but I told him if he did put me there to please pitch me. I think he may have resented that because after our conversation I hardly pitched.

"Right before the June 15 trading deadline my agent Dick Moss and I went to see [Expo g.m.] John McHale. We asked him to trade me. I wasn't pitching much, but I was throwing well when I did and I was 2–0. He told us he couldn't make a deal for me because I was too old [thirty-four] and on account of my broken ankle the year before. I couldn't believe it. They wouldn't trade me, use me, or sign me. I was in my option year. Finally when Montreal got into its first pennant race, they had no choice; they had to pitch me. I go 10–3 and all of a sudden the Expos want to talk contract two weeks before I could declare free agency. On the last day of the season, John McHale stopped by my locker and said, 'Don't leave town without talking to me.' I called my agent and he said, 'Bullshit, you're coming home.' I live in California. That was the last time I spoke to McHale.

"I heard other offers from clubs, offers that matched the Yankees. But even though the money those teams offered was the same, the contract wasn't the same as the one New York wanted to give me. The guaranteed language and the signing bonus were structured by my agent. Things were in it that we really wanted, especially the no-trade clause. My wife and I wanted to be able to buy a summer home here. We knew there's a big turnover on this club and we wanted to be sure we'd be here for a while. I didn't want to take the money, pitch a year, and then get uprooted by a trade. That clause was a big reason why we took George Steinbrenner's offer."

Within weeks of the signing of Watson and May, a center fielder arrived in the form of Ruppert Jones. He had come over from the Seattle Mariners in exchange for Jim Beattie, Juan Beniquez, Jerry Narron, and minor league pitcher Rick Anderson. Jones had been the best ballplayer Seattle had ever owned. When the franchise was founded, he had been the first player drafted onto their roster, plucked from the farm system of the Kansas City Royals. Jones's game was a happy marriage of speed and power. He had just completed the season among the league leaders in runs scored with 109, while stealing 33 bases and smashing 21 home runs. In the outfield, he covered vast stretches of territory with long graceful strides. This was an athlete of immense ability.

Jones would anchor a Yankee outfield that had fallen into disarray with the departure of Mickey Rivers. Jackson would be in right, while Piniella and Gamble were expected to platoon in left. Roy White, the left fielder for fourteen years, was headed for Japan. White had spent the entire season in quiet frustration. He was used sporadically, batted .215 as a consequence, and was discarded. When the summer was over, White declared his free agency. The Yankees made no attempt to sign him. A career of clutch performances at bat and in the field was conveniently forgotten.

The team did sign Jim Spencer and Bucky Dent before they had a chance to go into the re-entry draft. Dent had batted only .230, but had sparkled in the field and would have received a king's ransom had he left New York and signed with the California Angels. Spencer had wound up with an impressive season, hitting .288 with 23 home runs in only 295 at-bats. His signing, coupled with the presence of Bob Watson on the Yankee roster, made Chris Chambliss expendable. The New York front office had decided that Chambliss would be the bait used to capture a first-rate major league catcher.

The Toronto Blue Jays coveted Chambliss. They offered New York minor league outfielder Ted Wilborn, left-handed pitcher Tom Underwood (a Billy Martin suggestion), and the catcher the Yankees most desired: Rick Cerone. Of all the newly acquired ballplayers, Cerone came under the closest scrutiny. The others were expected to strengthen the ball club; he was being asked to replace a legend.

"You were constantly reminded of that," Cerone admitted, "because someone always asked you about it. But I didn't look at myself as the replacement for Thurman [Munson]. He died in August. In the two months after his death, the Yankees used two catchers—Jerry Narron and Brad Gulden—and if they had been happy with them they wouldn't have traded for me. So I felt I was replacing those guys, rather than stepping in for Munson. I didn't want to add that kind of pressure to my job. It was an honor to be mentioned with Thurman. I knew I couldn't replace him or make people forget about him. What I could do is make them respect me. By catching 150 games and having a good year for the Yankees in '80, I gained that respect."

Dick Howser, having been the Yankee third base coach, was a known commodity around the clubhouse. There was hardly a player who didn't like him. Howser was considered a knowledgeable baseball man and was an excellent communicator. He had no trouble getting close to players without allowing them to take advantage of him. If anyone mistook his openness for a weakness, they were in for a surprise. Howser didn't mind taking a back step if it was called for, but when it came time to make a stand, he could be as tough as hickory.

Players who liked him as a coach loved him as a manager. Bucky Dent was a Dick Howser fan. He remembered the new manager "came in and let us play our game. It was that simple. Dick [Howser] was very secure. He was always giving credit to the players, always building up their confidence. He gave me back mine. I had a bad year in 1979, but Dick came to me and said, 'Go play ball; you're my shortstop.' That's all I needed to hear. I didn't have to worry about being pinch-hit for, wasn't always looking over my shoulder. Charlie Lau was our hitting coach. He was a hard worker and put a lot of time in with me. I ended up having one of my better years, and it started with Dick telling me he knew I could do the job."

Jackson and Howser quickly formed a mutual admiration society. Jackson had often spoken about what it meant to play for a skipper who was not afraid to show an appreciation for his talents. Howser was never silent on the subject of his right fielder. He knew the team couldn't win without Jackson and said so. Jackson responded with a great year: 41 home runs, 111 RBI, and a first-time-ever .300 batting average.

Managing a winning ball club requires more than just an occasional stroking of the team's stars. Bobby Brown was a young man who had become a Yankee yo-yo, bouncing up and down between the parent club and the minor leagues, never quite living up to his unquestioned potential. He was able to find himself under Howser. When Ruppert Jones went out during the season, first with a blocked intestine and later with a severe shoulder injury, Brown replaced him. He couldn't match Jones in the field, but he did manage to bat .260 while hitting 14 home runs and stealing 27 bases. These were very close to the numbers expected of Jones.

Howser's finest achievement was his handling of Gossage and Davis. Howser recognized the value of keeping the healed Goose strong. He initiated a strategy that has since become common practice in the major leagues: saving the top bull in the pen for the final closeout. Davis was utilized in the sixth, seventh, and, occasionally, the eighth inning. Gossage came on only in the eighth or ninth, and was rarely used unless the game was tied or the Yankees were ahead. Pitching this way, the Goose stayed fresh all season and led the league in saves.

The 1980 Yankees were a team blessed with a mother lode of talent. When Graig Nettles was bowled over by hepatitis in midseason, Howser didn't panic. He also remained unrattled through Jones's two sessions on the disabled list, Dent's and Randolph's assorted hurts, and Jackson's debilitating bout with sinusitus.

Howser's calm was a luxury bought by team depth. The Yankees had so many good players on the field and on the bench that they were able to move as exacting a critic as Earl Weaver to comment, "Every time we play New York, it's like they have sixty guys in the dugout. They just keep throwing ballplayers at you."

Weaver's Orioles had gotten off to a tepid start and were nine and a half games behind the Bombers by late July. The Yankees had occupied the American League East penthouse since May 14, and didn't hit a serious slump until early August. Then they dropped six of eight meetings with Baltimore. As September rolled around, the two clubs stood eyeball to eyeball in the standings. The onrushing Orioles, always a dangerous team in any season's final month, ended up with 100 wins. It wasn't enough. The Yankees won 103.

Some old friends, the Kansas City Royals, were to be New York's opponents in the playoffs. This was a slightly different cast of Royals than the ones the Yankees had taken in the past. One of the new faces was Willie Wilson, a switch-hitting outfielder who ran the bases like a man being pursued by creditors. He had batted only four times against the Yankees in the 1978 playoffs. He had just finished the season batting .326 with 79 stolen bases. Another newcomer was Willie Aikens, a slugging first baseman picked up in a winter deal with the California Angels for Al Cowens. The Royals had expected him to deliver some left-handed power. They weren't disappointed. His numbers: .278, 20 home runs, and 98 RBI. U. L. Washington was a switch-hitting shortstop who forced Freddie Patek into free agency. Dan Quisenberry, a right-handed reliever with a strange sidearm delivery that looked hilarious only if you didn't have to hit against it, had tied Gossage for the league lead in saves with 33. An additional new face, Jim Frey, had replaced Whitey Herzog as manager of the Royals in the winter of 1979.

They joined catcher Darrell Porter, second baseman Frank White, center fielder Amos Otis, designated hitter Hal McRae, pitchers Dennis Leonard and Larry Gura, and the rest of the familiar K.C. gang to form a potent squad, winning their division by 14 games over Billy Martin's Oakland A's. They were a team with everything: pitching, defense, hitting, speed, power, and George Brett.

Brett had spent the summer trying to become the first major leaguer since Ted Williams in 1941 to bat .400. He missed by only 10 points, settling for a league-leading .390. In 117 games played he hit 24 home runs and gathered 118 RBI. Cecil Cooper of Milwaukee, finishing behind Brett, hit an eye-popping .352 and was never in the batting race. In a season crowded with robust hitting feats, the Royal third baseman's performance stood alone.

The Yankees were favored to beat Kansas City, it being generally conceded that New York had the best team in baseball. But the Royals weren't fazed by this prognostication. They had a confidence they had lacked in earlier playoff competition, and they had a strategy: "The idea," said their right fielder Clint Hurdle, "is to do anything we can to get an early lead and keep Gossage in the pen. He is the master of disaster."

Gossage had no opportunity to enter the first two games played in Kansas City and won by the Royals, 7–2 and 3–2. With New York groggy and ready to be taken, many people thought of playoffs past and wondered what K.C. could possibly do to blow the pennant this time. None of these pessimists wore a Royals uniform.

"We heard that," remembered George Brett, "from everybody. How the Yankees always found a way to beat us. People didn't realize something, though. These were not the same Yankees. Munson, Chambliss, Rivers, White, and Lyle weren't there anymore, and they used to kill us. This was a different group and we were very confident for that third game."

That contest was staged in Yankee Stadium on the evening of October 10. The Royals took a 1–0 lead in the fifth off Tommy John, but New York came back in the sixth, scoring two runs to go in front. In the seventh, Willie Wilson hit a two-out double, chasing John and summoning Gossage into the game. Upon reaching the mound, Gossage found Wilson on second, U. L. Washington up at the plate, and George Brett in the on-deck circle. Brett recalled, "U.L. hit a high chopper over the mound, and Randolph made a great play to get to it and make a throw. But with U.L.'s speed he just beat it out. I came up, first and third, two men out, we're one run down. I knew Gossage wasn't going to start me out with a changeup. I had faced him enough times to know he was going to be throwing something hard; in that sort of situation he had to go with his best pitch. I didn't know if it would be a fastball or a slider, so I just looked for something hard. The first pitch he threw me was right down the middle. I had come up trying to pull the ball because of the right field seats, figuring if I got it up into the air it was a bonus. Well, I did get it into the air for a three-run homer, and we ended up beating the Yankees 4–2. I got to tell you, I was here in '76, '77, and '78 as a member of those losing teams. Yankee fans were always noisy; they were noisy that night. So I guess the biggest thrill of all, in that moment, was getting a chance to hear just how quiet 56,000 people could get in this stadium. That was the most fun I had had in a long time."

The three-game sweep helped pave the way for Howser's firing. The Yankees were one of the few organizations in baseball with a history of firing managers after relatively successful seasons. Berra and Stengel had been canned after winning pennants. Howser was unseated after piloting his club to 103 victories and a division title. The incident used to hasten his departure was a minor one, blown all out of proportion by Steinbrenner until it had attained the size of the sinking of the *Lusitania*.

During the second game of the playoffs, the Yankees were down 3–2 in the eighth inning. Randolph led off the frame with a base hit. Two outs later, Bob Watson belted what looked to be a game-tying double until fate interceded. The ball caromed perfectly to left fielder Willie Wilson, who almost negated this piece of luck by getting off a weak rainbow of a throw to home in an effort to cut down Randolph. Brett, though, was able to cut off Wilson's errant toss. Wheeling around and making a perfect throw of his own, Brett nailed Randolph before he could score. The play all but killed any hopes the Yankees had for a rally.

Steinbrenner blamed third base coach Mike Ferraro for the eventual loss of the game, claiming Ferraro had no right to send Randolph in, and that the coach hadn't even noticed that Randolph had stumbled while rounding second. He also intimated that Ferraro had shown a similar lack of alertness throughout the season. Within a week of the Royals' sweep. Steinbrenner tried to hire former Red Sox manager Don Zimmer to replace Ferraro as third base coach.

The odor surrounding the proposed move was such that it wasn't very long before it reached the nostrils of Howser. His reaction was quiet but firm. "I should," he said, "be given the courtesy of approving or disapproving the coaches that are added to this ball club." With that statement, Howser had placed his head squarely on Steinbrenner's battered chopping block.

The interesting thing about the resultant flap between the manager and the owner is that it centered around a mistake allegedly made by Mike Ferraro. But if anyone had bothered to ask Willie Randolph, he would have discovered the third base coach hadn't erred. Two years after the incident, Willie Randolph said, "Mike [Ferraro] had nothing to do with the play, when you get down to it. I was going regardless of the third base coach. Not many people talk about the fact that I was stealing third on that play, but my back foot slipped from under me and I stopped. That's what's meant when we call it a game of inches. That split second hurt me because I got thrown out on a bang-bang play. But when the ball was hit, I figured there was no way I couldn't score. The way that ball bounced back to [Willie] Wilson was so unusual; most of the time a ball hit out there will roll around for days. When I rounded third, I wasn't even looking at Mike. I was going because I knew I could tie the game up. I was even laughing because I knew we had it. But then I felt the mood of the crowd change; you can sense that sometimes. Willie grabbed the carom and overthrew the cutoff man, but Brett was there. He made a perfect throw to [John] Wathan, and I was out. I was as shocked as anybody, but you couldn't blame anybody, especially Mike. I mean that's baseball."

Steinbrenner reacted immediately to Howser's questioning of the owner's authority. He labeled the manager a pop-off. Rumors started circulating that Howser's job was in jeopardy. These whispers drifted through the sports pages for six weeks. Then, on November 21, a press conference was called. The Yankees announced that Dick Howser had resigned. Steinbrenner explained that Howser was leaving to pursue a "spectacular real estate venture."

Couldn't have been that spectacular. By August 1981, Howser was back in baseball, managing the Kansas City Royals. As Willie Randolph would say, "That's baseball."

Gene Michael was named to succeed Howser for the upcoming season. Steinbrenner had gone two years without participating in a World Series. Fans of the Chicago Cubs, a team that hadn't played a serious game in October since 1945, could be forgiven if they didn't shed too many tears over the shipowner's plight. The most faithful among them had at that point waited thirty-five years for a pennant and were resigned, it seemed, to wait thirty-five more. Steinbrenner didn't have their patience. He couldn't bear watching the Series on television. It had become as much his stage as his team's. He wanted it back. Steinbrenner sensed that New York was one major star short of going all the way. He had a pretty good idea who that star was.

Dave Winfield was a big (6'6", 220 pounds), twenty-nine-year-old outfielder who had spent the last eight years playing championship-caliber ball for the usually last-place San Diego Padres. He was a right-handed power hitter with great speed, an incredible arm, and three Gold Gloves to his credit. Winfield had tired of playing for mediocre ball clubs. He was determined to join a contender and to receive a contract commensurate with his ability. He achieved both those goals by playing out his option and signing with the Yankees. It was a ten-year deal worth an estimated $2.3 million.

This Everest of baseball contracts was perused with great interest by Steinbrenner's resident superstar, the redoubtable Mr. Jackson. Jackson, entering his own option year, found himself besieged by reporters anxious for his reaction to his new teammate's sudden wealth. Jax didn't let them down. Over the next few weeks he was a font of newsy quotes. Each utterance treated the media to a different side of the Jackson persona. These diverse versions of the right fielder included:

1. The indifferent Reggie—Just before Winfield became a Yankee, Jackson told reporters, "If Winfield gets $2 million a year, it's none of my business."
2. The secure Reggie—Winfield has signed. Jackson, at his most magnanimous, responded, "He's entitled to the big money. He waited his turn on line and took his ticket. Now it's my turn. I'm not concerned about it."
3. The introspective Reggie—Shortly after the contract was announced, Jax wondered out loud, "I don't know if I'm secure enough to handle not having the largest numbers next to my name."
4. The simply complex Reggie—The right fielder decided, "I don't think I'm secure enough to kneel in the on-deck circle knowing I'm batting cleanup behind a guy making four times as much as I am."

The ball-playing Reggie showed up at spring training camp two days late, allowing both Winfield, who was there on time, and himself to make solo grand entrances. And giving Steinbrenner a severe case of apoplexy. He fined the right fielder $5,000.

Jackson was upset. He thought the fine was too stiff. He was also starting to wonder when Steinbrenner would get around to talking contract with him. The owner appeared to be in no great hurry. Jackson was thirty-five years old. Steinbrenner was leery about rewarding his middle-aged star with any sort of long-term commitment. Jackson was hurt and with good reason.

Jackson was no ordinary ballplayer. He was one of the few athletes—Muhammad Ali comes to mind here—with the ability to rise to an occasion and transcend it. People turned out in large numbers to watch him tap-dance along the precipice. For every dollar Steinbrenner had invested in him, Jackson had given the owner a tenfold return. He was coming off his greatest season and no one deserved a bigger contract. Steinbrenner had a chance to show a real appreciation for what Jackson had meant to the team. Instead, he was throwing the outfielder a lot of fake moves. It was making Jackson feel "like a piece of old luggage."

Winfield wasn't the only new Yankee in camp. Steinbrenner had also rescued Winfield's outfield partner, switch-hitting center fielder Jerry Mumphrey, from the oblivion of the last-place Padres. He came to New York in a trade for Ruppert Jones, outfielder Joe Lefebvre, and pitchers Tim Lollar and Chris Welsh. This was a high price to pay, too high as it turned out. Mumphrey was a good ballplayer; he had just finished the season hitting .298 with 52 stolen bases. But Jones was better. Jones had more power, was just as fast, possessed a better glove, and was two years younger than Mumphrey. Jones also had a startling ability to get on base. As sabermetrician Bill James pointed out in his 1982 *Baseball Abstract*, "If [Ruppert] Jones hits .250, and [Jerry] Mumphrey hits .300 they're even.... At .270 [Jones is] a better hitter than Mumphrey will ever be." Lollar and Welsh were two of the best young prospects in the Yankee organization, while Lefebvre had proven himself as a hard-nosed competitor during the 1980 season. He was an excellent fielder with an arm like Rocky Colavito's and a left-handed power stroke made for Yankee Stadium. He had shown so much native ability that many thought his future was in the infield, as Graig Nettles's eventual successor. Like most Yankee prospects, wherever his future was, it wasn't in New York.

When the season got under way, attention was focused on

the remarkable all-around play of Winfield and the lack of production of Jackson. Winfield was proving that, in the parlance of the locker room, he could do it all: hit for average and power, drive in runs, steal bases, intimidate base runners with his powerful arm, and make the most acrobatic catches in left field anyone could remember. Jackson, who had missed the first 12 games of the season with a pulled Achilles' tendon, couldn't buy a base hit. He was still unsigned, and his sudden, prolonged ineptitude at bat was verifying the owner's theory that his slugger was finished.

The Yankees were undaunted by Jackson's slump. They also were able to absorb injuries to Bob Watson and Rick Cerone. The team offense was producing just enough runs to back up their superb pitching staff. New York was on a roll.

Ron Davis had come up to the Yankees with a reputation as a sinkerball pitcher, "But," the reliever claimed, "I really wasn't. Jim Beattie and I had gone body-surfing in '79, and I dislocated my shoulder. It popped right back in but left me sore. I told Steamer [pitching coach Stan Williams] that I couldn't get anything on the ball coming over the top. So he taught me to drop down and make the ball sink. I had a good year in '79, so when the '80 season started I kept the sinker motion. But my shoulder had healed and the ball wouldn't drop. The hitters were whacking it. By July Stan said, 'Look, you've got your strength back so start coming over the top and drive the ball again.' That's what I did. I started to strike guys out. Everybody thought I had come up with something new, but I was just going back to my old style."

That old style paid big dividends for the Yankees during the 1981 season. Using his rising fastball, Davis began to strike out batters at a Gossage-like rate. He even managed to put together a skein that the Goose could envy. On May 3, Davis fanned the last five Oakland hitters he faced. The next day, against the Angels, he retired the first batter he faced, Don Baylor, on a pop fly, and then proceeded to strike out the next eight hitters. Davis had faced fourteen batters in two days. He struck out all but one. He and Gossage were the most frightening late-inning weapons in baseball. They were joined by left-hander Dave

LaRoche and right-hander George Frazier to give New York its deepest bullpen in years. Word flashed through the league: If you were going to beat the Yankees, you had to get them early.

Getting them early was no small accomplishment. Guidry, John, May, and Doug Bird were heading up a formidable starting pitching staff that had been strengthened with the blooming of rookie Dave Righetti.

With Winfield and Mumphrey hitting over .300, the team was able to stay close to the top of its division until May 29 when they started a run that netted them 11 wins in 12 games. On June 11, New York traded Bird and two minor leaguers— pitcher Mike Griffin and infielder Pat Tabler—to the Chicago Cubs for ace right-hander Rick Reuschel. Reuschel was a former 20-game winner and one of the most respected pitchers in the National League. The Yankees had assembled a pitching juggernaut. It seemed the only way to prevent them from winning would be to call off the season.

Which is precisely what happened within hours of the Reuschel swap. No, the rest of the league didn't give up and hand New York the pennant by default. Something far more serious occurred: The Players Union called a strike.

This action was taken due to the owners' insistence that clubs receive some form of adequate compensation for players lost through free agency. The players refused to part with even a portion of their hard-won rights. The ensuing impasse lasted until August 10, when a settlement was reached. It granted compensation, but in a form so modified it caused fans to wonder what all the fuss had been about.

Part of the beauty of a 162-game season is that a team can play horribly through its first 50 contests and still have time to get back in the pennant chase. The strike obliterated that possibility. When the shredded season resumed, a team that had slumped early, as had the Kansas City Royals who stood 12 games out of first when the strike was called, would have little more than 50 games to right itself. The owners didn't think that was fair. They also were interested in recouping some of their lost revenues. So they devised the concept of the split season. In its final form, the Yankees, Athletics, Phillies, and Dodgers were declared first-half champions of their respective divisions. Each team had been in first place on the day the strike commenced; New York had led Baltimore by two games. The format provided that these first-half winners would meet their division's second-half champion in a five-game series. The victor would advance to the regular league playoffs. Should a first-half champ win both halves, it would meet the club in its division with the next best overall record. This plan ensured the owners extra television revenues, allowed pretenders like the Cubs and Mets to think they had a shot at post-season play, and let the Yankees sleepwalk through the final two months of their schedule. They played below .500 in the second season. It shouldn't have been surprising. With post-season play assured, the club had nothing to play for.

Reggie Jackson did. Jackson returned from the two-month sabbatical determined to prove he wasn't through. He played with a vengeance. In 44 pre-strike games he had batted .199 with 6 home runs and 24 RBI. His post-strike numbers were slightly more Jacksonian: .272, 9 home runs, and 30 RBI. This output made no difference in his situation. Steinbrenner seemed no closer to making him an offer than he had at the height of Jackson's slump. This snubbing had a noticeable effect on the outfielder. He could still bring excitement to the plate, still bring the crowd to its feet. But there was a look in his eye that betrayed any smile he attempted. It wasn't fun anymore.

Jackson's favorite owner had also started to make life miserable for his latest manager. After watching six weeks of his team's less-than-scintillating play, Steinbrenner began to mumble that unless the club started to show some life, Michael might be out of a job. Most of Steinbrenner's recent managers had heard this tune before. Billy Martin could always be counted on to challenge Steinbrenner to carry out his threat. Dick Howser would act as though he hadn't heard a thing. Michael opted for the Martin Method. He called a press conference, announced that he was tired of Steinbrenner's talk, and said that if the owner wanted to dismiss him, he should go ahead and get it over with. Michael didn't have to say it twice. That media gathering had been called on August 28. By September 6, Michael was gone, and Bob Lemon was back as his successor in the Yankee dugout.

The team did not play a more inspired brand of baseball under Lem. It finished the second season with a record of 25–26. This created a worry throughout the organization that the split season had dulled New York's competitive edge. They would be facing the Milwaukee Brewers in the playoff for the division title. The Brewers had just withstood the challenges of three clubs—Boston, Detroit, and Baltimore—to earn that honor. This was no time for the Yankees to go soft.

The fears proved to be unfounded. When it came time for the Yankees to play some serious baseball, they were ready to rumble. They took a hard-fought five-game series from Milwaukee, then scorched the Oakland A's in three straight to win the American League pennant. When they won the first two games of the World Series against the Dodgers, they looked invincible.

Dave Righetti was scheduled to start game three in Los Angeles. He had joined the club in late May and was an immediate sensation, winning eight while losing four and posting an ERA of 2.06. He had gone 3–0 in post-season play, including a 3–0 shutout of the Brewers. Righetti's eventual selection as Rookie of the Year was a foregone conclusion. He was now expected to use his amazing left arm to throw one more handful of earth on the Dodgers' grave.

But L.A. had a rookie phenom of its own: Fernando Valenzuela. He had won 13 games and led the league in shutouts, innings pitched, complete games, and strikeouts. He had been the winning pitcher in the Dodgers' pennant clinching victory against the Montreal Expos.

Just as Los Angeles had let Guidry off the hook in '78, so too did the Yankees allow a beatable Valenzuela to come out on top in this contest. Valenzuela threw 145 pitches, surrendering nine hits and seven walks. But he escaped with a 5–4 complete game victory. It turned the Series around. The Dodgers took the next three games, wrapping up the Series with a 9–2 bloodletting in the sixth game in New York. The humiliation of '78 had been avenged. Reggie Jackson, the unchallenged Mr. October, had his World Series participation limited by injury to three games. He batted .333, with one home run and one run batted in.

When the Series was over, Steinbrenner issued his apology to the city of New York on behalf of the team. It was as predictable as it was tasteless. He ended it by saying, "... and we will be at work immediately to prepare for 1982." The owner started those preparations by signing four men the Yankees could have lost to free agency: Ron Guidry, Willie Randolph, Lou Piniella, and Bobby Murcer.

Reggie Jackson would have liked to have joined that group. He wasn't invited. Weeks passed without a sign of even passing interest from the owner. Jackson, meanwhile, was doing everything he could to create the proper atmosphere for his return. He offered to move to first base or become a designated hitter. Word got around that he would accept a three-year deal instead of the five-year pact he had hoped for. He was even willing to settle for less than Winfield had received. For a man of Jackson's immense pride and ego, these were not small concessions.

They didn't make a dent in the owner. Steinbrenner had spent a lot of time meditating on the team's future and had come away with a grab bag filled with plans, none of which included Number Forty-four.

Chapter
ELEVEN

...and a pall fell over the House That Ruth Built.

—Ervin Bauer, baseball analyst

IT must have been the snow that verified the strangeness of the day. This crystalline intruder had visited the city uninvited, just in time to lend confusion to the traditional rites of spring. Snow in New York in April. Something was amiss. It made the Stadium as cold as an owner's heart.

The Yankees and the Texas Rangers had gathered in the Bronx for practice on the day before their Opening Day game, a clash that would be aborted by foul weather. Most of the major New York reporters were present. There were enough names and stories to keep them busy.

Lee Mazzilli, the former Met darling, was in his new Ranger uniform. An informal press conference assembled around his locker. He was still in a daze over being ripped from the womb of Shea Stadium and discarded in a strange city on a strange team in a league full of strangers. The reporters cloaked their questions with a compassionate deference to the young outfielder's obvious pain. These queries were asked in hushed tones usually reserved for a chapel. The last question put to him was a frivolous "Who's the real Italian Stallion, you or Rick Cerone?" An exasperated Mazzilli replied, "Phil Rizzuto." He dashed off to the safety of the shower.

There were other familiar profiles to be found on the Rangers' generally faceless roster: former Mets Jon Matlack and Doug Flynn; Buddy Bell, Nettles's successor as the best third baseman in the business; former Yankee George Medich; Gold Glove catcher Jim Sundberg; and Charlie Hough, the ex-Dodger reliever who delivered the last and longest of Jackson's three home runs on that epic October evening in 1977. Mickey Rivers, though a member of the team, was not there. He was laid up with a knee injury that canceled him out for most of the season.

The Yankees, the New Faces of 1982, took the field just as Texas finished its workout. Gossage, Guidry, May, Frazier, Righetti, and Mike Morgan struggled to work out, keep warm, and protect their most fragile commodities: their throwing arms.

Tommy John wondered out loud if Steinbrenner's early spring training camp this year had been such a good idea, questioning if it might not leave the team overworked. Guidry, due to pitch the opener, opined that the early reporting was probably good for him. He reasoned that it could help him get his slider going early. When asked about the snow, he offered, "The maximum amount of snow I can pitch in is three feet. Above that I have trouble bringing my arm around." The twinkle never left his eye.

Bobby Murcer was at his locker preparing to join his mates on the diamond. Over the winter he had signed a three-year contract for $1 million. He kidded with a writer, "Yes, yes, it was a wonderful contract. A million dollars a year for three years." After a pause for laughter, Murcer put on his most incredulous look and said, "Well, gee, that's what I thought I signed. Maybe I should go see George [Steinbrenner]." Murcer didn't think the cold weather would be a problem at all. "Hell," he cracked, "you've never played in Candlestick Park like I did. Those wonderful crowds of people, all eighty-five of them, used to freeze to death watching the Giants play baseball."

Around the batting cage, Cerone, Rivers, Randolph, Watson,

Nettles, Winfield, Dent, Gamble, Piniella, Mumphrey, Andre Robertson, and the two newest additions, Dave Collins and Ken Griffey, waited their turns. The banter was loose, most of it centering around home runs. They joked about how everyone claimed the team needed power, how Steinbrenner wanted power, and how they would supply power. Gamble kept pulling the ball short of the seats. "I can't get it up," he wisecracked. That touched off a brief spate of predictably blue humor. Finally, Gamble put one in the right field stands. "There it is, that's what George [Steinbrenner] is looking for. Where is he? That's what he wants, and I got it for him. Let's talk money now. Where's my 3 million?" More laughter. Gamble spews out his comments with the rapidity of a tommy gun. He is the Richard Pryor of baseball.

If power was what Steinbrenner was looking for, he could not have been happy with the lack of it that day. Gamble's homer came after twenty minutes of BP. It was the only ball the Yankees hit over the fence fair all day.

Steinbrenner may have been there to see it. Several sightings of him were reported. Each one had him dressed in a trench coat, wearing dark glasses, prowling around the stands or in the executive box. Nobody claimed they actually saw him; they just heard of his presence.

There was another presence reported there. And that was no rumor. Though his physical shell was some three thousand miles from the vicinity, the shadow of Reggie Jackson, as tall and as wide as six stone slabs of Stonehenge, was cast across the proceedings. It blotted out the sun and gave birth to a small army of half-whispered doubts.

In the winter of 1971, the Baltimore Orioles, a team that could boast a quartet of All-Star outfielders and a minor league system as fertile as the great Yankee farms of the forties, had decided to undo their outfield logjam. They had unloaded thirty-five-year-old Frank Robinson, dealing him and reliever Pete Richert to the Los Angeles Dodgers for four players. The most notable of these was a young right-hander named Doyle Alexander.

The logic of this deal was impeccable. Baltimore still had

Merv Rettenmund, Paul Blair, and Don Buford to provide them with the best outfield in baseball. They had penciled in 1972 as the coming-out year for Don Baylor. Many writers and scouts had already christened Baylor "the next Frank Robinson."

Having considered the preceding data, and mindful of the fact that the Orioles had scored 742 runs the previous summer, the Baltimore front office had decided it could give up the old Frank Robinson. It would open up the outfield and allow them to receive an exceptional young pitcher (Alexander) without appreciably hurting the offense.

What they failed to realize was that Frank Robinson, with his reputation as a dangerous man in the clutch and with the threat of his power, *was* the Oriole offense.

He was the team's trigger, the straw that stirred the drink. Once he was gone, the Baltimore lineup was done in by a chain reaction. The resultant trauma was as clear as the print of the final statistics in *The Sporting News*. The 1972 Orioles batted .229 and suffered a loss of 223 runs scored from the previous season. Only their formidable pitching staff allowed them to finish as high as third.

During the winter of 1982, George Steinbrenner made a similar miscalculation. He allowed his thirty-five-year-old trigger-man to be carried off in the saddlebags of Gene Autry.

When Jackson departed to become an Angel, he left behind a group of talented ballplayers, seemingly able to form a potent lineup. But with him gone, they became a team without a personality.

In losing Jackson, the team had also lost the element of danger that had been so much of their identity. Jackson was Emperor of the Country of Big Swings. An intelligent, careful pitcher could make him seem a clown at the plate.

But in crucial situations, this clown became as wise as Shakespeare's fools. He would saunter from the on-deck circle, savoring his stage and his moment. Then he would take one practice swing. The man and the bat would spring forward as one in a dance to Mars. The body language was clear: "Let's get it on!" After these preliminaries, he would settle into the batter's box. His eyes would study the pitcher, and only the pitcher, with a gaze as heavy as death's touch. Looming over home plate he appeared dark and obdurate. Menacing. The moment his opponents dreaded had arrived. Reggie Jackson was about to kill their pleasure.

It was the announced plan of George Steinbrenner that the Yankees would be a running team in the 1982 season. This ignored a basic fact: Yankee Stadium is not a running team's ball park. It is not carpeted with Dacron sod, and it had that right field porch that turned ordinary left-handed hitters into fearsome sluggers.

Nevertheless, Steinbrenner traded two minor league pitchers to the Cincinnati Reds to secure the services of speedy outfielder Ken Griffey. Griffey had been one of the main cogs of the Big Red Machine. Despite a knee operation in 1979, he could still run. He could also hit the whey out of the ball, being one of the few active hitters with a lifetime batting average over .300. Jackson's right field spot would be his. It was anticipated that Griffey would not deliver as many home runs as Reggie Jackson. But he fit in with the current baserunning consciousness and was a better defensive player than the departed slugger. Steinbrenner also dipped into the market to sign free agent Dave Collins, another former Reds outfielder. Collins had stolen 79 bases in 1980, the last time a full season of baseball had been played. Randolph, Mumphrey, Griffey, Collins, and Winfield were supposed to steal 200 bases and drive their rivals batty with catch-as-catch-can baseball. At least one antagonist, Earl Weaver, was grateful for the change. "I'd rather see them sliding into second than circling the bases," he cracked.

Whether or not this new offense would have worked is a moot point. The running attack never materialized. New York didn't run during spring training. They also didn't score many runs or win many games. Jokes about "Georgeyball" began to appear in the press. Articles openly questioned the owner's sanity in using speed to replace rejected power.

The Yankee front-office party line held that the team hadn't lost any slugging. Jackson had only batted .237 with 15 home runs in the strike-shortened season. Management pointed to Dave Revering as the man who would better those figures. Joe

Pepitone, the Yankees' minor league batting instructor at the time, had worked with the first baseman on the art of pulling the ball. Revering had a torrid spring, batting .465. The experiment was deemed a success. The left-handed Revering, platooned most of his career, was going to be a full-time player.

Revering's good fortune was not shared by the rest of the team. The Yankees continued to look impotent in exhibition games. As losses piled up, beads of sweat began to glaze the Yankee logo. Moves were made to strengthen the club; they only helped to fracture its stability.

The first move came while the club was still in Florida. Though not the most important, it is at the top of a grim list:

MARCH 24—Yankees trade right-handed reliever Bill Castro to California for Butch Hobson. Castro had no chance to make the team, but Hobson is a man without a position. An elbow injury has robbed him of his usefulness at third, and he has never played first. He could be the right-handed DH, but the club already has Piniella and Watson for that role. Hobson's career stats outside of Fenway Park are not good. It is an acquisition that makes no sense.

MARCH 30—Doyle Alexander, after a contract dispute with the Giants, is shipped off to New York for three minor leaguers. The Yankees claim they need Alexander to replace the injured Rick Reuschel. It doesn't occur to them to give the responsibility to Gene Nelson, an impressive rookie right-hander. Nelson hears rumors he is being dealt to Seattle. When he questions management he is assured that he isn't going anywhere.

MARCH 31—The Yankees obtain Al Oliver, the .300-hitting first baseman, from Texas for Oscar Gamble. But Gamble vetoes the deal. Later, Steinbrenner chides Gamble for the failure of the Yankee offense, explaining that the acquisition of Oliver was part of his Master Plan. Somebody should remind Steinbrenner that you don't plan your offense around a player you haven't gotten yet, especially in today's age of no-trade clauses.

APRIL 1—Gene Nelson, who isn't going anywhere, is going to Seattle in a trade for lefty reliever Shane Rawley.

APRIL 10—With the Yankee opener delayed by snow, New York deals Ron Davis to Minnesota for switch-hitting shortstop Roy Smalley. Manager Bob Lemon says that Smalley will be platooned at short with the incumbent, Bucky Dent. Shock is not an adequate word to describe Dent's reaction.

The team opened on April 11, five days later than scheduled, with a doubleheader against the Chicago White Sox. New York dropped both games. Revering, the "everyday" first baseman, went hitless in five trips in the first contest and was benched. Up in the press box, Yankee officials evinced a calm sense of trepidation. A reporter asked one official if he could set up an interview with Steinbrenner. The man replied, "No way, not now. I wouldn't even ask him. Sorry."

The reasons for this cautious reading were obvious: the performance on the field and the empty seats in the Stadium. It had been wondered out loud what effect Jackson's absence would have on attendance. The crowd's numbers on that blustery Easter Sunday were announced at just over 31,000. That had to include a lot of no-shows. If there were 25,000 fans actually in attendance it was a lot. During the second game, the small gathering chanted, "We want Reggie! We want Reggie!" And it was only Opening Day.

The Yankees went on the road after the double loss and found small comfort away from the maddened crowd. They won a few, lost a few, and paddled through their games like an armless swimmer.

They returned to New York on April 22. Fans were in for a treat that day. They got to see a team that was expertly schooled in fundamentals, featuring tight pitching and defense. The offense was rich in variety: extra-base hits in the gaps, bunt singles, the hit-and-run, sacrifices, squeeze plays, stolen bases, and timely home runs. This was the team Yankee watchers were told to expect. The only problem was that all this marvelous baseball was being played by the Detroit Tigers. The Yankees were getting their heads kicked in.

When the series with the Bengals was over, Bob Lemon was fired. He had been publicly promised by Steinbrenner that, no matter what, he would manage for the whole season. Gene Michael, the Prodigal Son, was named as his replacement. Stick was replaced three months later by Clyde King. But Michael was lucky. He got his second chance to manage the Yankees just in time for Jackson's return.

On April 27, Jackson came home to the Bronx hitting a dismal .173. In 52 at-bats he had managed only 9 hits. All singles. He had driven in only four runs.

If he was depressed by those numbers he didn't act it. He stepped jauntily into the Stadium batting cage for some early, private licks and looked at the right field porch. It was dinner and Jackson was hungry. He deposited eight souvenirs into the farthest reaches of the ball park. When he was finished he stopped, turned, and surveyed the site of so much personal turmoil and triumph. Just like MacArthur in the Philippines. The second time.

That evening, about an hour before game time, the carnival that began with his afternoon arrival started to peak. The playing fields and stands were alive with a holiday atmosphere. The Stadium was packed, its diamond crawling with media types. Jackson made his entrance with exquisite timing. He walked into the midst of this Passion Play on a path of white towels strewn about for him by teammate Rod Carew. Jackson took batting practice again. This time it was more for the crowd than out of any real necessity. He was pumped. He hit nine more balls over the fence. The last one was a mortar shot that struck high atop the Stadium facade in right. It made the concrete tremble and was the sort of blast that had always served as Jackson's calling card.

Jackson's mesmerizing effect on the press was all-obscuring.

No better example of it could be found than in a little vignette played out that evening. As Jackson held court, all the reporters camped around the batting cage, hanging on every syllable. All were oblivious to the fact that off to the side, no more than two feet away, stood a pretty fair ballplayer. Fred Lynn was busy practicing his stroke, unhassled by anyone. It looked terrific.

The game was played under the dual threats of rain and Jackson's anticipated display of power. Both arrived together.

Guidry started for New York. He got Jackson, greeted by a long ovation, to pop up in the second. In the fifth, Jackson led off with a single, took second on a wild pitch, and scored on a suicide squeeze. That run broke a 1–1 deadlock.

Jackson delivered what everybody had come to see in the seventh. He hammered Guidry's first pitch into a majestic arc that split the night in two. The Stadium exploded. They cheered Jackson as he danced around the bases and forced him out of the visiting dugout for a curtain call. After the familiar song of "Reg-gie! Reg-gie!" subsided, the mood grew ugly.

The crowd, a mob now, shouted in unison, "Steinbrenner sucks!" The cry had started in such a simultaneous manner that it seemed to come from the mouth of a single giant. If the screamers had a rope, Steinbrenner would have been the latest in Stadium banners. One veteran reporter commented, "I have never seen anything like this, not in twenty-five years of covering baseball." It was that chilling. Shortly after Jackson's and the crowd's blasts, the sky opened up and released a downpour. The game was called after the Yankees batted in their half of the inning. New York lost 3–1. Only the gods could ring down the final curtain on Reggie's return.

Jackson left the Bronx and ended up with a typically Jacksonian season: 39 homers (tied for the league lead) and 101 RBI. He helped California to a division title and was missed in the Bronx. For more than just his bat.

Except for 1981, Jackson and Steinbrenner had been perfect foils for each other. The combination paid off in headlines and at the box office. It also managed to keep some heat off the rest of the team. Jackson was like a lightning rod. Whenever a bolt was thrown from the Stadium's executive heights, the right fielder usually bore the brunt of it. With Jackson gone, the lightning became napalm. The damage done was random, searing, and, in some cases, perhaps physically scarring.

When the team's performance continued to be lackluster, Steinbrenner charged that several members of the team "lacked mental toughness." In an interview with Maury Allen of the *New York Post*, Steinbrenner asserted, "I'm paying those guys a lot of money and they haven't produced. If they don't start producing, I promise there will be more fireworks by the Fourth of July than anybody can imagine." The players he was referring to were Dave Winfield, Dave Collins, and Ken Griffey.

More was to follow. More always followed. The Yankees had been asked to an early spring camp that year. They had worked— overworked according to some—long hard hours in preparation for a fast start a la the Oakland A's in 1981. The players had been promised days off once the season started.

Those promises were forgotten when the team struggled. Extra workouts were ordered. These put the club in a mutinous mood, and the rumblings of complaint started. Rich Gossage said, "They'll have us sleeping in the seats after the games soon." Oscar Gamble was even more vocal. "This workout stinks!" moaned the outfielder. "They tell us in spring they're going to give us time off. It's all a bunch of lies!" A couple of players talked about asking to be traded. One veteran mused, "They'd have to get at the back of a very long line." Steinbrenner ripped back, saying, "Don't tell me about mental fatigue, all of us get mental fatigue. But we press on."

Steinbrenner later peppered the headlines with vilifying comments about his famous employees. He called Dave Winfield "an outstanding athlete, but he's not a superstar in the sense that Reggie Jackson is. Winfield can't carry a team on his back the way Reggie does." Then why, one wanted to ask, was Jackson in Anaheim? Steinbrenner characterized Shane Rawley as "the worst deal we ever made." Graig Nettles, not especially sparkling in the field of late, was "in the twilight of his career." And Lou Piniella "might have the American League record for hitting into double plays."

He saved the worst for Doyle Alexander. After a bad outing against the Seattle Mariners, an angry Alexander got into a losing battle with a brick wall. He came away with a broken finger on his pitching hand and missed nine weeks. When Alexander came off the disabled list, he was asked to go to the minors to pitch himself into shape. He went, as did Rudy May, another injured returnee. Both pitched a game. The front office asked them to go down for at least one more outing. Alexander balked. Wrongly. He was a finesse pitcher and needed the work. When he finally rejoined the team, his rhythm was out of kilter. His best pitch was a changeup that needed a lot of work to be effective. He didn't get it, moving in and out of the starting rotation. After six losses in a row, Steinbrenner ordered him to undergo a medical exam, saying, "I'm afraid some of our players might get hurt playing behind him." Alexander one-upped him. "I want to make it clear," he retorted, "that I'm seeing a medical doctor, not a psychiatrist. I realize a lot of people around here have gone crazy, but I'm not there yet."

Rudy May had also been a target. He had vetoed a winter trade that would have sent him to the Royals for Hal McRae. It didn't please Steinbrenner that McRae was on his way to leading the league in runs batted in. But May didn't actually squelch the deal. "I did not veto it," he claimed. "I have a no-trade clause in my contract. I wanted to be compensated for giving that up. I asked for a figure that I didn't think was too high. They said no. They also said if I didn't okay the trade they wouldn't use me because they were going to go with the kids. I still wouldn't give up my clause. Now, when I come to the Stadium, I leave my head in the car. The other day I shut out Detroit for five innings until I came out. I didn't even know I was starting until I got to the ball park. It's a tough situation, but what can you do? If I ask to be traded now, they take it personally. They think it's more important to be a Yankee than to be a ballplayer. Meanwhile, I'm in my option year, I'm thirty-seven years old, and I'm not getting any stats. And I'm not going to because they won't use me. You think that game against Detroit makes any difference? It doesn't. I'm bitter about it, but I still smile because there's nothing I can do about it."

But there was. May was injured on June 4. He suffered a partially torn muscle near the chest area. Upon returning, May was still used haphazardly but more than he expected. The Yankees were lucky to have him. Next to the Goose, he was the best pitcher on the team.

The club, torn by dissension, began to get hit by injuries. Hard. Nettles, Mumphrey, and Cerone were struck by the Curse of the Left Thumb. Each suffered a fracture of that digit and missed a total of nineteen weeks of action.

These injuries hurt the team. Even more harmful were the continued misguided maneuverings of the front office.

Bob Watson, the ideal right-handed hitter for Yankee Stadium, was packed off to Atlanta for a minor league pitching prospect. Larry Milbourne, symbol of the depth that had been this team's strength, was included in a package to Minnesota that fetched catcher Butch Wynegar (to cover Cerone's absence) and pitcher Roger Erickson. Wynegar did an excellent job until he was felled by menigoencephalitis (a virus that affects the nervous system) and missed six weeks in late July and August.

In an attempt to get some power, the Yankees sent "regular" first baseman Dave Revering to Toronto for John Mayberry. New York may have been the only team in the majors that didn't know that Mayberry had lost his bat speed and was no longer the slugger he had been.

Winfield became involved in an imbroglio with Steinbrenner over promised contributions the Yankees hadn't made to his foundation. Steinbrenner countered that he wasn't satisfied with the makeup of the foundation's board of directors and wanted some changes made before he sent his check. This dispute was resolved. Winfield went through the first part of the season having to absorb the derisive cries of "Reg-gie! Reg-gie! Reg-gie!" with each at bat. He silenced these by consciously sacrificing average for power. Winfield went on a rampage that produced 37 homers and 106 RBI. He had a magnificent season.

The team didn't. The summer took on an air of high comedy. In the span of a season they had three managers (Lemon, Michael, and Clyde King), five pitching coaches (Jeff Torborg, Jerry Walker, Stan Williams, Clyde King, and Sammy Ellis), and three hitting coaches (Mickey Vernon, Joe Pepitone, and Lou Piniella). In one year the New York Yankees had as many pitching coaches as the Baltimore Orioles have had during the entire life of their franchise.

The running game that was supposed to ravage the league never got out of the gate. The team's whippets had been assured they would receive the green light as soon as the season commenced. It was never flashed. For some unfathomable reason, Yankee management refused to use the one weapon they had taken pains to secure during the off-season. They had turned away the team's best slugger, built an offense around the stolen base, and then refused to use it.

Collins was supposed to lead the Go-Go Yankees. He had been promised upon signing that he would play as often as Winfield. He was begging for playing time at midseason. Collins was an outfielder, but had taken hundreds of ground balls at first base during the opening week of spring training. Then that experiment was dropped. He eventually played some first during the season; he wasn't really ready. Through no fault of his own.

Mumphrey, Randolph, Griffey, Collins, and Winfield. They were supposed to average 40 stolen bases each. Not one of them had as many as 40 attempts. It wasn't their doing. A healthy running game must be used often to be effective. It requires a commitment. The New York management didn't seem interested in making any.

The hazy leadership affected the guys in the dugout. Only a few players knew what was expected of them, knew what their role on the club would be. Perhaps the best way to summarize the mess that passed for the 1982 season in the Bronx is to tell the stories of three men: Bucky Dent, Tommy John, and Dave Righetti.

When Bucky Dent was born, the baseball muses did not huddle around his crib and bless him with inordinate tools. His first major league manager, Chuck Tanner, once said of him, "He doesn't have a whole lot of size or great speed, and he doesn't carry a big bat. All he can do is beat you."

It started with his older brother Jim, who served as the young

Bucky's football and baseball coach. It was Jim who impressed "not just on me, but on all the kids, the importance of fundamentals. My brother had excellent coaching when he was a player, and he shared what he learned with us. The one thing I remember is he taught us to play every sport the right way."

This was the foundation on which Dent's athletic schooling was built. His education continued when he signed a contract to play with the Chicago White Sox. "I played in the minor leagues for three years under the same manager, Joe Sparks," he explains, "who was an excellent teacher and terrific disciplinarian. We had a young team, and we all moved up in the organization with him. From A ball right to Triple A. That's very unusual and was a great experience. We won the championship in every league we played in. Goose [Gossage], Terry Forster, Lamar Johnson, Jerry Hairston, and Bill Sharp were on those teams. Joe taught me basics. When I got to the big leagues with Chicago in 1973, Dick Allen was at first base. People always talk about Dick's power. He was strong, as strong as anybody I've ever seen. But he was much more than that. He was the best ballplayer I've ever seen. There wasn't anything he couldn't do: hit home runs, hit for average, field, steal bases. He could go from first to third with anyone. He used to talk to me, point things out. He was a good man that way. Al Monchak was a coach with the club, and he polished me up. He spent time with me, telling me how to play the position and just talking baseball. I think that's very important for a young player. He never let a day go by without telling me something about the game. Even if I played great he'd say, 'I think you should position yourself this way on that play.' He taught me little things to improve my defense. In my rookie year, Chuck Tanner pulled me from a game for taking a relay throw wrong. Al came to me and said, 'You know why Chuck took you out?' I told him I didn't. He said, 'Well, he wants me to tell you he never wants to see you make a relay like that again.' Till today, I don't think I've ever made that mistake again."

Dent never made the same mistake twice. It was one of his strengths as a ballplayer. For five years he gave the Yankees his heart at short, becoming one of the most respected infielders in the game. It was not Dent's nature to chatter on about the great Yankee tradition. But this was the club he had idolized as a youth, the only team he wanted to play for. If Billy Martin had NY stenciled on his heart, Bucky Dent had pinstripes for veins.

So one can imagine his hurt when he found his job had been taken from him.

Dent was a pro. Had he been beaten out of his position by a better player, it would have been acceptable. He would have sat on the bench, staying ready, and would have been the first one to lead the congratulations when his replacement made a good play or got a clutch base hit.

But Dent didn't lose his job; he hadn't been beaten out. The position had been taken from him because Steinbrenner had made the mistake of letting Jackson go, and then had compounded the error by trading Ron Davis to get Roy Smalley. Smalley was supposed to replenish some of the power Jackson had packed off in his California-bound luggage.

The Yankees had won the last two years with timely hitting. But more important was their pitching and defense. Dent was a key member of that tight infield, and Davis was the guy who saved the Goose for the eighth and ninth innings. He made Gossage all the more formidable, making the entire staff immeasurably stronger. But Davis had taken New York to salary arbitration and had had a poor World Series. And New York needed to find someone who could hit home runs.

The opening plan to platoon Dent and Smalley was a canard that would have obviously hurt both men. Each had been used to playing regularly. Smalley could not field the position as well as Dent. But he did have a lot more power, came at a big price, and was a switch-hitter. It was only a matter of time before the job was all his. This angered Dent and put Smalley, an intelligent and sensitive young man, in an awkward position. "Bucky Dent has earned the shortstop's job here," he said, "and he deserves it."

Dent got a reprieve when Nettles was injured in late April. Smalley shifted to third, and Dent went back to short.

He pressed. The tension exerted by the mind games management had played on him were proving to be too great. He had suffered a loss of self-esteem, and it showed between the white lines. In five games the normally sure-handed Dent made five errors. His batting average was whittled away until it was nonexistent. He tried to tough it out through the hurt and the bullshit. But he kept tripping over his own pain. Soon he was sharing the shortstop job again, with rookie Andre Robertson and Larry Milbourne. When Nettles returned, Smalley went back to short. Dent rode the bench.

He began to turn inward. At that point, he could have destroyed himself. It would have been easy enough for him to lock himself up in his private hell and put an out-to-lunch sign on the bars. But Bucky Dent never took the easy way.

He came to the park early and did his homework, keeping himself ready for that day of deliverance when he would be needed. Gradually the pride, never really lost, resurfaced, and he realized that he was still Bucky Dent. They could never take that away from him.

On the evening of Thursday, July 25, his mood seemed lighter than ever before. He had acquired a peace that cast a glow around him. Dent had won. He had decided not to let his situation run him. Dent had found the will to play his game. That evening he made a rare start against the Detroit Tigers. He went hitless in four trips. No big deal. What was of greater consequence was his showing in the field. He was loosey-goosey, and his play that evening was as smooth as a Red Smith phrase.

A perfect example was the double play he started. The twin-killing was vintage Randolph-Dent. There was an effortlessness to their collaboration that spoke of the poetry of physical harmony. Each time they repeated it, as they did that night, it became a videotaped replay of an earlier marvel. The completion of such plays usually incurred nothing more than politely enthusiastic applause and knowing grins. More celebrative outbursts are reserved for those miracles that surprise.

Dent that evening gave everybody a reminder of what he was all about. His play at short had always been a clinic on positioning and technique. He is a craftsman. Unlike Garry Templeton, the erratically brilliant shortstop with the Padres who is so overloaded with talent he occasionally short-circuits, Dent had carved out a career with sweat, smarts, and sheer desire. He built a reputation on pages torn from the bible of Smith, Barney, chapter one, verse one, from the prophet John Houseman: "He earned it."

For the next two weeks he played more than he had. He again did all the little things that add up to victory, showing the world he could not be beaten. Those two weeks turned out to be the final notes in his Yankee swan song. Each one was clear, strong, and defiant.

Several clubs had tried to deal for Dent. Earlier in the season, Baltimore had offered pitcher Jim Palmer for him, and the White Sox were willing to part with pitcher Dennis Lamp and third baseman Jim Morrison. The Yankees turned both offers down.

But on Sunday, August 8, they traded him to Texas for Lee Mazzilli. Only the day before, Dent had been told by the owner that there were no plans to trade him. He was later told that the deal had been set since Friday night.

As he prepared to leave the Stadium that afternoon, he was asked how he felt. Dent looked at the reporter. He was obviously overwhelmed with emotion. But he was still a professional. As dry-eyed and sure as if he had just tossed out a runner from the hole, he said, "I played with a lot of guys here that I respect. I feel it's been an honor. I had a lot of great moments and a lot of fun. That's about it." Not long after, he was gone.

The owner should have been there to see him off. Steinbrenner spent a lot of time talking about Yankee tradition, Yankee pride, and Yankee honor. He missed a chance to see them as they walked out the clubhouse door.

Tommy John was also supposed to become an ex-Yankee that weekend, but New York had turned down the Angels' offer of pitcher Bruce Kison for him. "They don't want to get Kison," one press box wag noted, "until they're absolutely sure he's hurt."

While Ron Guidry may have been more scintillating, John had been the Yankees' best starting pitcher over the last three years. Like Dent, the lefty was a finesse player. He didn't overwhelm anybody; he just beat them. During those years (1979–81) his Yankee record was 52–26. No pitcher in the American League had won more games during that time.

John relied on a sinkerball to retire batters. This type of hurling demanded a delicate touch. It is absolutely necessary that a proponent of this style get to toil on a regular basis.

John had been working steadily at the start of the season. He pitched well, as well as ever. But he wasn't winning. He wasn't winning because the Yankees' restructured offense wasn't scoring any runs for him. Then he got banged around a few times, and the whispers started: T.J. has lost it; age is catching up to him. It didn't matter that he was sound of mind and body. His birth certificate made him thirty-eight, and he was working for an organization that was turning panic into an art form.

The club started moving him in and out of the rotation. It was the worst thing they could have done. The touch needed to be a sinkerballer can be easily mislaid during these travels. John's record suffered. Finally, he was asked to stay in the bullpen.

As John later explained on the "Late Night with David Letterman" TV show, "It would have been fine if they sat me down and could show me five guys on our roster who were pitching better than me." But they couldn't, so he balked.

There was a fellow who pitched for the Yankees in the fifties and sixties. His name was Whitey Ford. There would be times in his career when he was treated rudely by opponents. Nobody put him in the bullpen. That Yankee management knew better. They trusted history and talent. That sort of patience had become an interloper in the present administration.

When pressed on the bullpen matter, John became publicly critical of the way the pitching staff was being handled. It was an unusual outburst for John. He questioned the sanity of the Yankee six-man rotation, asking sarcastically, "Why don't we go to seven? That way we could all put aside a certain day of the week to pitch and spend the rest of the week with our families."

John had a heated discussion with Yankee vice-president Bill Bergesch shortly after these comments appeared in the news.

John had heard that Bergesch had made a statement to the effect that John should be grateful for all George Steinbrenner had done for him. The pitcher viewed this as an obvious reference to Steinbrenner's support during his young son Travis's recovery from a near-fatal accident the year before.

That was too much. John met with Bergesch in a room near the Yankee clubhouse. The pitcher exploded, "Don't you ever mention Travis John's name again!" One person, who heard the outburst, said, "I never, ever saw T.J. that angry." A teammate, joking with a writer, referred to John as "our radical." He said it with approval.

John had placed himself in an untenable position with the ball club. He requested that he be traded, preferably to the California Angels. That first transaction for Bruce Kison did not go through, but John did get his wish on August 31. He was dealt to the Angels for three minor leaguers to be named later.

Before he left, he characterized the experience of playing for the Yankees that season by saying, "Mr. Steinbrenner said it takes a very, very special person to play in New York City for the New York Yankees under the present management. He is right."

If Yankee brass looked at Tommy John as part of their pitching past, then they should have viewed Dave Righetti as the pitching future.

Righetti had come to New York from Texas as the centerpiece of the Sparky Lyle deal. It took him three years to get his act together, but when he did he looked like the second coming of Sandy Koufax. During his first full season with the club, he went 8–4 with a 2.06 ERA, pitching 105 innings and allowing only 75 hits and 38 walks. He struck out 89. Righetti added two victories in the first tier of the playoffs against Milwaukee and another in the league championship series against Oakland. When the season was over he was voted Rookie of the Year.

Counting minor league games, the playoffs, and the World Series, Righetti made 25 starts. He only pitched badly in one of them—that World Series game against Valenzuela. Only two innings pitched kept him from qualifying for the ERA title.

His was an arm of rare splendor. It, as well as the pitcher it was attached to, should have been treated like a national treasure.

The Baltimore Orioles have not been the best organization in baseball for the last twenty-five years by accident. They have won that reputation by committing themselves to plans that work.

No Oriole prospect is inserted into the regular lineup until he is ready; no regular is traded until his replacement is sure. Over the last two decades, Baltimore has almost never traded a useful starting pitcher. Exceptions (e.g., Milt Pappas) were sacrificed only when the commodity received in return (Frank Robinson) was judged to be integral to the team. They erred in letting Robby go to L.A. That forced them to give up a hurler (Pat Dobson) to get a power hitter (Earl Williams) to replace him. Yet even Dobson was expendable because Doyle Alexander had already shown he could replace him. The only other times they would trade a pitcher is when he lost his effectiveness (Mike Cuellar), or if they got a more desirable arm in return (Torrez for Holtzman; Holtzman, Jackson, and Alexander for May, Martinez, Pagan, and McGregor).

One thing the Orioles never do is trade away good young pitching. They bring their kids along slowly, with great respect for the fragility of their art. Scott MacGregor, Mike Flanagan, and Dennis Martinez, three pitchers who were expected to lead the Orioles into the late eighties, spent their first years with the club as mop-up men, long relievers, and spot starters. Their stats were unimportant. They were learning how to pitch in the big leagues and how to win. When it came time for them to take their places on the starting staff, they were ready. They weren't rushed, and they weren't dissected the moment they went a few starts between wins.

Dave Righetti reported to spring training in 1982 with slight regard for the sophomore jinx. He had proven to himself that he could pitch, realizing it the previous September when he had faced the Red Sox and "reached back and threw the ball past Yastrzemski, Rice, and Evans, and the rest of them. They just couldn't hit it. I said to myself, 'Hey, this is nice. If I can keep throwing like this, stay healthy, and learn, then maybe those things they've been saying about me will come true.' It's one thing to read things in the paper, but you have to find out for yourself. Papers tend to build you up too much or put you down too low. You don't know what to believe. You might not be as good as they write you are. But when you're out there and doing it you realize maybe you can pitch here. I know I started to notice that I could do things other guys couldn't."

That sort of confidence is a huge part of any successful pitcher's artillery. It is a winner's arrogance that enables him to thrive in the hot spotlight of the crucial moment while others search anxiously for the cooling shadows of self-doubt. This is not to be confused with the insecure prattling that passes for strong ego. It is usually a quiet thing, an admission to oneself: "I'm as good as anybody."

The Yankee front office, unknowingly, did their best to strip Righetti of that hard-won worth. He remembered, "I had one bad game last season [1981], and only one. That doesn't happen very often. So I was left alone; you leave a good thing alone. Then I had a good game in spring training my first time out. My next game wasn't very good. Boom! The front office talked about sending me down to the minors, and then everyone was suddenly there to help me or hurt me. I thought, 'Wow! Nice patience.' It was strange for me, but it was something I had to deal with. I think it's good I took care of it now, instead of ten years from now like some of the guys this year. Some of these guys came up in different organizations. They did well, and when they did badly they were left to work their way out of it. They could go into a slump. You're not allowed to go into too many slumps around here."

Righetti had a horrendous spring and when the season commenced he didn't seem the same pitcher as he had been the previous year. He appeared hesitant on the mound, as if he weren't sure what to throw. He grew worse with each game. Watching him pitch was akin to watching a man cross a tightrope in newly sharpened spikes. His control disappeared. In one game he threw 96 pitches in four innings. This was becoming a common outing for him. After the games, he would meet the press and thrash out the evening. He could never quite find the words to express what was so mysteriously wrong. Even victory brought little solace. After one win, an affair in which he was forced to wiggle out of trouble all evening long, he was asked, "Was this a good outing for you?" "I won," he replied, incredulously. It was as though he wanted to scream, "What else do I have to do?"

He was demoted to Columbus on June 27. No Rookie of the Year had ever received a similar comedown in the season following his reception of the award. At least it got him away from the media and the sophomore jinx headlines. It also got him away from the often conflicting varieties of "good advice" that besieged him at every turn. The move reunited Righetti with pitching coach Sammy Ellis and helped him get his breath. When he came back, he seemed to have regained some of that lost confidence. Righetti finished with a winning record (11–10). The Yankees were lucky he was such a unique young man; he gave them a reprieve. They had juggled a piece of Ming china and dropped it. It proved too tough to break.

It was a very dull season at Yankee Stadium, except for the front-office histrionics which had become a big bore. Dave Winfield and Rich Gossage had MVP-quality seasons. Jerry Mumphrey hit well, though he was shaky in the field. Willie Randolph had a steady year, and Lou Piniella hit over .300. Shane Rawley, the "worst trade we ever made," pitched well once he became a starter. Guidry had an uneven year but finished at 14–8. Griffey hit .277 with a post–All-Star break surge and gave New Yorkers a glimpse of the player he really was. And only Bob Stanley of the Red Sox stood in George Frazier's way as the best long man in the league.

It was a dispirited team. Their bench had been splintered; they lacked the role players they once had in abundance. In September, the Yankees lost nine in a row. It was their longest losing streak since 1953 and the second longest in the club's history. They finished the season 79–83. They fell to sixth place, 16 games out of first, 1 game out of last. They barely beat out the Toronto Blue Jays. Stadium attendance fell by over

800,000 from the last full season. The Mets were once again a threat to take back the city.

The fans were haunted by living ghosts. Jackson and John made it to the playoffs with the Angels. When the Yankees first got into the free-agent market, it was explained that players would be bought only until the Yankee farm system was once again flourishing. In 1982, the rosters of many major league clubs were speckled with the names of dazzling young performers whose common thread was that they were no longer Yankees: Tim Lollar, Willie McGee, Damaso Garcia, Jim Beattie, Gene Nelson, Chris Welsh, Pat Tabler. The list could go on; it reads like a litany of broken promises.

Throughout the dismal first part of the season, many fans were taken with the delusion that this team was going to come back and make a fight of it. It was heard on the streets all the time: "It's going to be like '78, bad start, great finish." They were blinded by Yankee mystique.

That wondrous gang that had brought so much to so many had been broken up. Cerone, Randolph, Nettles, Piniella, Gamble, Guidry, May, Frazier, and Gossage were still there. They weren't men to mess with in a big game. Griffey had the tradition of the Big Red Machine behind him, and Winfield could play.

But Thurman Munson was dead, alas. Chambliss, Jackson, Dent, Rivers, Beattie, Lyle, Stanley, Doyle, Heath, and Johnson were playing in other cities. Roy White was in Japan. Paul Blair was a coach at Fordham University. Jim Spencer and Don Gullett had retired, and Ed Figueroa was pitching in Mexico. They hadn't been just a group of talented ballplayers. They were that rarest of a rare breed: champions. And now, they were gone. Alas again.

EPILOGUE

It's only a game.

—Anonymous

The fan just could not believe it. After sitting through the accident that was the 1982 baseball season in the Bronx, he had sworn he wouldn't come back. He couldn't bear the pain. But as winter loosened its grip on the city, and the seductive promises of spring crept back into the air, he realized he was kidding himself.

No matter what had gone on during the summer of his discontent, this was still *his* team. It had been the team of his father and of his father before him. Nothing could erase that.

This obvious fact hadn't struck him at first; he was still cursing himself for surrendering to the pinstriped siren's call as he took the long train ride uptown. When he reached the Stadium, he sneaked to the advance ticket window, plunked down his money, and made his purchase—all the while asking, "Why?"

He got the answer during the trip back to Manhattan. As the train pulled out along the platform of the el, just before it entered the blackened tunnel, he caught a glimpse of that dazzling palace of a ball park. Just the sight of it could still make him tremble. He closed his eyes. The present moment slipped away.

He was sitting in the Stadium, on an evening that could never end. A game was in progress. He didn't care about the score. Lyle, Gossage, and McDaniel were casually throwing in the bullpen. Guidry and Ford sat nervelessly in the home team dugout. Nettles and Kubek stood nearby discussing their last double play. In the batter's box, Munson started his swing as Mantle and finished it as Jackson. *Crack!* The ball was lofted deep into the night. It drifted past a solitary cloud, hung among the stars, and descended. It came to rest in the welcoming folds of the fan's warmest memories.

He opened his eyes. The visions had left. He was back in a subway car, surrounded by strangers. Reaching into his pocket, he grabbed a fistful of tickets and held on tightly.